The FDA and Worldwide Quality System Requirements Guidebook for Medical Devices

Second Edition

Also available from ASQ Quality Press:

ISO 13485:2003: Medical devices—Quality management systems—Requirements for regulatory purposes
ISO

Safe and Sound Software: Creating an Efficient and Effective Quality System for Software Medical Device Organizations
Thomas H. Faris

Development of FDA-Regulated Medical Products: Prescription Drugs, Biologics and Medical Devices
Elaine Whitmore

Measurement Matters: How Effective Assessment Drives Business and Safety Performance
Brooks Carder and Patrick Ragan

The Internal Auditing Pocket Guide: Preparing, Performing, Reporting and Follow-up, Second Edition
J.P. Russell

5S for Service Organizations and Offices: A Lean Look at Improvements
Debashis Sarkar

Managing Service Delivery Processes: Linking Strategy to Operations
Jean Harvey

The Executive Guide to Understanding and Implementing Lean Six Sigma: The Financial Impact
Robert M. Meisel, Steven J. Babb, Steven F. Marsh, and James P. Schlichting

Lean Kaizen: A Simplified Approach to Process Improvements
George Alukal and Anthony Manos

Root Cause Analysis: Simplified Tools and Techniques, Second Edition
Bjørn Andersen and Tom Fagerhaug

The Certified Manager of Quality/Organizational Excellence Handbook: Third Edition
Russell T. Westcott, editor

Enabling Excellence: The Seven Elements Essential to Achieving Competitive Advantage
Timothy A. Pine

To request a complimentary catalog of ASQ Quality Press publications, call 800-248-1946, or visit our Web site at http://www.asq.org/quality-press.

The FDA and Worldwide Quality System Requirements Guidebook for Medical Devices

Second Edition

COMPILED AND WRITTEN BY

Amiram Daniel
&
Ed Kimmelman

ASQ Quality Press
Milwaukee, Wisconsin

American Society for Quality, Quality Press, Milwaukee 53203

Printed in the United States of America
14 5 4

Library of Congress Cataloging-in-Publication Data

Daniel, Amiram.
The FDA and worldwide quality system requirements guidebook for medical devices / compiled and written by Amiram Daniel & Ed Kimmelman.—2nd ed.
p. cm.
Rev. ed. of: FDA and worldwide quality system requirements guide book for medical devices / Kimberly A. Trautman. c1997.
ISBN 978-0-87389-740-2 (alk. paper)
1. Medical instruments and apparatus industry—Law and legislation—United States. 2. Quality control—Law and legislation—United States. 3. Medical instruments and apparatus industry—United States—Quality control. 4. Medical instruments and apparatus industry—Law and legislation. 5. Quality control—Law and legislation. 6. Medical instruments and apparatus industry—Quality control. I. Kimmelman, Ed. II. Trautman, Kimberly A., 1964—FDA and worldwide quality system requirements guide book for medical devices. III. Title.

KF3827.M4T73 2008
344.7304′2—dc22 2008013052

Publisher: William A. Tony
Acquisitions Editor: Matt Meinholz
Project Editor: Paul O'Mara
Production Administrator: Randall Benson

ASQ Mission: The American Society for Quality advances individual, organizational, and community excellence worldwide through learning, quality improvement, and knowledge exchange.

Attention Bookstores, Wholesalers, Schools, and Corporations: ASQ Quality Press books, videotapes, audiotapes, and software are available at quantity discounts with bulk purchases for business, educational, or instructional use. For information, please contact ASQ Quality Press at 800-248-1946, or write to ASQ Quality Press, P.O. Box 3005, Milwaukee, WI 53201-3005.

To place orders or to request a free copy of the ASQ Quality Press Publications Catalog, including ASQ membership information, call 800-248-1946. Visit our Web site at www.asq.org or www.asq.org/quality-press.

Quality Press
600 N. Plankinton Avenue
Milwaukee, Wisconsin 53203
Call toll free 800-248-1946
Fax 414-272-1734
www.asq.org
http://www.asq.org/quality-press
http://standardsgroup.asq.org
E-mail: authors@asq.org

Printed on acid-free paper

CONTENTS

DETAILED ANALYSIS OF THE REQUIREMENTS AND GUIDANCES

ADDITIONAL SUBJECTS

INTRODUCTION

It has been more than 11 years since the U.S. Food and Drug Administration (FDA) published its Medical Devices: Current Good Manufacturing Practice (CGMP) Final Rule: Quality System Regulation (QSReg) (October 1996). Through the QSReg, FDA profoundly changed its approach. It focused its attention on the various processes contained within a compliant quality management system (QMS), with a new emphasis on the design and development process. By doing so it moved much closer to the approach taken by the International Organization for Standardization (ISO) quality system standard ISO 9001:2000, which was being developed concurrently with the new regulation. After publication of the new QSReg, the QMS standard for medical device organizations, ISO 13485:2003, and an associated guidance document, ISO/TR 14969:2004, were published.

Since the publication of ISO 13485:2003, FDA has been asked why it hasn't simply adopted this international standard as its quality system regulation. FDA explains that it is constrained from doing so by the statutes under which it operates. In addition, it is discouraged from further revising the QSReg by the complicated process for such revision and by the impact on other FDA compliance activities. FDA correctly maintains that there are few substantive differences between the QSReg and the Standard. The text in this book confirms that there are no conflicting requirements between the QSReg and the Standard, and that an effective QMS can be constructed by combining requirements of both documents or following either.

In 1997, the American Society for Quality (ASQ) published the first edition of *The FDA and Worldwide Quality System Requirements Guidebook for Medical Devices*, compiled by Kimberly A. Trautman, FDA GMP/Quality Systems Expert. The *Guidebook* has served the medical device industry as a definitive source of "FDA thinking" on quality system processes. There are well-worn, dog-eared, and annotated copies of this book on the desks of medical device manufacturers in the United States and around the world.

In the years since the first edition was published, regulatory agencies in key countries and regions have incorporated the requirements contained in the ISO 13485:2003 standard into their quality system regulations. In addition, Global Harmonization Task Force (GHTF) study groups have been effective in developing guidance documents intended to harmonize the regulation of medical devices sold in the international market.

This new and expanded second edition of the *Guidebook* maintains the organizational approach of the first edition and includes the requirements and guidance contained in the QSReg, the ISO 13485:2003 standard, the ISO/TR 14969:2004 guidance document, and, as appropriate, the GHTF guidance documents. The organization of the book is based on the order of requirements in the QSReg. For each substantive requirement section, there is:

A verbatim statement of the QSReg and the U.S. Food, Drug, and Cosmetic Act requirement.

A description of the comparable requirement in ISO 13485:2003, including, as appropriate, brief excerpts from the Standard, focusing on any additions to or differences from the requirements contained in the QSReg.

FDA Guidance. Excerpts of the FDA responses to relevant comment groups contained in the preamble to the QSReg, as well as excerpts from various FDA guidance documents related to QMSs. These guidance documents can be searched by accessing the FDA Web site, http://www.accessdata.fda.gov/scripts/cdrh/cfdocs/cfggp/search.cfm, and clicking on the Office of Compliance page or a page from other FDA offices of interest.

AAMI/ANSI/ISO TR 14969:2004. A description of the relevant guidance contained in ISO/TR 14969:2004, including, as appropriate, excerpts from the TR, focusing on any additions to or differences from the guidance in the preamble and other FDA guidance documents.

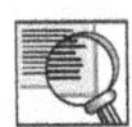

GHTF Guidance. Excerpts from relevant GHTF guidances (if useful). A number of original GHTF guidance documents have been retired since the publication of ISO/TR 14969:2004. The contents of the TR cover many of the topics discussed in these original guidances. Access to GHTF guidances is available from its Web site, http://www.GHTF.org.

"Authors' Notes," which include guidance derived from the authors' 60 years of regulatory compliance experience.

The second edition also addresses a number of additional topics:

- The incorporation of risk management into the medical device organization's QMS
- QMS issues related to combination products
- The key process interactions within a QMS
- Effective presentation of and advocacy for a QMS during FDA inspections and third-party assessment
- Future FDA compliance and standards activities

The discussion of requirements contained in ISO 9001 has been eliminated in this edition. ISO 13485:2003 is based on the requirements contained in ISO 9001, but it stands independent of ISO 9001 in order to fulfill its objective of being a model for device quality system regulation around the world.

Immediately following this introduction is a side-by-side, at-a-glance comparison of the FDA Quality System Regulation and the ISO Quality Standard 13485:2003.

The reader should note the following for the purposes of this book:

- When the term "Standard" is used, it refers to ISO 13485:2003.
- When the term "QSReg" is used, it refers to the FDA Quality System Regulation, 1996. "QSReg" is used in this book instead of "QSR" to avoid any confusion with QSR meaning either the "Quality System Regulation" or the "Quality System Record" required by § 820.186 of the QSReg.
- When the term "TR" is used, it refers to the ISO/TR 14969:2004 technical report.
- When the term "Statute" is used, it refers to the U.S. Food, Drug, and Cosmetics Act.

This guidance book is a resource for manufacturers of medical devices, those who provide support services to these manufacturers, and the users of medical devices. It provides up-to-date information concerning required and recommended quality system practices. It should be used as a companion to the regulations/standards themselves and the texts on the specific processes and activities contained within the QMS.

Another useful guidance book is published by the Canadian Standards Association: *The ISO 13485 Essentials: A Practical Handbook for Implementing the ISO 13485 Standard for Manufacturers of Medical Devices.* This handbook is part of a series of guidances published by the Canadian Standards Association. A complete listing of these handbooks and the Canadian standards relevant to health and safety can be found at http://www.csa.ca/electronic_catalogue/health_and_safety.pdf.

Users should ensure that their organization possesses the most up-to-date, relevant regulations and standards.

An At-a-Glance Comparison of the 1996 QSReg and ISO 13485:2003

This at-a-glance comparison of the 1996 QSReg and the ISO 13485:2003 Standard is intended to align the comparable subclauses of the two documents and quickly highlight their similarities and differences. Additional, more detailed comparisons are explained in the subpart chapters that follow.

QSReg, 21 CFR § 820	ISO 13485:2003	Authors' notes
§ 820.1 Scope (a) Applicability (c) Authority (d) Foreign manufacturers (e) Exemptions or variances	1 Scope 1.1 General	The scope section of each document sets out its objective. For the ISO 13485, the objective is to harmonize regulation around the world. An attempt was made by FDA during the revision of the GMPs, while the 1996 version of ISO 13485 was being developed, to incorporate the requirements that were included in that version of the Standard. While the agency could not revise the format of the regulation to follow that of the Standard, many of the requirements were included. This section of the regulation contains some additional regulatory issues that are not appropriate for the Standard.
§ 820.1 Scope (a) Applicability (b) Limitations	1.2 Application	The applicability guidance is essentially the same in both documents, as both allow the QMS to exclude requirements associated with activities not performed by the organization. The Standard explicitly limits those exclusions to those associated with product realization. Because of this approach, it will be necessary for registrars to explain in detail the scope of any certificates of compliance with ISO 13485:2003. They will have to clearly spell out any exclusions.
§ 820.3 Definitions	3 Terms and definitions	The Standard clearly spells out the new meanings of the words "supplier" and "organization."
	3.1 Active implantable medical device 3.2 Active medical device 3.3 Advisory notice	
§ 820.3 Definitions (b) Complaint . . .	3.4 Customer complaint	The regulatory definition is a bit broader, as it covers products that have not as yet been placed on the market but have been released for distribution. This means that a lot of a product that has been released for distribution could be included in the activities associated with a customer complaint, even though no part of the lot has reached the customer.

QSReg, 21 CFR § 820	ISO 13485:2003	Authors' notes
§ 812.3(c) Component . . .		
§ 812.3(d) Implant . . .	3.5 Implantable medical device	The definition in the Standard explicitly includes eye implants.
Federal Food, Drug, and Cosmetics Act, Section 201 (k) The "label" . . . (m) The term "labeling" . . .	3.6 Labeling	The definition in the statute is a bit more detailed, but the definition in the Standard should cover all that is included in the definitions of "label" and "labeling" in the regulation.
§ 820.3 Definitions (f) Design input . . .	7.3.2 Design and development inputs	The definition of "design and development inputs" in the Standard is actually incorporated into the requirements section. It is also a bit more explicit.
§ 820.3 Definitions (g) Design output . . .	7.3.3 Design and development outputs	The definition of "design and development outputs" in the Standard is actually incorporated into the requirements section. It is also a bit more explicit. While the regulation doesn't explicitly include examples of design output, it is clear that FDA considers items like the product and component specifications, manufacturing procedures, engineering drawings, and logbooks to be part of the design output.
Federal Food, Drug, and Cosmetics Act, Section 201 (h) The term "device" . . .	3.7 Medical device	No significant difference in the definitions.
§ 820.3 Definitions (h) Design review . . .	7.3.4 Design and development review	The definition of "design and development review" in the Standard is actually incorporated into the requirements section. Otherwise there is no significant difference.
	3.8 Sterile medical device	

QSReg, 21 CFR § 820	ISO 13485:2003	Authors' notes
§ 820.3 Definitions (i) Device History Record . . . (j) Device Master Record . . . (k) Establish . . . (l) Finished device . . . (m) Lot or batch . . .		
§ 820.3 Definitions (n) Management with executive responsibility . . .	ISO 9000:2000, 3.2.7 Top management	The intent of both definitions is the same.
§ 820.3 Definitions (o) Manufacturer . . . (p) Manufacturing material . . .		
§ 820.3 Definitions (q) Nonconformity . . .	ISO 9000:2000, 3.6.2 Nonconformity	The definitions are identical.
§ 820.3 Definitions (r) Product . . .	ISO 9000:2000, 3.4.2 Product	The definition in the Standard more clearly reflects the process approach of this document, and it is a bit more detailed.
§ 820.3 Definitions (s) Quality . . .	ISO 9000:2000, 3.1.1 Quality	No significant difference. The definition in the regulation reflects the objective of the regulation, that is, the assurance of product safety and effectiveness.
§ 820.3 Definitions (t) Quality audit . . .	ISO 9000:2000, 3.9.1 Audit	The definition in the regulation imposes the requirement related to defined intervals, and it includes activities that occur after the audit is actually performed.

QSReg, 21 CFR § 820	ISO 13485:2003	Authors' notes
§ 820.3 Definitions (u) Quality policy . . .	ISO 9000:2000, 3.2.4 Quality policy	No significant difference in the definitions.
§ 820.3 Definitions (v) Quality system . . .	ISO 9000:2000, 3.2.2 System	The definition in the regulation is more instructive, but it is consistent with the intent of the Standard.
§ 820.3 Definitions (w) Remanufacturer . . .		
§ 820.3 Definitions (x) Rework . . .	ISO 9000:2000, 3.6.7 Rework	No significant difference in the definitions.
§ 820.3 Definitions (y) Specification . . .	ISO 9000:2000, 3.7.3 Specification	The regulation requires documentation of specifications.
§ 820.3 Definitions (z) Validation . . . (1) Process validation . . . (2) Design validation . . .	ISO 9000:2000, 3.8.5 Validation	No significant difference, but neither definition is very informative. The regulatory definition is more detailed in that it breaks out and defines "process validation" and "design validation." Normally, validation is performed on the final product or on the final process for manufacturing, monitoring, testing, and supporting the product.
§ 820.3 Definitions (aa) Verification . . .	ISO 9000:2000, 3.8.4 Verification	No significant difference. The Standard is more detailed.
§ 820.5 Quality system	4 Quality management system 4.1 General requirements	No significant differences.

QSReg, 21 CFR § 820	ISO 13485:2003	Authors' notes
	4.2 Documentation requirements 4.2.1 General	The Standard lists the required QMS documentation in this clause, while the QSReg indicates the documentation requirements in the various sections throughout the regulation. There is no significant difference in the documentation requirements for the two documents, except that the QSReg implicitly recognizes that the extent of QMS documentation will reflect the size and complexity of the organization. It also implicitly recognizes that some documentation may not be needed due to the expertise (either through training or education or through experience) of the personnel.
	7 Product realization 7.1 Planning of product realization	The QSReg doesn't specifically recognize the concept of product realization, even though it includes requirements related to essentially all of the processes associated with it. The QSReg also requires, either implicitly or explicitly, in various sections planning associated with these requirements. The Standard recognizes that risk management is a process that is conducted throughout the product realization process, while the QSReg refers to risk management only in the section related to design validation. FDA, however, recognizes the wisdom of the Standard's risk management requirements and will seek records associated with risk management consistent with the requirements set out in the Standard.
	4.2.2 Quality manual	The QSReg has no requirement for a Quality Manual. Such a manual would be helpful in explaining the nature and extent of the QMS to an FDA investigator during an inspection. It would also be useful in the training of personnel with regard to the QMS of the organization and their place within that system. The Quality Manual could be used as the repository of some of the individual QMS documentation required by the QSReg (e.g., the organizational structure and interrelationships, and the highest-level procedures in a small organization dealing with items like document control, record keeping, and training).

QSReg, 21 CFR § 820	ISO 13485:2003	Authors' notes
§ 820.20 Management responsibility (a) Quality policy . . .	5 Management responsibility 5.1 Management commitment	No significant differences in management responsibilities; the QSReg spells some of them out in subsequent sections of the regulation.
	5.3 Quality policy	No significant differences.
	5.4 Planning 5.4.1 Quality objectives	No significant differences.
	5.2 Customer focus	The Standard distinctly focuses on meeting customer requirements in addition to meeting regulatory requirements. The QSReg is entirely focused on meeting those requirements that have as their objective the design, manufacture, distribution, and support of safe and effective medical devices. The Standard includes requirements for determining customer requirements during the entire product realization process, while the QSReg includes requirements that identify product and process requirements focused on ensuring safe and effective medical devices.
§ 820.20(b) Organization (1) Responsibility and authority	5.5 Responsibility, authority, and communication 5.5.1 Responsibility and authority	No significant differences.
§ 820.20(b) Organization (1) Responsibility and authority	5.5.3 Internal communications	No significant differences; the QSReg implicitly requires the necessary communication processes that make for successful interrelationships.

QSReg, 21 CFR § 820	ISO 13485:2003	Authors' notes
§ 820.20(b)(2) Resources	6.2 Human resources 6.2.1 General 6.2.2 Competence, awareness, and training	No significant differences.
§ 820.20(b)(3) Management representative	5.5.2 Management representative	No significant differences, except the requirements in the Standard reflect the focus on meeting customer requirements.
§ 820.20(c) Management review	5.6 Management review 5.6.1 General	No significant differences.
	5.6.2 Review input	The requirements for review input spelled out in the Standard are logical and would be expected by an FDA investigator during an inspection that focused on management responsibilities.
	5.6.3 Review output	The requirements for review output spelled out in the Standard are logical and would be expected by an FDA investigator during an inspection that focused on management responsibilities.
	8.5 Improvement 8.5.1 General	There is no one section of the QSReg that corresponds directly with subclause 8.5.1 of the Standard. The intents of the two documents as they relate to improvement of the QMS through the use of corrective and preventive action are consistent.

QSReg, 21 CFR § 820	ISO 13485:2003	Authors' notes
§ 820.20(d) Quality planning	5.4.2 Quality management system planning	The QSReg contains the prescriptive requirement for a quality plan and quality system procedures. It is not clear what the FDA is looking for in a quality plan. It seems to be a combination of a high-level quality planning document containing policy and key objectives (with a mandate to drive those objectives down into the organization) and a set of high-level procedures that illustrate how that plan will be met. It may also be a quality plan established on a product-by-product basis. Both the QSReg and the Standard require the establishment of these kinds of procedures; only the QSReg gives them special standing as quality system procedures.
§ 820.20(e) Quality system procedures	4 Quality management system 4.2 Documentation requirements 4.2.1 General	There is no separate section in the Standard specifically targeted at quality system procedures. The documentation requirements are covered in the general QMS requirements. There is no substantive difference in the documentation requirements.
§ 820.22 Quality audit	8.2.2 Internal audit	No significant differences.
§ 820.25 Personnel (a) General	6.2 Human resources 6.2.1 General 6.2.2 Competence, awareness, and training	No significant differences.
§ 820.25(b) Training	6.2 Human resources 6.2.1 General 6.2.2 Competence, awareness, and training	No significant differences.

QSReg, 21 CFR § 820	ISO 13485:2003	Authors' notes
§ 820.30 Design controls (a) General	1.2 Application	There is no comparable section in the Standard. The QSReg limits the applicability of design controls to more high-risk medical devices, while the Standard applies them to all medical devices. The regulation excludes all Class I devices other than those specifically listed in the § 820.30(a) from the requirement to establish procedures for design control. The Standard recognizes such regulatory exclusions.
§ 820.30(b) Design and development planning	7.3.1 Design and development planning	The overall objectives related to design control planning are consistent in the two documents.
§ 820.30(c) Design input	7.3.2 Design and development inputs	No significant differences.
§ 820.30(d) Design output	7.3.3 Design and development outputs	The intents of the two documents are consistent with each other, with the QSReg containing specific requirements associated with the approval and release of design outputs.
§ 820.30(e) Design review	7.3.4 Design and development review	The intents of the two documents are consistent with each other, with the Standard illustrating in more detail the objectives of the design review, and the QSReg including prescriptive design review process requirements not contained in the Standard.
§ 820.30(f) Design verification	7.3.5 Design and development verification	The intents of the two documents are consistent with each other, with the QSReg including prescriptive design verification process requirements not contained in the Standard.

QSReg, 21 CFR § 820	ISO 13485:2003	Authors' notes
§ 820.30(g) Design validation	7.3.6 Design and development validation	The intents of the two documents are consistent with each other. The QSReg seems to indicate that risk analysis is a design validation process. This is not consistent with the teachings of the Standard, which calls for risk management activities throughout the product realization process. See the chapter in this book related specifically to risk management. The Standard addresses a scenario not addressed by the QSReg (e.g., where final assembly of the medical device is accomplished upon delivery to the customer). The QSReg contains a number of design validation process requirements not included in the Standard.
§ 820.30(h) Design transfer	7.3.1 Design and development planning	There is no comparable section in the Standard addressing design transfer directly. Design transfer is addressed in a note in section 7.3.1 of the Standard.
	7.5.1 Control of production and service provision	No significant differences.
§ 820.30(i) Design changes	7.3.7 Control of design and development changes	The Standard contains requirements related to the effect of design changes on a product already delivered to customers and records of design changes that do not appear in the QSReg.
§ 820.30(j) Design History File	7.3.1 Design and development planning	While the Standard requires the creation of design control documentation and records, the QSReg requires the establishment of a Design History File (DHF), which either contains or refers to all the documents and records associated with the application of the design control processes to a particular product.
§ 820.40 Document controls	4.2.3 Control of documents	The requirements are essentially the same, except that the QSReg has the specific requirement to communicate changes to documents to the affected personnel. The Standard requires the organization to define a retention period for "obsoleted" documents.

QSReg, 21 CFR § 820	ISO 13485:2003	Authors' notes
§ 820.50 Purchasing controls	7.4 Purchasing 7.4.1 Purchasing process	No significant differences.
§ 820.50(a) Evaluation of suppliers, contractors, and consultants	7.4 Purchasing 7.4.1 Purchasing process	No significant differences.
§ 820.50(b) Purchasing data	7.4.2 Purchasing information	The intents of both documents are consistent with each other. The Standard contains a requirement associated with the organization ensuring the adequacy of purchasing requirements prior to communicating them to the supplier. The QSReg contains a requirement that the organization obtain, where possible, the agreement of the supplier to notify the organization of changes to the product or service so that the organization can assess the potential effect on the quality of the medical device.
§ 820.60 Identification	7.5.3 Identification and traceability 7.5.3.1 Identification	The Standard addresses the identification and traceability of product returned to the organization in order to ensure it is distinguished from normal product.
§ 820.65 Traceability	7.5.3.2 Traceability	The Standard includes some general requirements associated with traceability not found in the QSReg. The requirements for implantable and active implantable devices found in both documents are supplementary and shall be incorporated into the QMS of an organization supplying such medical devices.
§ 820.70 Production and process control	7.5 Production and service provision	The intents of both documents are consistent with each other, with each of the documents providing details of control or the types of processes that must be controlled in a way that supplements the other. It is suggested that the sections be read together in order to get a complete list of processes and process controls that are to be included in the QMS.

QSReg, 21 CFR § 820	ISO 13485:2003	Authors' notes
§ 820.70(a) General	7.5 Production and service provision 7.5.1 Control of production and service provision 7.5.1.1 General requirements	The intents of both documents are consistent with each other, with each of the documents providing details of control or the types of processes that must be controlled in a way that supplements the other. It is suggested that the sections be read together in order to get a complete list of processes and process controls that are to be included in the QMS.
	7.5.1.3 Particular requirements for sterile medical devices	This section requires the establishment of process parameters for sterilization processes and records traceable to each batch of medical devices that were subjected to sterilization.
	7.5.4 Customer property	Aside from the general controls exerted by the organization over purchased product, the QSReg does not specifically address the issue of care exercised over customer property when it is being held or processed by the organization.
	8.2.3 Monitoring and measurement of processes	The intents of the two documents are consistent with each other, even though the QSReg is far more detailed and has a product focus.
§ 820.70(b) Production and process changes		There is no specific section of the Standard that addresses production and process changes.
§ 820.70(c) Environmental control	6.4 Work environment	The intents of both documents are consistent with each other; the Standard specifically calls for control of used product to prevent contamination of other products, the manufacturing environment, or personnel.
§ 820.70(d) Personnel	6.2 Human resources 6.2.1 General 6.2.2 Competence, awareness, and training	No significant differences.
	6.3 Infrastructure 6.4 Work environment	The intents of the two documents are consistent with each other.

QSReg, 21 CFR § 820	ISO 13485:2003	Authors' notes
§ 820.70(e) Contamination control	6.4 Work environment	The intents of both documents are consistent with each other; the Standard specifically calls for control of used product to prevent contamination of other products, the manufacturing environment, or personnel.
	7.5.1.2.1 Cleanliness of product and contamination control	This section of the Standard introduces cleanliness controls related to product that is to be sterilized.
§ 820.70(f) Buildings	6.3 Infrastructure	The intents of the two documents are consistent with each other.
§ 820.70(g) Equipment	6.3 Infrastructure	The intents of the two documents are consistent with each other; the QSReg contains a number of specific requirements related to the creation of maintenance schedules, inspections, and adjustment of equipment.
§ 820.70(h) Manufacturing material	6.3 Infrastructure	The intents of the two documents are consistent with each other; the QSReg contains a number of specific requirements related to manufacturing materials.
§ 820.70(i) Automated processes	7.5.2 Validation of processes for production and service provision	No significant differences.
§ 820.72 Inspection, measuring, and test equipment	7.6 Control of monitoring and measuring equipment	The intents of the two documents are consistent with each other, with the Standard providing generalized guidance as to the control of monitoring and measuring devices and the QSReg focusing more specifically on the process of calibration of such equipment.
	8 Measurement, analysis, and improvement 8.1 General	There is no one section of the QSReg that corresponds to clause 8.1 of the Standard. It is clear from a reading of the overall QSReg that the objectives of this clause of the Standard and the QSReg are consistent with each other.
§ 820.75 Process validation	7.5.2 Validation of processes for production and service provision 7.5.2.1 General requirements	No significant differences. The QSReg contains a number of prescriptive requirements associated with documentation of validation activities. There are no specific requirements related to process validation of sterilization processes in the QSReg.

QSReg, 21 CFR § 820	ISO 13485:2003	Authors' notes
§ 820.80 Receiving, in-process, and finished device acceptance (a) General	8.2.4 Monitoring and measurement of product	The intents of the two documents are consistent with each other, even though the QSReg is far more detailed and prescriptive. The acceptance records requirements of the QSReg would appear to satisfy the implantable and active implantable requirements of the Standard.
§ 820.80(b) Receiving acceptance activities	7.4.3 Verification of purchased product	The Standard contains requirements related to the scenario where the organization seeks to verify purchased product at the supplier's location.
	8.2.4 Monitoring and measurement of product	The Standard has no separate subclause targeted at receiving acceptance activities. See comments related to § 820.80(a).
§ 820.80(c) In-process acceptance activities	8.2.4 Monitoring and measurement of product	The Standard has no separate subclause targeted at in-process acceptance activities. See comments related to § 820.80(a).
§ 820.80(d) Final acceptance activities	7.5 Production and service provision 7.5.1 Control of production and service provision 7.5.1.1 General requirements	The Standard has no separate subclause targeted at final acceptance activities. See comments related to § 820.80(a).
	8.2.4 Monitoring and measurement of product	The Standard has no separate subclause targeted at final acceptance activities. See comments related to § 820.80(a).
§ 820.80(e) Acceptance records	8.2.4 Monitoring and measurement of product 8.2.4.1 General requirements	This section of the Standard has no additional requirements for final acceptance records beyond those applied to acceptance activities in general. See text related to QSReg § 820.80(a).
§ 820.86 Acceptance status	7.5.3 Identification and traceability 7.5.3.3 Status identification	The QSReg contains a number of prescriptive requirements associated with the records of acceptance status.

QSReg, 21 CFR § 820	ISO 13485:2003	Authors' notes
§ 820.90 Nonconforming product (a) Control of nonconforming product	8.3 Control of nonconforming product	The intents of the two documents are consistent with each other. The QSReg provides more detail as to the items to be recorded in a nonconforming product situation. It explicitly addresses the subject of the need for an investigation in such a situation. The Standard addresses the handling of already-released product that is subject to a finding of nonconformity. The Standard provides requirements related to rework of nonconforming product.
§ 820.90(b) Nonconforming review and disposition	8.3 Control of nonconforming product	The intents of the two documents are consistent with each other. The QSReg provides more detail as to the items to be recorded in a nonconforming product situation. It explicitly addresses the subject of the need for an investigation in such a situation. The Standard addresses the handling of an already-released product that is subject to a finding of nonconformity. The Standard provides requirements related to rework of nonconforming product.
§ 820.100 Corrective and preventive action	8.5 Improvement 8.5.1 General	The QSReg treats corrective actions and preventive actions in one subsection. There is no equivalent combined section in the Standard. The General subsection of the Standard deals with the general subject of improvement and focuses on improvements necessary to maintain the effectiveness of the QMS to meet customer requirements, including regulatory requirements.
	8.5.2 Corrective action	The intents of the two documents are consistent with each other. The requirements as set out by the QSReg are more prescriptive.
	8.5.3 Preventive action	The intents of the two documents are consistent with each other. The requirements as set out by the QSReg are more prescriptive.

QSReg, 21 CFR § 820	ISO 13485:2003	Authors' notes
§ 820.120 Device labeling	7.3.2 Design and development inputs	The TR contains recommendations related to labeling in the local language and the use of symbols.
	7.5.1.1(g) the implementation of defined operations for labeling . . .	No significant differences.
	7.5.5 Preservation of product	While the intents of the two documents are consistent with each other, the QSReg contains many prescriptive requirements related to label control and the handling, storage, packaging, preservation, and distribution of product not specifically called out in the Standard.
§ 820.130 Device packaging	7.3.2 Design and development inputs	The TR recommends a number of considerations during the design and development of packaging materials. It recommends that the packaging be compatible with the product, any sterilization requirements, and other cleanliness requirements. It references ISO 11607 for additional guidance related to packaging of terminally sterilized medical devices.
	7.5.1.1(g) the implementation of defined operations for labeling and packaging	No significant differences.
	7.5.5 Preservation of product	While the intents of the two documents are consistent with each other, the QSReg contains many prescriptive requirements related to label control and the handling, storage, packaging, preservation, and distribution of a product not specifically called out in the Standard.
§ 820.140 Handling	7.2 Customer-related processes 7.2.1 Determination of requirements related to the product 7.2.2 Review of requirements related to the product	The closest the QSReg gets to determining customer requirements related to the product in 820.30(c) design inputs. The customer requirements referred to in clause 7.2 of the Standard refer to those requirements associated with getting the product to the customer. This includes items associated with order handling and what were referred to in early versions of ISO 9001 as contract review. These are not focuses of the QSReg.

QSReg, 21 CFR § 820	ISO 13485:2003	Authors' notes
	7.5.5 Preservation of product	While the intents of the two documents are consistent with each other, the QSReg contains many prescriptive requirements related to label control and the handling, storage, packaging, preservation, and distribution of a product not specifically called out in the Standard.
§ 820.150 Storage	7.5.5 Preservation of product	While the intents of the two documents are consistent with each other, the QSReg contains many prescriptive requirements related to label control and the handling, storage, packaging, preservation, and distribution of product not specifically called out in the Standard.
§ 820.160 Distribution	7.2 Customer-related processes 7.2.1 Determination of requirements related to the product 7.2.2 Review of requirements related to the product	The closest the QSReg gets to determining customer requirements related to the product in 820.30(c) design inputs. The customer requirements referred to in clause 7.2 of the Standard refer to those requirements associated with getting the product to the customer. This includes items associated with order handling and what were referred to in early versions of ISO 9001 as contract review. These are not focuses of the QSReg.
	7.5 Production and service provision 7.5.1 Control of production and service provision 7.5.1.1 General requirements	The Standard contains no requirements in § 7.5.1.1 in addition to those contained in the QSReg.
	7.5.5 Preservation of product	While the intents of the two documents are consistent with each other, the QSReg contains many prescriptive requirements related to label control and the handling, storage, packaging, preservation, and distribution of product not specifically called out in the Standard.

QSReg, 21 CFR § 820	ISO 13485:2003	Authors' notes
§ 820.170 Installation	7.2 Customer-related processes 7.2.1 Determination of requirements related to the product 7.2.2 Review of requirements related to the product	The closest the QSReg gets to determining customer requirements related to the product in 820.30(c) design inputs. The customer requirements referred to in clause 7.2 of the Standard refer to those requirements associated with getting the product to the customer. This includes items associated with order handling and what were referred to in early versions of ISO 9001 as contract review. These are not focuses of the QSReg.
	7.5.1.2.2 Installation activities	No significant differences.
§ 820.180 General requirements [related to control of records]	4.2.4 Control of records	No significant differences in the general requirements associated with control of records, except that the QSReg contains requirements for communications with FDA.
§ 820.181 Device Master Record	7.3.3 Design and development outputs 7.3.7 Design and development changes 7.5.1 Control of production and service provision 7.5.1.1 General requirements	The QSReg requires the establishment of a Device Master Record (DMR). The Standard has no requirement for such a named file even though it requires the individual documents and records that would be contained within that file. The DMR may be a separate file of documents and records, or it may be a document containing references to the various elements of the DMR.
§ 820.184 Device History Record	7.5.1 Control of production and service provision 7.5.1.1 General requirements	The QSReg requires the establishment of a Device History Record (DHR) for each lot of devices or unit manufactured. The Standard does not require the establishment of such a named file even though it requires the individual records that would be contained within that file. The DHR may be a separate file containing the records, or it may be a document that references the location of these records.

QSReg, 21 CFR § 820	ISO 13485:2003	Authors' notes
§ 820.186 Quality System Record	4 Quality management system 4.2 Documentation requirements 4.2.1 General	The QSReg requires the establishment of a Quality System Record, which may be a separate file containing the required documents or a document referencing the required contents. The Standard does not require the establishment of such a named file even though it does require the establishment of the various documents that would be included in that file.
§ 820.198 Complaint files	7.2.3 Customer communication	The requirement in the Standard goes beyond the communication of information related to complaints; it includes communication associated with general product information and information related to order handling and amendment of orders.
	8.2 Monitoring and measurement 8.2.1 Feedback	The QSReg contains prescriptive requirements regarding the handling of complaints and other user input that would be useful in conducting corrective or preventive action. These requirements are not spelled out in detail in the Standard, but compliance with the requirements set out in the QSReg would satisfy the requirements of the Standard.
	8.5 Improvement 8.5.1 General	The requirements of the QSReg are significantly more prescriptive related to the handling and documentation of complaints.
§ 820.200 Servicing	7.5.1.2.3 Servicing activities	No significant differences.
§ 820.250 Statistical techniques	8 Measurement, analysis, and improvement 8.1 General	No significant differences.
	8.2.3 Monitoring and measurement of processes	The intents of the two documents are consistent with each other, even though the QSReg is far more detailed and has a product focus.
	8.2.4 Monitoring and measurement of product	
	8.4 Analysis of data	There is no one section of the QSReg that corresponds directly with subclause 8.4 of the Standard. Requirements for analysis of data related to various elements of the QMSs are contained in a number of QSReg sections. The intents of the two documents as they relate to analysis of data are consistent with each other.

DETAILED ANALYSIS OF THE REQUIREMENTS AND GUIDANCES

SUBPART A

General Provisions

FDA Quality System Regulation—1996[1]

§ 820.1 Scope

§ 820.1(a) *Applicability.*

(1) Current good manufacturing practice (CGMP) requirements are set forth in this quality system regulation. The requirements in this part govern the methods used in, and the facilities and controls used for, the design, manufacture, packaging, labeling, storage, installation, and servicing of all finished devices intended for human use. The requirements in this part are intended to ensure that finished devices will be safe and effective and otherwise in compliance with the Federal Food, Drug, and Cosmetic Act (the act). This part establishes basic requirements applicable to manufacturers of finished medical devices. If a manufacturer engages in only some operations subject to the requirements in this part, and not in others, that manufacturer need only comply with those requirements applicable to the operations in which it is engaged. With respect to class I devices, design controls apply only to those devices listed in Sec. 820.30(a)(2). This regulation does not apply to manufacturers of components or parts of finished devices, but such manufacturers are encouraged to use appropriate provisions of this regulation as guidance. Manufacturers of human blood and blood components are not subject to this part, but are subject to part 606 of this chapter.

(2) The provisions of this part shall be applicable to any finished device as defined in this part, intended for human use that is manufactured, imported, or offered for import in any State or Territory of the United States, the District of Columbia, or the Commonwealth of Puerto Rico.

(3) In this regulation the term "where appropriate" is used several times. When a requirement is qualified by "where appropriate," it is deemed

1. The text in this section is quoted directly from the Quality System Regulation (QSReg).

to be "appropriate" unless the manufacturer can document justification otherwise. A requirement is "appropriate" if non-implementation could reasonably be expected to result in the product not meeting its specified requirements or the manufacturer not being able to carry out any necessary corrective action.

§ 820.1(b) ***Limitations.*** The quality system regulation in this part supplements regulations in other parts of this chapter except where explicitly stated otherwise. In the event that it is impossible to comply with all applicable regulations, both in this part and in other parts of this chapter, the regulations specifically applicable to the device in question shall supersede any other generally applicable requirements.

§ 820.1(c) ***Authority.*** Part 820 is established and issued under authority of sections 501, 502, 510, 513, 514, 515, 518, 519, 520, 522, 701, 704, 801, 803 of the act (21 U.S.C. 351, 352, 360, 360c, 360d, 360e, 360h, 360i, 360j, 360l, 371, 374, 381, 383). The failure to comply with any applicable provision in this part renders a device adulterated under section 501(h) of the act. Such a device, as well as any person responsible for the failure to comply, is subject to regulatory action.

§ 820.1(d) ***Foreign manufacturers.*** If a manufacturer who offers devices for import into the United States refuses to permit or allow the completion of a Food and Drug Administration (FDA) inspection of the foreign facility for the purpose of determining compliance with this part, it shall appear for purposes of section 801(a) of the act, that the methods used in, and the facilities and controls used for, the design, manufacture, packaging, labeling, storage, installation, or servicing of any devices produced at such facility that are offered for import into the United States do not conform to the requirements of section 520(f) of the act and this part and that the devices manufactured at that facility are adulterated under section 501(h) of the act.

§ 820.1(e) ***Exemptions or variances.***

(1) Any person who wishes to petition for an exemption or variance from any device quality system requirement is subject to the requirements of section 520(f)(2) of the act. Petitions for an exemption or variance shall be submitted according to the procedures set forth in Sec. 10.30 of this chapter, the FDA's administrative procedures. Guidance is available from the Center for Devices and Radiological Health, Division of Small Manufacturers Assistance, (HFZ-220), 1350 Piccard Dr., Rockville, MD 20850, U.S.A., telephone 1-800-638-2041 or 1-301-443-6597, FAX 301-443-8818.

(2) FDA may initiate and grant a variance from any device quality system requirement when the agency determines that such variance is in the best interest of the public health. Such variance will remain in effect only so long as there remains a public health need for the device and the device would not likely be made sufficiently available without the variance.

AAMI/ANSI/ISO 13485:2003[2]

Reference § 1 Scope

§ 1.1 General

This subclause describes the QMS as a collection of interacting processes (that is, uses the process approach) and states the two basic objectives of the Standard:

- To set out the requirements for a QMS that maximizes the probability that medical devices produced by the organization will meet customer and regulatory requirements
- To serve as a model for regulation of medical device organization QMSs around the world

The Standard is based on the requirements set out in ISO 9001, but it stands independently in that it contains only those requirements consistent with regulatory objectives. Certification of a QMS's compliance with ISO 9001 alone will not serve as certification of the compliance of that QMS with the requirements of the ISO 13485:2003 Standard.

Reference § 1.2 Application

The requirements of the Standard apply to medical device organizations of all types and sizes. The following exclusions are permitted:

- If regulatory requirements in the countries in which the organization's devices are manufactured and/or sold permit the exclusion of design control requirements, then design controls included in the Standard may be excluded from the organization's QMS, even though design and development are performed within the organization
- If the organization does not perform certain product realization activities covered within clause 7 of the Standard because those activities are not relevant to the medical device provided by the organization, then the organization may exclude requirements related to those activities from its QMS

If the product realization activities are relevant to the medical device provided by the organization but are being performed by suppliers outside the organization, the organization's QMS must describe the nature and kinds of control being exerted to ensure that the resulting medical devices meet specifications.

---

2. The text in this section explains the requirements content of the Standard section but does not quote those requirements directly. The text focuses on the differences and agreements between the content of this section and the comparable section in the QSReg.

FDA Guidance[3]

QSReg Preamble

Comment group 1. The title of the regulation, . . . has been changed from the "Current Good Manufacturing Practices (CGMP)" regulation to the "Quality System" regulation. This revision follows the suggestion underlying many comments on specific provisions that FDA generally harmonize the CGMP requirements and terminology with international standards. ISO 9001:1994, ISO/CD 13485, and EN 46001 employ this terminology to describe the CGMP requirements. In addition, this title accurately describes the sum of the requirements, which now include the CGMP requirements for design, purchasing, and servicing controls. CGMP requirements now cover a full quality system.

FDA notes that the principles embodied in this quality system regulation have been accepted worldwide as a means of ensuring that acceptable products are produced. . . .

FDA, however, did not adopt ISO 9001:1994 verbatim. . . . FDA along with health agencies of other governments does not believe that for medical devices ISO 9001:1994 alone is sufficient to adequately protect the public health. . . . FDA has worked closely with the GHTF and TC 210 to develop a regulation which is consistent with both ISO 9001:1994 and ISO/CD 13485. FDA made several suggestions to TC 210 on the drafts of the ISO/CD 13485 document in order to minimize differences and move closer to harmonization. In some cases, FDA has explicitly stated requirements that many experts believe are inherent in ISO 9001:1994. Through the many years of experience enforcing and evaluating compliance with the original CGMP regulation, FDA has found that it is necessary to clearly spell out its expectations. This difference in approach does not represent any fundamentally different requirements that would hinder global harmonization. . . .

Comment group 2. One comment suggested that the term "purchasing" in the scope be deleted because it could be interpreted to mean the purchase of finished medical devices by health care institutions and medical professionals, instead of the purchase of components and manufacturing materials as intended.

FDA agrees and has deleted the term "purchasing" throughout the regulation when used in this context.

Comment group 3. . . . The quality system regulation provides a framework of basic requirements for each manufacturer to use in establishing a qual-

3. The graphic rules in this section denote text that is excerpted directly from the preamble to the QSReg or the indicated FDA guidance document.

ity system appropriate to the devices designed and manufactured and the manufacturing processes employed. Manufacturers must adopt current and effective methods and procedures for each device they design and manufacture to comply with and implement the basic requirements. The regulation provides the flexibility necessary to allow manufacturers to adopt advances in technology, as well as new manufacturing and quality system procedures, as they become available.

During inspections, FDA will assess whether a manufacturer has established procedures and followed requirements that are appropriate to a given device under the current state-of-the-art manufacturing for that specific device. . . .

Comment group 4. . . . FDA has retained the concept of distinguishing between devices for the traceability requirements in Sec. 820.65. As addressed in the discussion under that section, FDA believes that it is imperative that manufacturers be able to trace, by control number, any device, or where appropriate component of a device, that is intended for surgical implant into the body or to support or sustain life whose failure to perform when properly used in accordance with instructions for use provided in the labeling can be reasonably expected to result in a significant injury to the user.

The deletion of the terminology [critical device] will bring the regulation in closer harmony with ISO 9001:1994 and the quality system standards or requirements of other countries.

Finally, FDA notes that eliminating the term "critical device" and the list of critical devices does not result in the imposition of new requirements. In fact the new regulation is less prescriptive and gives the manufacturer the flexibility to determine the controls that are necessary commensurate with risk. The burden is on the manufacturer, however, to describe the types and degree of controls and how those controls were decided upon. Such determinations are made in accordance with standard operating procedures (SOP's) established by the manufacturer.

Comment group 5. . . . FDA has added the sentence, "If a person engages in only some operations subject to the requirements in this part, and not in others, that person need only comply with those requirements applicable to the operations in which he or she is engaged." This sentence was added to clarify the scope of the regulation and the responsibility of those who fall under this regulation. The wording is the same as that used in the drug CGMP.

Comment group 6. . . . FDA has experienced problems or has concerns with the class I devices listed and has determined that design controls are needed for the listed devices. Further, placing the list in the regulation establishes the requirements related to those devices, and is convenient for use by persons who are not familiar with, or who do not have access to, the preamble. Further, FDA notes that individual sections of a regulation may be revised independent of the remainder of the regulation.

Comment group 7. . . . FDA believes that because of the complexity of many components used in medical devices, their adequacy cannot always be assured through inspection and testing at the finished device manufacturer. This is especially true of software and software-related components, such as microprocessors and microcircuits. Quality must be designed and built into components through the application of proper quality systems.

However, FDA notes that the quality system regulation now explicitly requires that the finished device manufacturer assess the capability of suppliers, contractors, and consultants to provide quality products pursuant to Sec. 820.50 Purchasing controls. These requirements supplement the acceptance requirements under Sec. 820.80.

Manufacturers must comply with both sections for any incoming component or subassembly or service, regardless of the finished device manufacturer's financial or business affiliation with the person providing such products or services. FDA believes that these purchasing controls are sufficient to provide the needed assurance that suppliers, contractors, and consultants have adequate controls to produce acceptable components.

. . . FDA will continue to focus its inspections on finished device manufacturers and expects that such manufacturers will properly ensure that the components they purchase are safe and effective. Finished device manufacturers who fail to comply with Secs. 820.50 and 820.80 will be subject to enforcement action. FDA notes that the legal authority exists to cover component manufacturers under the CGMP regulation should the need arise.

Comment group 8. . . . Sec. 820.1(a)(2) . . . include[s] the District of Columbia and the Commonwealth of Puerto Rico, as in the original CGMP regulation. . . .

Comment group 10. . . . The consequences of the failure to comply, and the legal authority under which regulatory action may be taken, are included in the regulation [820.1(c)] so that the public may be fully apprised of the possible consequences of noncompliance and understand the importance of compliance. FDA notes that the agency exercises discretion when deciding whether to pursue a regulatory action and does not take enforcement action for every violation it encounters. Further, FDA generally provides manufacturers with warning prior to initiating regulatory action and encourages voluntary compliance. The agency also notes, however, that violations of this regulation need not be intentional to place the public at serious risk or for FDA to take regulatory action for such violations. . . .

Comment group 11. . . . FDA has moved the provision related to foreign manufacturers into a separate section and has modified the language. The language in the regulation reflects the language in section 801(a) of the act (21 U.S.C. 381(a)). . . . The agency believes that it is imperative that foreign facilities be inspected for compliance with this regulation and that they be held to the same high standards to which U.S. manufacturers are held. . . .

FDA intends to continue scheduling inspections of foreign manufacturers in advance to assure their availability and avoid conflicts with holidays and shut down periods. However, the language pertaining to the "scheduling" of such inspections has been deleted to allow flexibility in scheduling methods.

FDA disagrees that, as written, the language would prohibit inspections by third parties. FDA may use third party inspections, as it uses other compliance information, in setting its priorities and utilizing its resources related to foreign inspections. In this regard, FDA looks forward to entering into agreements with foreign countries related to CGMP inspections that would provide FDA with reliable inspectional information.

Comment group 12. . . . Currently, FDA is required by section 520(f)(2)(B) of the act to respond within 60 days of receipt of the petition [for exemption or waiver], unless the petition is referred to an advisory committee.

. . . Over the past 18 years, since the CGMP regulation first became effective, FDA has only received approximately 75 petitions. It is FDA's opinion that few petitions have been received because of the flexible nature of the CGMP regulation. FDA has attempted to write the current regulation with at least the same degree of flexibility, if not more, to allow manufacturers to design a quality system that is appropriate for their devices and operations and that is not overly burdensome.

Guidelines for the submission of petitions for exemption or variance are available from the Division of Small Manufacturers Assistance (the DSMA). The petition guidelines state that FDA will not process a petition for exemption or variance while an FDA inspection of a manufacturer is ongoing. Until FDA has approved a petition for an exemption or variance, a manufacturer should not deviate from the requirements of this regulation. FDA must first have the opportunity to ensure that the manufacturer has established that an exemption or variance is warranted, to carry out its obligation of ensuring that devices are safe and effective.

Comment group 13. . . . The regulation provides the "basic" requirements for the design and manufacture of medical devices. . . . the requirements are written in general terms to allow manufacturers to establish procedures appropriate for their devices and operations.

Also, . . . , a manufacturer need only comply with those requirements applicable to the operations in which he or she is engaged. However, because the regulation requirements are basic, they will apply in total to most manufacturers subject to the regulation. The extent of the documentation necessary to meet the regulation requirements may vary with the complexity of the design and manufacturing operations, the size of the firm, the importance of a process, and the risk associated with the failure of the device, among other factors. Small manufacturers may design acceptable quality systems that require a minimum of documentation and, where possible, may automate documentation. In many situations, documentation may be kept at a minimum by combining many of the recordkeeping requirements of the regulation, for example, the production SOP's, handling, and storage procedures. When manufacturers believe that the requirements are not necessary for their operations, they may petition for an exemption or variance from all or part of the regulation pursuant to section 520(f)(2) of the act.

In addition, FDA has added a variance provision in Sec. 820.1(e)(2) under which the agency can initiate a variance when it is in the best interest of the public health. Under this provision, for instance, the agency may initiate and grant a variance to manufacturers of devices during times of product shortages, where the devices are needed by the public and may not otherwise be made available, if such manufacturers can adequately assure that the resulting devices are safe and effective. The agency envisions this provision as a bridge, providing a manufacturer with the time necessary to fulfill the requirements in the regulation while providing important and needed devices to the public. Thus, the variance would only be granted for a short period of time, and only while the devices remained necessary and in short supply. Under this provision, FDA will require a manufacturer to submit a plan detailing the action it is taking to assure the safety and effectiveness of the devices it manufactures and to meet the requirements of the regulation. . . .

"Guideline for the Manufacture of In Vitro Diagnostic Products," January 10, 1994

A copy of this guidance document may be found at http://www.fda.gov/cdrh/comp/918.pdf.

This guideline is applicable to manufacturers of all in vitro diagnostic reagents and systems, but is not intended to apply to manufacturers of IVD instrumentation. As such, this guideline applies to clinical chemistry and clinical toxicology devices, hematology and pathology devices, and immunology and microbiology devices.

This guideline provides general guidance on the application of the medical device good manufacturing practice (GMP) regulation, 21 CFR Part 820, to processes commonly used in the manufacture of IVDs. It includes methods and procedures for meeting requirements of the medical device GMP regulation. . . . This guideline will be used as a reference by FDA investigators during GMP inspections of manufacturer's facilities. When manufacturers elect not to rely upon this guideline, FDA expects that their choice of procedures and processes will be equivalent to ensure the safety and effectiveness of their IVDs.

This guideline has been issued to address several areas concerning the application of the GMP regulation to IVDs. Foremost, the guideline will assist IVD manufacturers in complying with the GMP regulation and also help ensure uniform application of the GMP regulation by FDA. It is understood that this guideline is an attempt to reduce instances of failure to comply with the GMP regulation as reflected in FDA's experience with legal actions, recalls, results of GMP inspections, and data from the Center for Devices and Radiological Health (CDRH) Device Experience Network (DEN). . . .

This guidance document is supported by the FDA Office of IVD Devices Evaluation and Safety. While it was issued in 1994, there is no indication that it has been amended or withdrawn.

The document addresses a number of issues that have special relevance to the manufacture of IVD reagents and other "noninstrument" devices:

- Product and process specifications
- Process validation
- Production and process controls
  - —Sterilization and microbiological reduction techniques
  - —Lyophilization
  - —Filtration
  - —Filling processes
- Environmental control
  - —Airborne and other contamination
  - —Air pressure
  - —Filtration
- Personnel attire
- Cleaning and sanitation
- Components
- Finished IVD inspection and testing
- Stability studies and expiration dating
- Complaints and failure investigations
- Trend analysis

Appendix I in this guidance document contains a listing of reference documents that relate to IVD reagent quality system processes.

AAMI/ANSI/ISO TR 14969:2004[4]

Reference § 1 Scope

§ 1.1 General

The Technical Report (TR) is intended to provide guidance in the application of the requirements of the ISO 13485:2003 Standard. It does not add to these requirements. Guidance contained in the TR is also not intended to be used for QMS certification purposes.

The term "should" is intended as guidance indicating a recommended approach that does not exclude other approaches. The terms "can" and "might" are intended as guidance to indicate possible alternative approaches, with no recommendation intended.

4. The text in this section explains the guidance content of the TR section without quoting it directly. The text focuses on the differences between the content of this section and the comparable section in the QSReg preamble.

Reference § 1.2 Application
§ 1.2.1 General

The TR strongly recommends that if any of the product realization activities (see text related to QSReg § 820.5) are excluded from the QMS, the justification for the exclusion should be explained in the organization's Quality Manual.

Reference § 1.2.2 Exclusions

The regulatory exclusion of design controls is to be taken independently of the exclusion of the requirements for other product realization activities. This design control exclusion is both product and market dependent.

Reference § 1.2.3 Non-applicability

The TR illustrates the non-applicability of product realization controls by outlining a number of examples (for example, the non-applicability of sterile handling requirements for products intended to be provided nonsterile, or the non-applicability of installation and servicing requirements for single-use devices).

Reference § 1.2.4 Example

The TR provides another, more detailed example related to the exclusion of design controls. In this example, it is not relevant that the organization outsources the design and development if the regulations do not provide the exclusion for the specific product involved.

Authors' Notes

The TR discusses at length the process approach and its objective of ensuring that activities conducted within the QMS are targeted at meeting customer requirements, including regulatory requirements. The TR embraces the concept of "Plan, Do, Check, Act."

It is important to keep in mind that the organization still has the responsibility to plan for those product realization activities that remain after the appropriate ones are excluded.

FDA Quality System Regulation—1996

§ 820.3 Definitions

(a) **Act** means the Federal Food, Drug, and Cosmetic Act, as amended (secs. 201–903, 52 Stat. 1040 et seq., as amended (21 U.S.C. 321–394)). All definitions in section 201 of the act shall apply to the regulations in this part.

(b) **Complaint** means any written, electronic, or oral communication that alleges deficiencies related to the identity, quality, durability, reliability, safety, effectiveness, or performance of a device after it is released for distribution.

(c) **Component** means any raw material, substance, piece, part, software, firmware, labeling, or assembly which is intended to be included as part of the finished, packaged, and labeled device.

(d) **Control number** means any distinctive symbols, such as a distinctive combination of letters or numbers, or both, from which the history of the manufacturing, packaging, labeling, and distribution of a unit, lot, or batch of finished devices can be determined.

(e) **Design history file (DHF)** means a compilation of records which describes the design history of a finished device.

(f) **Design input** means the physical and performance requirements of a device that are used as a basis for device design.

(g) **Design output** means the results of a design effort at each design phase and at the end of the total design effort. The finished design output is the basis for the device master record. The total finished design output consists of the device, its packaging and labeling, and the device master record.

(h) **Design review** means a documented, comprehensive, systematic examination of a design to evaluate the adequacy of the design requirements, to evaluate the capability of the design to meet these requirements, and to identify problems.

(i) **Device history record (DHR)** means a compilation of records containing the production history of a finished device.

(j) **Device master record (DMR)** means a compilation of records containing the procedures and specifications for a finished device.

(k) **Establish** means define, document (in writing or electronically), and implement.

(l) **Finished device** means any device or accessory to any device that is suitable for use or capable of functioning, whether or not it is packaged, labeled, or sterilized.

(m) **Lot** or **batch** means one or more components or finished devices that consist of a single type, model, class, size, composition, or software version that are manufactured under essentially the same conditions and that are intended to have uniform characteristics and quality within specified limits.

(n) **Management with executive responsibility** means those senior employees of a manufacturer who have the authority to establish or make changes to the manufacturer's quality policy and quality system.

(o) **Manufacturer** means any person who designs, manufactures, fabricates, assembles, or processes a finished device. Manufacturer includes but is not limited to those who perform the functions of contract sterilization, installation, relabeling, remanufacturing, repacking, or specification development, and initial distributors of foreign entities performing these functions.

(p) **Manufacturing material** means any material or substance used in or used to facilitate the manufacturing process, a concomitant constituent, or a byproduct constituent produced during the manufacturing process, which is present in or on the finished device as a residue or impurity not by design or intent of the manufacturer.

(q) **Nonconformity** means the no-fulfillment of a specified requirement.

(r) **Product** means components, manufacturing materials, in-process devices, finished devices, and returned devices.

(s) **Quality** means the totality of features and characteristics that bear on the ability of a device to satisfy fitness-for-use, including safety and performance.

(t) **Quality audit** means a systematic, independent examination of a manufacturer's quality system that is performed at defined intervals and at sufficient frequency to determine whether both quality system activities and the results of such activities comply with quality system procedures, that these procedures are implemented effectively, and that these procedures are suitable to achieve quality system objectives.

(u) **Quality policy** means the overall intentions and direction of an organization with respect to quality, as established by management with executive responsibility.

(v) **Quality system** means the organizational structure, responsibilities, procedures, processes, and resources for implementing quality management.

(w) **Remanufacturer** means any person who processes, conditions, renovates, repackages, restores, or does any other act to a finished device that significantly changes the finished device's performance or safety specifications, or intended use.

(x) **Rework** means action taken on a nonconforming product so that it will fulfill the specified DMR requirements before it is released for distribution.

(y) **Specification** means any requirement with which a product, process, service, or other activity must conform.

(z) **Validation** means confirmation by examination and provision of objective evidence that the particular requirements for a specific intended use can be consistently fulfilled.

  (1) **Process validation** means establishing by objective evidence that a process consistently produces a result or product meeting its predetermined specifications.

  (2) **Design validation** means establishing by objective evidence that device specifications conform to user needs and intended use(s).

(aa) **Verification** means confirmation by examination and provision of objective evidence that specified requirements have been fulfilled.

U.S. Federal Food, Drug, and Cosmetic Act

§ 201(h) Device

The term "device" . . . means an instrument, apparatus, implement, machine, contrivance, implant, in vitro reagent, or other similar or related article, including any component, part, or accessory, which is—

(1) Recognized in the official National Formulary, or the United States Pharmacopeia, or any supplement to them,
(2) Intended for use in the diagnosis of disease or other conditions, or in the cure, mitigation, treatment, or prevention of disease, in man or other animals, or
(3) Intended to affect the structure or any function of the body of man or other animals, and which does not achieve any of its principal intended purposes through chemical action within or on the body of man or other animals and which is not dependent upon being metabolized for the achievement of any of its principal intended purposes.

AAMI/ANSI/ISO 13485:2003

Reference § 3 Terms and definitions

In general, there are no significant differences among the lists of definitions in the QSReg and the relevant U.S. statutes and the Standard.

One difference is in the use of the term "organization" in the Standard. This term is equivalent to the term "manufacturer" in the QSReg. It is the unit to which the Standard applies.

The regulatory definition of "complaint" or "customer complaint" is a bit broader than the one in the Standard in that the QSReg applies the term to a product that has been released for distribution as well as a product that has been delivered to customers. That means that the product that is still within the manufacturer's control can be involved in complaint handling activities, even if no lots of the product or only certain lots of the product have actually reached the customer.

The Standard definition of "active implantable device" explicitly includes a device "intended to replace an epithelial surface or the surface of the eye."

The QSReg defines the term "establish" to include the activities of "define, document, and implement." The Standard does not include such a definition.

Reference § 3.7 Medical device

There is no significant difference between the definition of "device" in the Statute and the definition of "medical device" in the Standard.

Reference § 3.8 Sterile medical device

The Standard defines a sterile medical device as one that meets the requirements for sterility, and suggests that the requirements for sterility may be found in national or regional regulations.

FDA Guidance

QSReg Preamble

Note: References in the preamble to international quality system standards are to the then-existing versions of those standards. In most cases these references are still current, but it would be wise to confirm that fact, if these references are being used to establish or revise a QMS.

DEFINITIONS

Comment group 14. . . . a communication would be considered a "complaint" only if the communication alleged some deficiency related to the identity, quality, durability, reliability, safety, effectiveness, or performance of the device after it is released for distribution. The definition is now very similar to the definition used in ISO/CD 13485.

The regulation addresses service requests and in-house indications of dissatisfaction under Sec. 820.100 Corrective and preventive action. This section requires manufacturers to establish procedures to identify quality problems and process the information received to detect and correct quality problems. Information generated in-house relating to quality problems should be documented and processed as part of this corrective and preventive action program.

With respect to service requests, Sec. 820.200 Servicing states that a service report that represents an event which must be reported to the FDA under part 803 or 804 (21 CFR part 803 or 804) shall automatically be considered a complaint. All other service reports must be analyzed for trends or systemic problems and when found, these trends or systemic problems must be investigated according to the provisions of Sec. 820.100 Corrective and preventive action.

Comment group 15. . . . FDA . . . has deleted the words "used during device manufacturing" from the definition [of component] because it was not intended to differentiate between distributors and manufacturers. Further, FDA deleted the term "packaging" to clarify that every piece of packaging is not necessarily a component. Only the materials that are part of the "finished, packaged, and labeled device" are considered to be components.

Comment group 16. . . . The control number is the means by which the history of the device, from purchase of components and materials through distribution, may be traced, where traceability is required. The definition does not require that a manufacturer be able to trace the device whenever control numbers are used. In fact, the definition itself does not establish any requirements. The agency notes, however, that the manufacturer's traceability procedures should ensure that a complete history of the device, including environmental conditions which could cause the device to fail to conform to its specified requirements, can be traced and should facilitate investigation of quality problems and corrective action. FDA notes, however, that the level of detail required for this history is dependent on the nature of the device, its intended use, and its complexity. . . .

FDA has also amended the definition for added flexibility, to state that symbols may be used and has included the term "unit" for any device that is not manufactured as a lot or batch.

Comment group 18. . . . FDA . . . require[s] that the [design history] file describe the design history, as it may not be necessary to maintain a record of every step in the design phase, although the "entire history" should be apparent from the document. Section 820.30(j) further delineates what should be in the design history file (the DHF), specifically records sufficient to verify that the design was developed in accordance with the design and development plan and other applicable design requirements of the regulation. . . .

Comment group 19. . . . The term "requirement" [as used in the definition of design input] is meant in the broadest sense, to encompass any internally or externally imposed requirements such as safety, customer-related, and regulatory requirements. All of these requirements must be considered as design inputs. How these requirements are handled and dealt with is up to the manufacturer.

Comment group 20. . . . FDA . . . has not deleted the phrase "results of a design effort at each design phase and at the end" from the definition. The intent was not to dictate when design phases would occur. Such phases will be defined in the design and development plan. For example, a manufacturer may only have a few design phases for a new type of syringe. Thus, design output would be the results of those few efforts. The results of each design phase constitute the total design output. The definition has been amended, however, to clarify that the finished design output is the basis for the DMR.

FDA disagrees . . . that the design output should be restricted to physical characteristics of the device. Design output is more than just the device specifications. Design output includes, among other things, the specifications for the manufacturing process, the quality assurance testing, and the device labeling and packaging. It is important to note that the design effort should not only control the design aspects of the device during the original development phase, but also all subsequent design and development activities including any redesign or design changes after the original design is transferred to production.

Comment group 21. . . . FDA agrees that the design review participants are typically not responsible for establishing solutions, although they may do so in many small operations. . . . FDA wants to make clear that although the design review participants need not propose solutions, they should ensure that solutions to any identified problems are adequate and implemented appropriately.

Regarding the scope of design review, each design review need not be "comprehensive" for the entire design process but must be "comprehensive" for the design phase being reviewed. However, at the end of the design process when the design is transferred to production, all aspects of the design process should have been reviewed. . . .

Comment group 22. . . . FDA . . . has amended the definition to be consistent with the requirements set forth in Sec. 820.181. . . . the DMR requirements in Sec. 820.181 state that the DMR "shall include or refer to the location of" the required information. . . .

Comment group 24. . . . The term "establish" is only used where documentation is necessary. FDA also notes that the quality system regulation is premised on the theory that adequate written procedures, which are implemented appropriately, will likely ensure the safety and effectiveness of the device. ISO 9001:1994 relies on the same premise. The 1994 version of ISO 9001 broadly requires the manufacturer to "establish, document, and maintain a quality system," which includes documenting procedures to meet the requirements.

The definition has been amended, however, in response to general comments received, to clarify that a "document" may be in writing or on electronic media, to allow flexibility for any type of recorded media.

Comment group 25. . . . The agency had intended the new definition to make explicit the application of the regulation to the manufacture of sterile devices that have yet to be sterilized. . . .

To better clarify its intent, FDA has amended the definition to add that all devices that are capable of functioning, including those devices that could be used even though they are not yet in their final form, are "finished devices." For example, devices that have been manufactured or assembled, and need only to be sterilized, polished, inspected and tested, or packaged or labeled by a purchaser/manufacturer are clearly not components, but are now in a condition in which they could be used, therefore meeting the definition of "finished device."

The distinction between "components" and "finished devices" was not intended to permit manufacturers to manufacture devices without complying with CGMP requirements by claiming that other functions, such as sterilization, incoming inspection (where sold for subsequent minor polishing, sterilization, or packaging), or insertion of software, will take place. The public would not be adequately protected in such cases if a manufacturer could claim that a device was not a "finished" device subject to the CGMP regulation because it was not in its "final" form.

. . . it is not necessary for a device to be in commercial distribution to be considered a finished device. . . . FDA notes that the term "accessory" is described in Sec. 807.20(a)(5) (21 CFR 807.20(a)(5)).

Comment group 26. . . . FDA has modified the definition [of lot or batch] to make clear that a lot or batch may, depending on circumstances, be comprised of one finished device. Whether for inspection or for distribution, a lot or batch is determined by the factors set forth in the definition; of course, a manufacturer may determine the size of the lot or batch, as appropriate.

Comment group 27. . . . FDA . . . has modified the definition [of executive management] by deleting the second half, which appeared to bring executive authority and responsibility too far down the organization chart. The term was intended to apply only to management that has the authority to bring about change in the quality system and the management of the quality system. Although such management would clearly have authority over, for example, distribution, those who may have delegated management authority over distribution would not necessarily have authority over the quality system and quality policy. Accordingly, the definition has been modified to include only those who have the authority and responsibility to establish and make changes to the quality policy and quality system. . . . In addition, the term "executive management" has been changed to "management with executive responsibility," to harmonize with ISO 9001:1994.

Comment group 28. . . . FDA's Compliance Policy Guide (CPG) 7124.28 contains the agency's policy regarding the provisions of the act and regulations with which persons who recondition or rebuild used devices are expected to comply. This CPG is in the process of being revised in light of FDA's experience in this area. FDA is not including the terms "servicer" or "refurbisher," as they relate to entities outside the control of the original equipment manufacturer, in this final regulation, even though it believes that persons who perform such functions meet the definition of manufacturer. Because of a number of competitive and other issues, including sharply divided views by members of the GMP Advisory Committee at the September 1995 meeting, FDA has elected to address application of the CGMP requirements to persons who perform servicing and refurbishing functions outside the control of the original manufacturer in a separate rulemaking later this year, with another opportunity for public comment.

FDA agrees that the term "remanufacturing" should be added to the definition of "manufacturer" and has separately defined the term. A remanufacturer is defined as "any person who processes, conditions, renovates, repackages, restores, or does any other act to a finished device that significantly changes the finished device's performance or safety specifications, or intended use."

However, FDA disagrees that contract sterilizers, installers, specification developers, repackagers, relabelers, and initial distributors should be deleted from the definition, primarily because all such persons may have a significant effect on the safety and effectiveness of a device and on the public health. All persons who perform these functions meet the definition of manufacturer, and therefore should be inspected to ensure that they are complying with the applicable provisions. For example, a specification developer initiates the design requirements for a device that is manufactured by a second party for subsequent commercial distribution. Such a developer is subject to design controls. Further, those that perform the functions of contract sterilization, installation, relabeling, remanufacturing, and repacking have routinely been considered to be manufacturers under the original CGMP definition, and the agency has treated them as such by inspecting them to ensure that they comply with the appropriate portions of the original CGMP. By explicitly including them in the definition of "manufacturer" the agency has simply codified its longstanding policy and interpretation of the original regulation.

The phrase "processes a finished device" applies to a finished device after distribution. Again, this phrase has been part of the CGMP regulation definition of "manufacturer" for 18 years.

Comment group 29. . . . depending on the manufacturing material and the device, the degree of control that is needed will vary. . . . the regulation requires manufacturers to assess, assure acceptability of, and control manufacturing materials to the degree necessary to meet the specified requirements. The agency notes that international standards such as ISO 8402:1994 include manufacturing material in their definition of "product," to which all requirements apply, and notes that FDA has added the same definition in Sec. 820.3(r) in its effort toward harmonization.

FDA amended the definition of manufacturing material to read "a concomitant constituent, or a byproduct constituent produced during the manufacturing process" to help clarify this definition. These terms refer to those materials or substances that naturally occur as a part of the material or during the manufacturing process which are intended to be removed or reduced in the finished device. For example, some components, such as natural rubber latex, contain allergenic proteins that must be reduced or removed from the finished devices. The definition has been modified to include "concomitant constituents" to clarify the meaning.

. . . FDA notes that cleaning agents, mold release agents, lubricating oils, latex proteins, and sterilant residues are just some examples of manufacturing materials.

Comment group 30. . . . the definition from ISO 8402:1994 for "nonconformity" was added to ensure that the requirements in the regulation, especially those in Secs. 820.90 Nonconforming product and 820.100 Corrective and preventive action are understood. FDA emphasizes that a "nonconformity" may not always rise to the level of a product defect or failure, but a product defect or failure will typically constitute a nonconformity.

Comment group 31. . . . FDA has added a definition of "product" to conform to the definition in ISO 8402:1994 and to avoid the necessity of repeating the individual terms throughout the regulation. Whenever a requirement is not applicable to all types of product, the regulation specifically states the product(s) to which the requirement is applicable.

It should be noted that the regulation has acceptance requirements for incoming "product" and other requirements for "product," which by definition includes manufacturing materials. Manufacturing materials should be controlled in a manner that is commensurate with their risk as discussed above. However, for manufacturing materials that are "concomitant constituents," FDA realizes that incoming acceptance, identification, etc., may not be feasible. The important control measure for "concomitant constituents" is the reduction or removal requirement found in Sec. 820.70(h).

Comment group 32. . . . FDA . . . believes that the definition [of quality] is closely harmonized to that in ISO 8402:1994. FDA believes that the definition appropriately defines quality in the context of a medical device and believes that the phrase from ISO 8402:1994, "stated and implied needs," has the same meaning as the phrase "fitness-for-use, including safety and performance" in the context of the Quality System regulation. Further, "quality" is not just "defined by the manufacturer" but is also defined by customer need and expectation.

Comment group 33. . . . while the quality audit is an audit of the "entire" quality system, audits may be conducted in phases, with some areas requiring more frequent audits than other areas, and that each audit need not review the whole system. The frequency of internal quality audits should be commensurate with, among other things, the importance of the activity, the difficulty of the activity to perform, and the problems found. To avoid any misunderstanding, the word "entire" before quality system has been deleted.

FDA emphasizes that if conducted properly, internal quality audits can prevent major problems from developing and provide a foundation for the management review required by Sec. 820.20(c), "Management review."

. . . On occasion, manufacturers have attempted to prevent FDA investigators from reviewing such quality assurance procedures and results (for example, trend analysis results) by stating that they are part of the internal quality audit report and not subject to review during a CGMP inspection. FDA disagrees with this position. To clarify which records are exempt from routine FDA inspection, FDA has added Sec. 820.180(c).

Comment group 34. . . . FDA agrees that all company personnel must follow the quality policy. However, the definition is intended to make clear that the quality policy must be established by top management. . . .

Comment group 36. . . . The definition of "record" was deleted because it seemed to add more confusion than clarity. The definition was intended to clarify that "records" may include more than the traditional hardcopy procedures and SOP's, for example, plans, notes, forms, data, etc. FDA was trying to clarify that "records" could be written, electronic, optical, etc., as long as they could be stored and controlled. FDA could not adopt the ISO 8402:1994 definition because of how the term "record" is used in the act, which is broader than the ISO definition. Therefore, FDA will allow the act and case law to continue to define the term.

Comment group 38. FDA added the definition of "remanufacturer" to codify FDA's longstanding policy and interpretation of the original CGMP. . . . FDA has always considered remanufacturers in fact to be manufacturers of a new device.

Comment group 39. . . . FDA . . . has changed the term [reprocessing/ refurbishing] to "rework," adopted the ISO 8402:1994 definition, and added that "rework" is performed according to specified DMR requirements before the device is released for distribution.

Comment group 40. . . . FDA notes . . . that servicing performed by manufacturers and remanufacturers is subject to the requirements in Sec. 820.200 Servicing. These requirements are a codification of longstanding interpretations of the original CGMP, Sec. 820.20(a)(3), and current agency policy.

Comment group 41. . . . FDA . . . modified the requirements of the regulation to reflect that, in many cases, testing and inspecting alone may be insufficient to prove the adequacy of a process. One of the principles on which the quality systems regulation is based is that all processes require some degree of qualification, verification, or validation, and manufacturers should not rely solely on inspection and testing to ensure processes are adequate for their intended uses.

Comment group 42. . . . FDA has amended the definition [of specification] to make clear that it applies to the requirements for a product, process, service, or other activity. . . . a specification can be developed for anything the manufacturer chooses. . . .

Comment group 43. . . . FDA has adopted the ISO 8402:1994 definition of validation. "Validation" is a step beyond verification to ensure the user needs and intended uses can be fulfilled on a consistent basis. FDA has further distinguished "process validation" from "design validation" to help clarify these two types of "validation." The "process validation" definition follows from FDA's "Guidelines on General Principles of Process Validation" (Ref. 10). The definition for "design validation" is consistent with the requirements contained in Sec. 820.30 Design controls.

The ISO 8402:1994 definition of "verification" has been adopted. "Verification" is confirmation by examination and provision of objective evidence that specified requirements for a particular device or activity at hand have been met.

"Guideline for the Manufacture of In Vitro Diagnostic Products," January 10, 1994

Appendix II in this guidance document contains a list of definitions specific to IVD reagent devices. While it was issued in 1994, there is no indication that it has been amended or withdrawn. A copy of this guidance document may be found at http://www.fda.gov/cdrh/comp/918.pdf.

Authors' Notes

There are no significant differences between the individual definitions contained in the lists of defined terms in the QSReg and those in the Standard. Refer to the "Authors' Notes" contained in the "at-a-glance comparison" in the introduction.

Among the more poorly understood QMS terms are "validation" and "verification." It is important to understand that both verification and validation are confirmatory activities—they confirm that what you believe to be a fact is actually a fact, or that what you believe the component dimensions or product performance to be is, in fact, the truth. They are not intended to be activities in which you characterize the performance of a component or product. Too many times organizations launch into design validation before they have fully characterized the performance of a product. As a result, the validation fails and has to be repeated, or shortcuts are taken that impair the value of the validation activity.

There is no definition of "sterile medical device" in either the Statute or the QSReg.

SUBPART B

Quality System Requirements

FDA Quality System Regulation—1996

§ 820.5 Quality system

Each manufacturer shall establish and maintain a quality system that is appropriate for the specific medical device(s) designed or manufactured, and that meets the requirements of this part.

AAMI/ANSI/ISO 13485:2003

Reference § 4 Quality management system
§ 4.1 General requirements

The Standard requires the establishment of a QMS that complies with the requirements of the Standard. The Standard focuses on the QMS being a collection of interrelated processes and includes requirements associated with their identification, sequence, interrelationships, and the monitoring of their effectiveness. The Standard also includes requirements associated with planning at the QMS level and the achievement of the planned results.

The Standard requires that when any process that can affect the product's conformity with requirements is outsourced, the QMS must have identified provisions for maintaining control over such processes.

FDA Guidance

QSReg Preamble

Comment group 44. Several comments . . . recommended that the quality system requirements be harmonized with international standards and focus on requiring that a system be established that is appropriate to the specific device and that meets the requirements of the regulation.

FDA agrees in part with the comments and has modified the language as generally suggested by several comments to require that the quality system be "appropriate for the specific medical device(s) designed or manufactured, and meets the requirements of this part." This is essentially the requirement of the original CGMP regulation with the added reference to design control.

. . . As previously noted, the quality system regulation is premised on the theory that the development, implementation, and maintenance of procedures designed to carry out the requirements will assure the safety and effectiveness of devices. Thus, the broad requirements in Sec. 820.5 are in a sense the foundation on which the remaining quality system requirements are built.

QUALITY SYSTEM

AAMI/ANSI/ISO TR 14969:2004

Reference § 4 Quality management system
§ 4.1 General requirements

The TR notes that processes such as internal and external audits of the QMS are useful in assessing the effectiveness of the QMS, and processes like management review, corrective actions, and preventive actions are useful in maintaining the continuing effectiveness of the QMS.

The TR lists a number of internal factors (for example, changes to product, personnel, facilities, and manufacturing and control processes) and external factors (for example, product-related adverse events, customer feedback, and changes to regulatory requirements) that can alter the effectiveness of the QMS. The TR also lists a number of continuing activities that can be used to track these factors, emphasizing that actions that result from these activities should be based on objective information and data.

Authors' Notes

The objectives of the QSReg and the Standard are the same. While both recognize that the QMS is a compilation of interrelated processes, the Standard provides a differently organized description of the process requirements of such a QMS.

The Standard divides the process requirements into five process areas related to:

- The QMS in general (for example, control of documents and records).
- Management of the QMS (for example, management commitment, customer focus, quality policy, quality planning, and organization).
- Resource management (for example, provision of resources, human resources, infrastructure, and work environment).
- Product realization. "Product realization" is a term coined by the drafters of ISO 9001:2000. While it is not defined anywhere in the international quality system standards, it includes those processes involved in:
  - —Understanding the requirements associated with the product supplied by the manufacturer.
  - —Procuring the products and services needed to supply the finished product to the customer.
  - —Designing and developing the product.
  - —Manufacturing the product.
  - —Controlling the monitoring and measurement equipment used in manufacturing the product.
- Measurement, analysis, and improvement (for example, handling nonconformities, handling customer feedback (including complaints), and employing corrective actions, preventive actions, and statistical techniques).

The Standard requires the establishment of a Quality Manual, which provides the overall description of the organization's QMS. While the QSReg doesn't require such a manual, it does require a listing of the documentation associated with the QMS. We suggest that the Quality Manual meet the requirements of both the QSReg and the Standard. We also suggest that the Manual be organized based on the structure of the Standard. Do not be surprised if an FDA investigator, upon determining that your organization is certified to the Standard, asks to see your organization's Quality Manual during an inspection. We recommend that the investigator be given the Manual to assist him or her in conducting an efficient inspection.

We have experienced the use of the Quality Manual in the United States as a sales aid for providing a potential customer with an overview of a company's QMS. Such use does not obligate the company to treat the Manual as a "controlled document," but if the Quality Manual is established as part of a QMS that is compliant with the Standard, then it will have to be controlled as other documentation is controlled.

FDA Quality System Regulation—1996

§ 820.20 Management responsibility

§ 820.20(a) *Quality policy.* Management with executive responsibility shall establish its policy and objectives for, and commitment to, quality. Management with executive responsibility shall ensure that the quality policy is understood, implemented, and maintained at all levels of the organization.

AAMI/ANSI/ISO 13485:2003

Reference § 5 Management responsibility
§ 5.2 Customer focus

The Standard requires top management to ensure that customer requirements are determined, understood, and met by the organization.

Reference § 5 Management responsibility
§ 5.3 Quality policy

The Standard contains no additional requirements related to the quality policy beyond those set out in the QSReg.

FDA Guidance

QSReg Preamble

Comment group 45. . . . [As it relates to the responsibility for establishing the quality policy] FDA has deleted the term "executive management" and replaced it with "management with executive responsibility," which is consistent with [the Standard's term "top management"]. Management with executive responsibility is that level of management that has the authority to establish and make changes to the company quality policy. The establishment of quality objectives, the translation of such objectives into actual methods and procedures, and the implementation of the quality system may be delegated. The regulation does not prohibit [such] delegation. However, it is the responsibility of the highest level of management to establish the quality policy and to ensure that it is followed. (See United States v. Dotterweich, 320 U.S. 277 (1943), and United States v. Park, 421 U.S. 658 (1975).)

. . . It is without question management's responsibility to undertake appropriate actions to ensure that employees understand management's policies and objectives. Understanding is a learning process achieved through training and reinforcement. Management reinforces understanding of policies and objectives by demonstrating a commitment to the quality system visibly and actively on a continuous basis. Such commitment can be demonstrated by providing adequate resources and training to support quality system development and implementation. In the interest of harmonization, the regulation has been amended to be very similar to [the Standard].

AAMI/ANSI/ISO TR 14969:2004

Reference § 5 Management responsibility
§ 5.2 Customer focus

The Standard requires top management to ensure that customer requirements are determined, understood, and met by the operations of the organization. Secs. 7.2 and 8.2.1 illustrate the processes for determining the relevant customer requirements.

Reference § 5 Management responsibility
§ 5.3 Quality policy

The TR reinforces the objective that the Standard describes a QMS that is intended to meet customer requirements (that is, considering the regulatory agency as one of the organization's customers) by suggesting that the quality policy explicitly reflect the policy to meet customer requirements.

The TR suggests that the quality policy reflect and be consistent with the organization's business policies, and it recommends that the quality policy be periodically reviewed when other policies are being reviewed to ensure that it remains consistent with the current goals and objectives of the organization.

The TR suggests a number of ways the organization can show its commitment to the quality policy (for example, publication and posting of signed copies of the policy, and group discussions of the policy with employees and customers) in addition to top management showing its commitment by its decisions and actions.

Authors' Notes

We strongly suggest that the organization's quality policy explicitly state a commitment "to consistently produce safe and effective medical devices" in addition to commitments to meet customer requirements and support a competitively successful and profitable business.

FDA Quality System Regulation—1996

§ 820.20(b) ***Organization.*** Each manufacturer shall establish and maintain an adequate organizational structure to ensure that devices are designed and produced in accordance with the requirements of this part.

§ 820.20(b)(1) ***Responsibility and authority.*** Each manufacturer shall establish the appropriate responsibility, authority, and interrelation of all personnel who manage, perform, and assess work affecting quality, and provide the independence and authority necessary to perform these tasks.

AAMI/ANSI/ISO 13485:2003

Reference § 5 Management responsibility
§ 5.5.1 Responsibility and authority

The Standard incorporates the requirement for an adequate organizational structure into its discussion of responsibility and authority.

The Standard includes a note alerting the reader to the probability that there will be national regulations that contain specific responsibilities and authorities related to certain jobs within the organization (for example, handling complaints and reporting to the regulatory agencies).

Reference § 5 Management responsibility
§ 5.5.3 Internal communication

The Standard requires top management to ensure that an effective communication process exists within the organization "regarding the effectiveness of the QMS."

FDA Guidance

QSReg Preamble

> **Comment group 46.** . . . FDA has retained the requirement for establishing an "adequate organizational structure" to ensure compliance with the regulation, because such an organizational structure is fundamental to a manufacturer's ability to produce safe and effective devices. The organizational structure should ensure that the technical, administrative, and human factors

functions affecting the quality of the device will be controlled, whether these functions involve hardware, software, processed materials, or services. All such controls should be oriented towards the reduction, elimination, or ideally, prevention of quality nonconformities. . . . The organizational structure established will be determined in part by the type of device produced, the manufacturer's organizational goals, and the expectations and needs of customers. What may be an "adequate" organizational structure for manufacturing a relatively simple device may not be "adequate" for the production of a more complex device, such as a defibrillator. . . .

Comment group 47. . . . FDA has retained the broad requirement that the necessary independence and authority be provided, as appropriate, to every function affecting quality. FDA emphasizes that it is crucial to the success of the quality system for the manufacturer to ensure that responsibility, authority, and organizational freedom (or independence) is provided to those who initiate action to prevent nonconformities, identify and document quality problems, initiate, recommend, provide, and verify solutions to quality problems, and direct or control further processing, delivery, or installation of nonconforming product.

Organizational freedom or independence does not necessarily require a stand-alone group, but responsibility, authority, and independence should be sufficient to attain the assigned quality objectives with the desired efficiency.

AAMI/ANSI/ISO TR 14969:2004

Reference § 5 Management responsibility
§ 5.5.1 Responsibility and authority

The TR suggests a number of mechanisms for documenting responsibilities and authorities within the QMS (for example, written position descriptions, documented procedures, and process maps).

Reference § 5 Management responsibility
§ 5.5.3 Internal communication

There should be active and open communications within all levels of the organization.

The information communicated should be clear and understandable to those personnel intended to use it. They should communicate top management's expectations regarding the nature of the QMS and the performance of and results from the QMS.

Examples of some communications mechanisms are posters and bulletin board postings, meetings, and memos. Where appropriate, rotation of personnel through various positions in the organization may help familiarize them with the needs of areas other than their own.

FDA Quality System Regulation—1996

§ 820.20(b)(2) ***Resources.*** Each manufacturer shall provide adequate resources, including the assignment of trained personnel, for management, performance of work, and assessment activities, including internal quality audits, to meet the requirements of this part.

AAMI/ANSI/ISO 13485:2003

Reference § 6 Resource management
§ 6.2 Human resources

The Standard states more explicitly than the QSReg the elements that describe "adequate" human resources by describing "competency" in terms of education, training, inherent skills, and experience.

In addition, the Standard outlines in § 6.2.2 the organization's responsibilities related to competency, awareness, and training (for example, determining competency requirements, establishing the actions needed to attain and ensure competency, and confirming the record-keeping requirements related to competency).

The Standard also addresses the need to make personnel aware of how their job performance can affect the organization's ability to meet its quality objectives.

A note in the Standard alerts the reader to the probability of national regulations related to determining training needs.

FDA Guidance

QSReg Preamble

Comment group 48. . . . Sec. 820.20(b)(2), "Resources," emphasizes that all resource needs must be provided for, including monetary, supplies, etc., as well as personnel resources. In contrast, Sec. 820.25(a) specifically addresses education, background, training, and experience requirements for personnel.

AAMI/ANSI/ISO TR 14969:2004

Reference § 6 Resource management
§ 6.2 Human resources

The TR points out that management review, corrective action, preventive action, and internal quality audit processes may provide input to human resource competency requirements.

Authors' Notes

Even though the guidance provided in the QSReg preamble states otherwise, § 820.20(b)(2) deals primarily with human resources and must be read in conjunction with the requirements described in § 820.25. Refer to the various subsections related to production and process control (§ 820.70) for discussions related to infrastructure resources.

FDA Quality System Regulation—1996

§ 820.20(b)(3) ***Management representative.*** Management with executive responsibility shall appoint, and document such appointment of, a member of management who, irrespective of other responsibilities, shall have established authority over and responsibility for:

(i) Ensuring that quality system requirements are effectively established and effectively maintained in accordance with this part; and
(ii) Reporting on the performance of the quality system to management with executive responsibility for review.

AAMI/ANSI/ISO 13485:2003

Reference § 5 Management responsibility
§ 5.5.2 Management representative

The Management Representative requirements in the QSReg and the Standard are the same, except that the Standard gives the Management Representative the additional responsibility of "promoting the awareness of regulatory and customer requirements throughout the organization."

Also, in a note, the Standard indicates that the Management Representative may be given QMS-related liaison responsibilities with external parties.

FDA Guidance

QSReg Preamble

Comment group 49. . . . The agency agrees that the responsibility need not be assigned to "executive" management and has modified the requirement to allow management with executive responsibility to appoint a member of management. When a member of management is appointed to this function, potential conflicts of interest should be examined to ensure that the effectiveness of the quality system is not compromised. . . . the requirement was amended to make clear that the appointment of [the management representative] must be documented. . . .

Comment group 50. . . . FDA notes . . . that information collected in complying with §§820.20(b)(3)(ii) and 820.100, Corrective and Preventive Action, should be used not only for detecting deficiencies and for subsequent correction of the deficiencies but also to improve the device and quality system.

AAMI/ANSI/ISO TR 14969:2004

Reference § 5 Management responsibility
§ 5.5.2 Management representative

The TR suggests that the Management Representative have the authority to delegate some of his or her Management Representative responsibilities.

Authors' Notes

One of the key jobs of the Management Representative is to ensure that top management fulfills its responsibilities related to the quality system. For example, the Management Representative may be responsible for developing the agendas for periodic and "special" management review meetings, riding herd on the timely completion of management review action items, and identifying situations where a member of top management may be showing less than satisfactory commitment to the quality policy or quality obligations and provide suggestions for improving the situation.

FDA Quality System Regulation—1996

§ 820.20(c) ***Management review.*** Management with executive responsibility shall review the suitability and effectiveness of the quality system at defined intervals and with sufficient frequency according to established procedures to ensure that the quality system satisfies the requirements of this part and the manufacturer's established quality policy and objectives. The dates and results of quality system reviews shall be documented.

AAMI/ANSI/ISO 13485:2003

Reference § 5 Management responsibility
§ 5.6 Management review
§ 5.6.1 General

There is no significant difference between the QSReg and the Standard in regard to the purpose of management reviews. The Standard explicitly includes in the management review purpose the discussion of opportunities for improvement and the need for changes in the QMS.

Reference § 5 Management responsibility
§ 5.6 Management review
§ 5.6.2 Review input

The Standard includes a prescriptive listing of items that shall be included as part of the management review (for example, output of internal QMS audits, customer feedback, and follow-up of action items from previous management reviews).

Reference § 5 Management responsibility
§ 5.6 Management review
§ 5.6.3 Review output

The Standard includes a prescriptive listing of several types of decisions and actions that may result from a management review (for example, actions to improve the effectiveness of the QMS, product or process improvements, and additional resource needs).

FDA Guidance

QSReg Preamble

Comment group 51. . . . FDA agrees that it will not request to inspect and copy the reports of reviews required by Sec. 820.20(c) when conducting routine inspections to determine compliance with this part. FDA believes that refraining from routinely reviewing these reports may help ensure that the audits are complete and candid and of maximum use to the manufacturer. However, FDA believes that it is important that the dates and results of quality system reviews be documented, and FDA may require that management with executive responsibility certify in writing that the manufacturer has complied with the requirements of Sec. 820.20(c). FDA will also review the written procedures required by Sec. 820.20(c), as well as all other records required under Sec. 820.20.

Comment group 52. . . . FDA believes that a manufacturer can establish procedures flexible enough for management to vary the way in which a review is conducted, as appropriate. Procedures should require that the review be conducted at appropriate intervals and should be designed to ensure that all parts of the quality system are adequately reviewed. A manufacturer may, of course, develop procedures that permit review of different areas at different times, so long as such reviews are sufficient to carry out the objectives of this section. If there are known problems, for example, a "sufficient frequency" may be fairly frequent. Further, because FDA will not be reviewing the results of such reviews, FDA must be assured that this function will occur in a consistent manner.

Comment group 53. . . . The purpose of the management reviews required by Sec. 820.20(c) is to determine if the manufacturer's quality policy and quality objectives are being met, and to ensure the continued suitability and effectiveness of the quality system. An evaluation of the findings of internal and supplier audits should be included in the Sec. 820.20(c) evaluation. The management review may include a review of the following: (1) The organizational structure, including the adequacy of staffing and resources; (2) the quality of the finished device in relation to the quality objectives; (3) combined information based on purchaser feedback, internal feedback (such as results of internal audits), process performance, product (including servicing) performance, among other things; and (4) internal audit results and corrective and preventive actions taken. Management reviews should include considerations for updating the quality system in relation to changes brought about by new technologies, quality concepts, market strategies, and other social or environmental conditions. Management should also review periodically the appropriateness of the review frequency, based on the findings of previous reviews. The quality system review process in Sec. 820.20(c), and the reasons for the review, should be understood by the organization.

The requirements under Sec. 820.22, Quality audit, are for an internal audit and review of the quality system to verify compliance with the quality system regulation. The review and evaluations under Sec. 820.22 are very focused. During the internal quality audit, the manufacturer should review all procedures to ensure adequacy and compliance with the regulation, and determine whether the procedures are being effectively implemented at all times. In contrast, as noted above, the management review under Sec. 820.20(c) is a broader review of the organization as a whole to ensure that the quality policy is implemented and the quality objectives are met. The reviews of the quality policy and objectives (Sec. 820.20(c)) should be carried out by top management, and the review of supporting activities (Sec. 820.22) should be carried out by management with executive responsibility for quality and other appropriate members of management, utilizing competent personnel as decided on by the management.

AAMI/ANSI/ISO TR 14969:2004

Reference § 5 Management responsibility
§ 5.6 Management review
§ 5.6.1 General

The TR indicates that management reviews can be conducted in a number of ways (for example, face-to-face, teleconference, or in segments focused on specific issues with varying attendees).

The records of a management review, including information on attendees, items discussed, decisions made or recommended, action items, and responsibilities, may be kept in any form (for example, notebook entries or formal written or electronic reports).

The TR notes that the frequency of management reviews can vary depending on the maturity of the QMS. If there is evidence that the QMS has been working effectively for a period of time, then once-a-year management reviews may be sufficient; if significant changes are made to the QMS or if a new QMS is being established, more frequent management reviews would be appropriate. The TR also allows for ad hoc management reviews to be conducted outside the planned intervals.

The TR recommends that attendees at the management review be authorized to take action on the items discussed.

Reference § 5 Management responsibility
§ 5.6 Management review
§ 5.6.2 Review input

The TR includes additional descriptive information related to the required inputs to a management review.

The TR recommends that individual problems be addressed as they occur, without waiting for the next scheduled management review. If an individual problem has significant QMS ramifications, it may be discussed at the management review, with the discussion focused on the issues and actions that may have to be taken at the QMS level. Minor details that do not have significant QMS consequences should not be discussed at the management review; individual QMS audit observations may be addressed at management reviews if they indicate a significant QMS issue as defined in the QMS Audit or Management Review procedure.

The TR recommends that any significant changes to regulatory requirements or any regulatory requirements that become relevant due to changes in the business objectives be discussed at a management review.

Reference § 5 Management responsibility
§ 5.6 Management review
§ 5.6.3 Review output

The TR suggests that one output of a management review could be discussion of the overall effectiveness of the QMS or the effectiveness of individual elements of the QMS. The output could also include recommendations for changing the frequency of management reviews and a listing of action items and how resources to accomplish those action items will be assigned.

Authors' Notes

It is generally a good idea to create a process for follow-up of action items identified during a management review. Many organizations assign the follow-up responsibility to the Management Representative, who works with management and the group responsible for the action item to ensure sufficient resources and effort to achieve timely completion. If additional consideration by top management is required, the Management Representative would arrange this as appropriate.

FDA Quality System Regulation—1996

§ 820.20(d) ***Quality planning.*** Each manufacturer shall establish a quality plan which defines the quality practices, resources, and activities relevant to devices that are designed and manufactured. The manufacturer shall establish how the requirements for quality will be met.

AAMI/ANSI/ISO 13485:2003

Reference § 5 Management responsibility
§ 5.4 Planning
§ 5.4.1 Quality objectives

The QMS system level planning described in this section is consistent with other types of planning done within the organization (for example, general business planning and marketing planning). This section calls for the establishment of quality objectives that are "measurable and consistent with the quality policy."

Reference § 5 Management responsibility
§ 5.4 Planning
§ 5.4.2 Quality management system planning

QMS planning is performed to ensure that the QMS meets the requirements set out in the Standard, to achieve the quality objectives identified, and to successfully manage any changes to the QMS.

FDA Guidance

QSReg Preamble

Comment group 54. [There is no current guidance relevant to the requirements set out in § 820.20(d). See "Authors' Notes" for this section.]

AAMI/ANSI/ISO TR 14969:2004

Reference § 5 Management responsibility
§ 5.4 Planning
§ 5.4.1 Quality objectives

The TR points out that while the QMS level quality objectives are "owned" by top management, the activities required to meet those objectives can be delegated within the organization.

Quality objectives must be achievable, even though their attainment may "stretch" the organization. The TR includes a list of outcomes that can be the subject of quality objectives (for example, meeting customer or regulatory requirements, reducing errors, or reducing complaint handling times).

It should be possible to trace quality objectives into the organization by seeing the relevance of group and individual quality objectives to the overall organization quality objectives.

Reference § 5 Management responsibility
§ 5.4 Planning
§ 5.4.2 Quality management system planning

The TR stresses that QMS level planning is an ongoing process that begins with the establishment of the QMS and continues throughout the life of the QMS to deal with external and internal changes that must be addressed by the organization.

The TR includes a list of typical inputs to QMS planning (for example, quality policy, quality objectives, regulatory requirements, and results from corrective and preventive actions). The TR also includes a list of typical outputs from the QMS planning activities (for example, the Quality Manual, gap analyses, and action plans).

The TR notes that the term "quality plan" usually relates to a plan for product realization of an individual product, rather than the planning associated with the QMS.

Authors' Notes

The Standard provides a more sophisticated set of requirements for quality planning than what is set out in the QSReg. The QSReg calls for a quality plan that is loosely related to a set of quality system procedures and product-related procedures. It can be argued that the FDA describes a system rather than a plan.

Rather than requiring a plan, the Standard sets out requirements for various kinds of quality planning that are to be performed within the QMS. Some of that planning is done at the QMS level (see ISO 13485:2003, § 5.4), and some is done as part of the processes that make up the QMS (for example, risk management planning for an individual product (see ISO 14971), product realization planning (see ISO 13485:2003, § 7.1), design and development planning for an individual product (see ISO 13485:2003, § 7.3.1), and QMS audit planning (see ISO 13485:2003, § 8.2.2(a))).

Discussion related to planning for the various processes within the QMS is contained in the sections of this book related to these individual processes.

We suggest that quality planning consistent with that described in the Standard provides significant benefits to the organization. If a quality plan is requested by an FDA investigator, the organization should provide examples of the various types of quality planning performed in compliance with the Standard.

FDA Quality System Regulation—1996

§ 820.20(e) ***Quality system procedures.*** Each manufacturer shall establish quality system procedures and instructions. An outline of the structure of the documentation used in the quality system shall be established where appropriate.

AAMI/ANSI/ISO 13485:2003

Reference § 4 Quality management system
§ 4.2 Documentation requirements
§ 4.2.1 General

There is no individual section of the Standard devoted to quality system procedures. The Standard requires that there will be quality system level procedures that describe processes such as design and development, calibration of monitoring and measurement equipment, corrective action, preventive action, and handling of nonconformities.

Whenever the Standard requires that a process or activity be documented, it assumes that the documentation must be implemented and maintained.

FDA Guidance

QSReg Preamble

Comment group 54. . . . Section 820.20(e) discusses "[a]n outline of the structure of the documentation used in the quality system." FDA believes that outlining the structure of the documentation is beneficial and, at times, may be critical to the effective operation of the quality system. FDA recognizes, however, that it may not be necessary to create an outline in all cases. For example, it may not be necessary for smaller manufacturers and manufacturers of less complicated devices. Thus, the outline is only required where appropriate.

AAMI/ANSI/ISO TR 14969:2004

Reference § 4 Quality management system
§ 4.2 Documentation requirements
§ 4.2.1 General

The TR indicates that documented quality system level procedures should be consistent with the quality policy of the organization and can be tailored in structure and detail to reflect the methods used and the qualifications of the individuals within the organization.

Authors' Notes

Most organizations have adopted a "pyramid" approach to documentation of processes, including quality system processes. The top of the pyramid, the policy level, contains written policies and the Quality Manual. The next level down is the quality system procedure level, and it contains procedures related to key QMS processes like risk management, design and development, handling of nonconformities, corrective action, preventive action, handling of complaints, and reporting of field problems to the FDA. Lower levels of the pyramid include specific work instructions (for example, how to conduct a design review, how to perform failure modes and effects analysis (FMEA), and how to calibrate measurement devices) and forms (for example, the management review report form, the calibration data report form, and the design review agenda form).

FDA Quality System Regulation—1996

§ 820.22 Quality audit

Each manufacturer shall establish procedures for quality audits and conduct such audits to assure that the quality system is in compliance with the established quality system requirements and to determine the effectiveness of the quality system. Quality audits shall be conducted by individuals who do not have direct responsibility for the matters being audited. Corrective action(s), including a reaudit of deficient matters, shall be taken when necessary. A report of the results of each quality audit, and reaudit(s) where taken, shall be made and such reports shall be reviewed by management having responsibility for the matters audited. The dates and results of quality audits and reaudits shall be documented.

AAMI/ANSI/ISO 13485:2003

Reference § 8 Measurement, analysis, and improvement
§ 8.2 Monitoring and measurement
§ 8.2.2 Internal audit

The QSReg and the Standard have essentially the same requirements and the same intent in regard to quality system audits.

The Standard explicitly states requirements that are implied by the QSReg:

- The internal audit program shall be planned based on the status and importance of the processes to be audited
- Selection of auditors shall be based on the skills and knowledge required for the audit
- Corrections and corrective actions resulting from audit observations shall be completed "without undue delay"

The Standard also contains a note referencing ISO 19011 as the source of guidance for the conduct of quality audits.

FDA Guidance

QSReg Preamble

Comment group 53. The requirements under Sec. 820.22 Quality audit are for an internal audit and review of the quality system to verify compliance with the quality system regulation. The review and evaluations under Sec. 820.22 are very focused. During the internal quality audit, the manufacturer should review all procedures to ensure adequacy and compliance with the regulation, and determine whether the procedures are being effectively implemented at all times. In contrast, as noted above, the management review under Sec. 820.20(c) is a broader review of the organization as a whole to ensure that the quality policy is implemented and the quality objectives are met. The reviews of the quality policy and objectives (Sec. 820.20(c)) should be carried out by top management, and the review of supporting activities (Sec. 820.22) should be carried out by management with executive responsibility for quality and other appropriate members of management, utilizing competent personnel as decided on by the management.

Comment group 55. . . . in response to general comments suggesting better harmonization [with the international quality system standard], FDA has added the requirement that the audit "determine the effectiveness of the quality system." . . . This requirement underscores that the quality audit must not only determine whether the manufacturer's requirements are being carried out, but whether the requirements themselves are adequate.

Comment group 56. Some comments stated that requiring "individuals who do not have direct responsibility for the matters being audited" to conduct the audits is impractical and burdensome, particularly for small manufacturers. FDA disagrees with the comments. Both small and large manufacturers have been subject to the identical requirement since 1978 and FDA knows of no hardship, on small or large manufacturers, as a result. Small manufacturers must generally establish independence, even if it means hiring outside auditors, because the failure to have an independent auditor could result in an ineffective audit.

Manufacturers must realize that conducting effective quality audits is crucial. Without the feedback provided by the quality audit and other information sources, such as complaints and service records, manufacturers operate in an open loop system with no assurance that the process used to design and produce devices is operating in a state of control.

Comment group 57. . . . It [is] the agency's intent that the provision requires that where corrective action [is] necessary, it would be taken and documented in a reaudit report. The provision has been rewritten to make that clear. New Sec. 820.22 also clarifies that a reaudit is not always required, but where it is indicated, it must be conducted. The report should verify that corrective action was implemented and effective. Because FDA does not review these reports, the date on which the audit and reaudit were performed must be documented and will be subject to FDA review.

Comment group 58. . . . FDA has decided not to review such evaluations [of suppliers] at this time and will revisit this decision after the agency gains sufficient experience with the new requirement to determine its effectiveness. A thorough response to the comments is found with the agency's response to other comments received on Sec. 820.50 Purchasing controls. FDA has moved the section regarding which reports the agency will refrain from reviewing from Sec. 820.22(b) to new Sec. 820.180(c), "Exemptions," under the related records requirements. FDA believes this organization is easier to follow.

Comment group 108. . . . FDA recognizes that quality audits of suppliers have a significant and demonstrated value as a management tool for corrective action, quality improvement, and overall assurance of component and service quality, and does not seek to undermine their value. Therefore, based on the concerns raised by the comments, FDA will not review supplier audit reports during a routine FDA inspection for compliance with part 820, as noted in Sec. 820.180(c), "Exceptions." The audit procedures, the evaluation procedures, and documents other than the supplier audit reports themselves that demonstrate conformance with Sec. 820.50 will be subject to review by an FDA investigator.

Comment group 182. . . . FDA . . . believes that the disclosure of the audit reports themselves would be counterproductive to the intent of the quality system. FDA has added Sec. 820.180(c), "Exceptions," to address which records FDA, as a matter of policy, will not request to review or copy during a routine inspection; such records include quality audit reports. FDA may request an employee in management with executive responsibility to certify in writing that the management reviews, quality audits, and supplier audits (where conducted) have been performed, among other things. FDA may also seek production of these reports in litigation under applicable procedural rules or by inspection warrant where access to the records is authorized by statute. Again, FDA emphasizes that its policy of refraining from reviewing these reports extends only to the specific reports, not to the procedures required by the sections or to any other quality assurance records, which will be subject to review and copying. . . .

AAMI/ANSI/ISO TR 14969:2004

Reference § 8 Measurement, analysis, and improvement
§ 8.2 Monitoring and measurement
§ 8.2.2 Internal audit

The TR recommends that the audit program and the individual audits be flexible to respond to inputs received from the process being audited, from other sources within the organization (for example, other company units and previous audit reports), and from external sources (for example, customers, suppliers, and external assessors).

The TR suggests that a series of smaller audits may be more effective and less disruptive to the organization than a single, comprehensive audit of a process. A series of audits makes the overall audit program more flexible and is also more likely to uncover minor deficiencies.

The TR recommends that the audit report be distributed to all affected parties, including management of the audited functional group(s) or process(es), for their review and action.

The TR suggests that target dates for the completion of corrections and corrective actions be included in the audit report(s) along with any response reports from the audit. Much of this information is an output of meetings that occur at the end or shortly after the completion of the audit. This practice and the inclusion of audit reports as input to management reviews can assist in avoiding undue delay in the completion of corrections and corrective actions.

The TR allows for special quality audits in addition to periodic audits when responding to contractual requirements, when significant changes are made to facilities or processes, and when confirming that nonconformities or safety issues have been effectively eliminated.

GHTF Guidance[5]

Study Group 4 (SG4) of the GHTF has published a series of guidance documents related to regulatory audits. These guidance documents provide insight into the audit approach recommended to regulatory agencies that are likely to inspect or audit medical device organizations. The overall objective of these guidance documents is to harmonize the inspection and audit approach to be used around the world and to increase the probability that regulatory agencies will accept the results of inspections by colleague agencies or private sector Conformity Assessment Bodies (CABs) and Notified Bodies (NBs).

The GHTF guidance documents include the following:

- GHTF.SG4.(99)28—Guidelines for Regulatory Auditing of Quality Systems of Medical Device Manufacturers—Part 1: General Requirements
- GHTF/SG4/N30R20:2006—Guidelines for Regulatory Auditing of Quality Systems of Medical Device Manufacturers—Part 2: Regulatory Auditing Strategy
- GHTF/SG4/N33R16—Guidelines for Regulatory Auditing of Quality Systems of Medical Device Manufacturers—Part 3: Regulatory Audit Reports
- GHTF/SG4/N(99)24R23:2002—Guidelines for Regulatory Auditing of Quality System of Medical Device Manufacturers—Supplement No. 4—Compilation of Audit Documentation (Clause 5.7)
- GHTF.SG4.(99)14—Audit Language Requirements
- GHTF-SG4-(00)3—Training Requirements of Auditors

Authors' Notes

In QSReg § 820.180(c) the FDA sets forth the policy statement that it will not request access to certain reports generated within the QMS, including, among others, internal audit reports and supplier audit reports. In the case of internal audits, the FDA will accept written documentation that a scheduled internal audit has been conducted and closed as satisfactory objective evidence of an effective internal audit process.

It is, however, important to understand that if the results of an internal audit lead to either a corrective action or a preventive action under the organization's corrective action and preventive action (CAPA) process, those audit results may become accessible to the FDA to allow the agency to assess the effectiveness of the corrective or preventive action. Some organizations have attempted, albeit unsuccessfully, to keep those results from the FDA by setting up a special CAPA

5. The text in sections entitled "GHTF Guidance" describes the contents of the specifically referenced guidance document. It is not quoted directly from the guidance except for text within quotation marks.

process under the internal audit process. The reader should be aware that audit reports may be subpoenaed under procedural rules related to litigation.

Not all deficiencies uncovered during an internal audit result in a corrective or preventive action under the CAPA process. Only those audit observations that are evidence of a systemic deficiency in the QMS or are directly related to the safety or effectiveness of the resulting medical device need be considered for CAPA processing. Randomly occurring deficiencies may be corrected, with the record of the correction maintained within the internal audit process. For example, if an internal auditor observes that a window is broken in the manufacturing area and the investigation indicates no systemic cause for the broken window, the window can be replaced as a "correction" within the internal audit process, without requiring the activity to be conducted under the CAPA process. Other examples are illustrated under § 820.100 of this text.

Many companies have revised their internal audit programs to recognize that their QMSs are compilations of interrelated processes that require the effective participation of more than one functional group. They are now auditing processes (for example, design and development, corrective action, and handling of nonconformities) with the individual audits involving input from a number of functional groups and having an increased focus on the interactions of the groups.

FDA Quality System Regulation—1996

§ 820.25 Personnel

§ 820.25(a) *General.* Each manufacturer shall have sufficient personnel with the necessary education, background, training, and experience to assure that all activities required by this part are correctly performed.

AAMI/ANSI/ISO 13485:2003

Reference § 6 Resource management
§ 6.2 Human resources
§ 6.2.1 General

There is no significant difference between the QSReg and Standard requirements in this section.

FDA Guidance

QSReg Preamble

Comment group 59. . . . Whether "sufficient" personnel are employed will be determined by the requirements of the quality system, which must be designed to ensure that the requirements of the regulation are properly implemented. In making staffing decisions, a manufacturer must ensure that persons assigned to particular functions are properly equipped and possess the necessary education, background, training, and experience to perform their functions correctly. However, FDA changed "ensure" to "assure" to address the concerns that people do make mistakes and management cannot guarantee that work is correctly performed all of the time. Further, FDA agrees that the manufacturer must determine for itself what constitutes "sufficient" personnel with proper qualification in the first instance. However, if the manufacturer does not employ sufficient personnel, or personnel with the necessary qualifications to carry out their functions, the manufacturer will be in violation of the regulation. FDA has often found that the failure to comply with this requirement leads to other significant regulatory violations. . . . the requirement covers all personnel who work at a firm [especially those who are employed in the act of manufacturing and associated activities, including housekeeping].

Authors' Notes

An FDA investigator or a third-party assessor will infer "insufficient personnel resources" from records that show a pattern of failure to meet targeted completion dates for various QMS activities (for example, completion of corrective actions, conduct of internal audits, and handling of complaints).

FDA Quality System Regulation—1996

§ 820.25(b) ***Training.*** Each manufacturer shall establish procedures for identifying training needs and ensure that all personnel are trained to adequately perform their assigned responsibilities. Training shall be documented.

(1) As part of their training, personnel shall be made aware of device defects which may occur from the improper performance of their specific jobs.

(2) Personnel who perform verification and validation activities shall be made aware of defects and errors that may be encountered as part of their job functions.

AAMI/ANSI/ISO 13485:2003

Reference § 6 Resource management
§ 6.2 Human resources
§ 6.2.2 Competence, awareness, and training

The Standard addresses the training topic in the context of ensuring that personnel are competent to perform their tasks within the QMS.

The requirements in the QSReg and the Standard are similar with a few minor exceptions. In § 6.2.2 (b) the Standard allows management to ". . . provide training or take other actions to satisfy these needs." Although the nature of the "other actions" is not specified, in part (c) the Standard requires the user to evaluate the effectiveness of such actions.

While the QSReg requires that "personnel performing work affecting product quality shall be competent," the Standard applies that requirement to all personnel whose work can affect the achievement of quality objectives.

Also, a note in the Standard recognizes that certain regional regulations mandate the creation of a documented training needs matrix.

PERSONNEL

FDA Guidance

QSReg Preamble

Comment group 60. FDA amended the requirement so that the training procedure includes the identification of training needs. . . . FDA notes . . . that a training program to ensure personnel adequately perform their assigned responsibilities should include information about the CGMP requirements and how particular job functions relate to the overall quality system. FDA further believes that it is imperative that training cover the consequences of improper performance so that personnel will be apprised of defects that they should look for, as well as be aware of the effect their actions can have on the safety and effectiveness of the device. In addition, FDA disagrees with comments that suggested that only "personnel affecting quality" should be required to be adequately trained. In order for the full quality system to function as intended, all personnel should be properly trained. Each function in the manufacture of a medical device must be viewed as integral to all other functions. . . .

AAMI/ANSI/ISO TR 14969:2004

Reference § 6 Resource management
§ 6.2 Human resources
§ 6.2.2 Competence, awareness, and training

The TR recognizes that most medical device organizations provide education and training to their personnel on issues related to the organization's business in general, on relevant safety regulations and requirements, on the nature and structure of its QMS (including its quality policy and objective(s)), and on the procedures and instructions relevant to the employees' responsibilities.

The TR emphasizes, in addition to the stated requirements, that attainment of competency for a task within the QMS can be achieved not only through formal training but by other means, such as academic degree (for example, lab technician), work experience, or inherent talent or skill. If training is the mechanism to be used to ensure competency, it may be carried out in a number of ways (for example, tutorial classroom training or on-the-job training) and may be conducted in stages (for example, initial training followed by refresher training). Records of the types and effectiveness of training should be kept, and planning for additional required training should be recorded.

Trainers should have the appropriate skills, qualifications, and experience, and they should keep records to provide objective evidence of their qualifications.

The TR also recommends that the competence of personnel and the effectiveness of the training activity be evaluated on a periodic basis. Such assessment can come from review of performance records, records of nonconformance and corrective action, and other records.

The TR points out that it might be necessary for people to be further qualified or formally certified for some tasks (for example, chemical or microbiological analysis, radiation activities, laser operation, welding, or soldering).

GHTF Guidance

There is no separate GHTF guidance document on training within the QMS, except as it relates to regulatory auditing. See GHTF guidance document GHTF-SG4-(00)3, Training Requirements for Auditors.

Authors' Notes

The negative effects of lack of competency can be felt throughout the QMS:

- Failure of proper control of suppliers (for example, a parts supplier using an obsolete version of an engineering drawing because the purchasing agent did not specify the version to be used)

- Failure to perform proper quality control (QC) (for example, the QC inspector failing to check for the latest version of the engineering drawing)
- Continuing failure of a high-volume production operation to manufacture products within specifications due to training provided by unqualified trainers
- Failure of a product to meet sterility requirements due to ineffective sterility validation designed by unqualified personnel

Provision of effective training is a key activity in ensuring the competency of personnel to perform their responsibilities. As a result, the training process should be included among the QMS processes subject to internal audit, with those audits focusing on the competency of the training personnel, the planning and execution of the training activity, and the means used to evaluate the effectiveness of the training.

SUBPART C

Design Controls

FDA Quality System Regulation—1996

§ 820.30 Design controls

§ 820.30(a) *General.*

(1) Each manufacturer of any class III or class II device, and the class I devices listed in paragraph (a)(2) of this section, shall establish and maintain procedures to control the design of the device in order to ensure that specified design requirements are met.

(2) The following class I devices are subject to design controls:

(i) Devices automated with computer software; and

(ii) The devices listed in the following chart.

Section	Device
868.6810	Catheter, Tracheobronchial Suction.
878.4460	Glove, Surgeon's.
892.5650	System, Applicator, Radionuclide, Manual.
892.5740	Source, Radionuclide Teletherapy.

AAMI/ANSI/ISO 13485:2003

Reference § 1.2 Application

The Standard allows the exclusion of design and development controls from the QMS if the relevant regulations allow for such exclusion. If an organization manufactures only Class I devices that are not specifically listed in the QSReg, then

DESIGN CONTROLS

any design and development processes conducted by the organization may be excluded from the QMS. It is important to note that design transfer requirements still apply to exempted Class I devices.

Reference § 7.3 Design and development

The overall objectives of the ISO 13485 standard and the FDA regulation related to design controls are the same.

FDA Guidance

QSReg Preamble

Since early 1984, FDA has identified lack of design controls as one of the major causes of device recalls. The intrinsic quality of devices, including their safety and effectiveness, is established during the design phase. Thus, FDA believes that unless appropriate design controls are observed during preproduction stages of development, a finished device may be neither safe nor effective for its intended use. The SMDA [Safe Medical Devices Act of 1976] provided FDA with the authority to add preproduction design controls to the device CGMP regulation. Based on its experience with administering the original CGMP regulation, which did not include preproduction design controls, the agency was concerned that the original regulation provided less than an adequate level of assurance that devices would be safe and effective. Therefore, FDA has added general requirements for design controls to the device CGMP regulation for all class III and II devices and certain class I devices.

FDA is not subjecting the majority of class I devices to design controls because FDA does not believe that such controls are necessary to ensure that such devices are safe and effective and otherwise in compliance with the act. However, all devices, including class I devices exempt from design controls, must be properly transferred to production in order to comply with Sec. 820.181 [Device Master Record requirements], as well as other applicable requirements. For most class I devices, FDA believes that the production and other controls in the new quality system regulation and other general controls of the act will be sufficient, as they have been in the past, to ensure safety and effectiveness.

Comment group 62. . . . The design control requirements are not intended to apply to the development of concepts and feasibility studies. However, once it is decided that a design will be developed, a plan must be established to determine the adequacy of the design requirements and to ensure that the design that will eventually be released to production meets the approved requirements.

Those who design medical devices must be aware of the design control requirements in the regulation and comply with them. Unsafe and ineffective devices are often the result of informal development that does not ensure the proper establishment and assessment of design requirements which are necessary to develop a medical device that is safe and effective for the intended use of the device and that meets the needs of the user.

However, FDA investigators will not inspect a device under the design control requirements to determine whether the design is appropriate or "safe and effective." Section 520(f)(1)(a) of the Act precludes FDA from evaluating the "safety or effectiveness of a device" through preproduction design control procedures. FDA investigators will evaluate the process, the methods, and the procedures that a manufacturer has established to implement the requirements for design controls. If, based on any information gained during an inspection, an investigator believes that distributed devices are unsafe or ineffective, the investigator has an obligation to report the observations to the Center for Devices and Radiological Health (CDRH).

Comment group 63. . . . It is not the intent of FDA to interfere with creativity and innovation, and it is not the intent of FDA to apply the design control requirements to the research phase. Instead, the regulation requires the establishment of procedures to ensure that whatever design is ultimately transferred to production is, in fact, a design that will translate into a device that properly performs according to its intended use and user needs.

To assist FDA in applying the regulation, manufacturers should document the flow of the design process so that it is clear to the FDA investigator where research is ending and development of the design is beginning.

Comment group 64. . . . FDA did not intend the design requirements to be retroactive, and Sec. 820.30 Design controls will not require the manufacturer to apply such requirements to already distributed devices. . . .

When changes are made to new or existing designs, the design controls of Sec. 820.30 must be followed to ensure that the changes are appropriate and that the device will continue to perform as intended. FDA notes that the original CGMP regulation contained requirements for specification controls and controls for specification or design changes under Sec. 820.100(a).

Comment group 65. . . . With respect to the new regulation, FDA believes that it is reasonable to expect manufacturers who design medical devices to develop the designs in conformance with design control requirements and that adhering to such requirements is necessary to adequately protect the public from potentially harmful devices. The design control requirements are basic controls needed to ensure that the device being designed will perform as intended when produced for commercial distribution. Clinical evaluation is an important aspect of the design verification and validation process during the design and development of the device. Because some of the device design occurs during the IDE [Investigation Device Exemption] stage, it is logical that manufacturers who intend to commercially produce the device follow design control procedures. Were a manufacturer to wait until all the IDE studies were complete, it would be too late to take advantage of the design control process, and the manufacturer would not be able to fulfill the requirements of the quality system regulation for that device.

Therefore, FDA has concurrently amended the IDE regulation, §812.1 Scope to state:

> (a) * * * An IDE approved under Sec. 812.30 or considered approved under Sec. 812.2(b) exempts a device from the requirements of the following sections of the Federal Food, Drug, and Cosmetic Act (the act) and regulations issued thereunder: * * * good manufacturing practice requirements under section 520(f) except for the requirements found in Sec. 820.30, if applicable (unless the sponsor states an intention to comply with these requirements under Sec. 812.20(b)(3) or Sec. 812.140(b)(4)(v)) and color additive requirements under section 721. (Emphasis added.)
>
> FDA does not expect any new information in IDE applications as a result of this amendment, nor will FDA inspect design controls during bioresearch monitoring inspections. FDA is simply making a conforming amendment to the IDE regulation to make clear that design controls must be followed when design functions are undertaken by manufacturers, including design activity which occurs under an approved IDE. FDA will evaluate the adequacy of manufacturers' compliance with design control requirements in routine CGMP inspections, including preapproval inspections for premarket approval applications (PMA's).

Comment group 67. . . . The Act and its legislative history make clear that FDA has the authority to impose those controls necessary to ensure that devices are safe and effective. The SMDA gave FDA explicit authority to promulgate design controls, including a process to assess the performance of a device (see section 520(f)(1)(A) of the act). The legislative history of the SMDA supports a "comprehensive device design validation regulation." H. Rept. 808, 101st Cong., 2d sess. 23 (emphasis added). Congress stated that the amendment to the statute was necessary because almost half of all device recalls over a 5-year period were "related to a problem with product design." Id. There is a thorough discussion on the evolution of and need for the design controls in the preamble to the November 23, 1993 (58 FR 61952), proposal.

Comment group 68. . . . FDA believes that, for the class I devices listed, design controls are necessary and has retained the requirements. Those relatively few devices, while class I, require close control of the design process to ensure that the devices perform as intended, given the serious consequences that could occur if their designs were flawed and the devices were to fail to meet their intended uses. In fact, some of the devices included on the list have experienced failures due to design related problems that have resulted in health hazards, injuries, or death. Further, verification, or even validation, cannot provide the assurance of proper design for some devices, especially those containing extensive software. Thus, all automated devices must be developed under the design control requirements.

Design Control Guidance for Medical Device Manufacturers, Issued 11 March, 1997

This guidance document can be found at http://www.fda.gov/cdrh/comp/designgd.html.

> This guidance is intended to assist manufacturers in understanding quality system requirements concerning design controls. . . .
>
> . . . Design controls make systematic assessment of the design an integral part of development. As a result, deficiencies in design input requirements, and discrepancies between the proposed designs and requirements, are made evident and corrected earlier in the development process. Design controls increase the likelihood that the design transferred to production will translate into a device that is appropriate for its intended use.
>
> In practice, design controls provide managers and designers with improved visibility of the design process. . . . Designers benefit both by enhanced understanding of the degree of conformance of a design to user and patient needs, and by improved communications and coordination among all participants in the process.
>
> The medical device industry encompasses a wide range of technologies and applications, . . . Given this diversity, this guidance does not suggest particular methods of implementation, . . . Rather, the intent is to expand upon the distilled language of the quality system requirements with practical explanations and examples of design control principles. Armed with this basic knowledge, manufacturers can and should seek out technology-specific guidance on applying design controls to their particular situation.
>
> . . . It is a well-established fact that the cost to correct design errors is lower when errors are detected early in the design and development process. . . .
>
> The guidance applies to the design of medical devices as well as the design of the associated manufacturing processes. The guidance is applicable to new designs as well as modifications or improvements to existing device designs. . . .
>
> Design controls are a component of a comprehensive quality system that covers the life of a device. The assurance process is a total systems approach that extends from the development of device requirements through design, production, distribution, use, maintenance, and eventually, obsolescence. . . .
>
> Design control does not end with the transfer of a design to production. Design control applies to all changes to the device or manufacturing process design, including those occurring long after a device has been introduced to the market. . . .

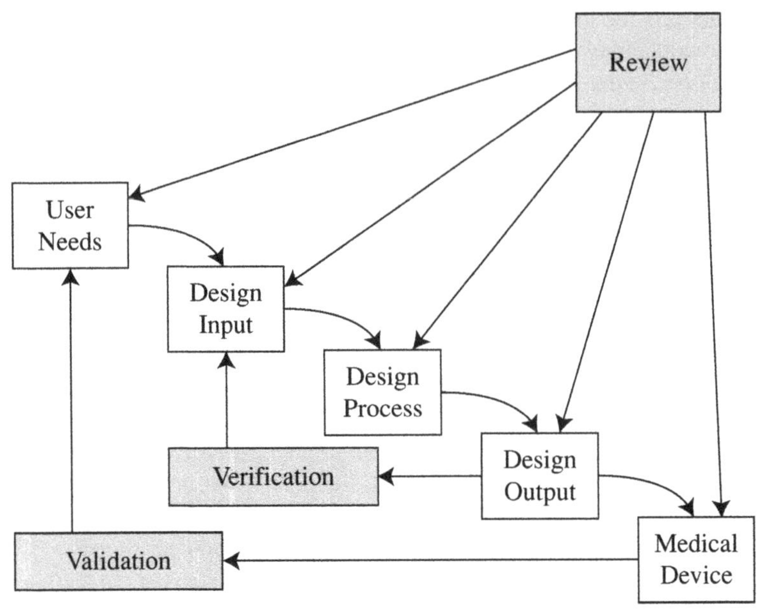

Figure 1 Application of design controls to waterfall design process.

. . . The simple example shown in Figure 1 illustrates the influence of design controls on a design process.

The development process depicted in the example is a traditional waterfall model. The design proceeds in a logical sequence of phases or stages. Basically, requirements are developed, and a device is designed to meet those requirements. The design is then evaluated, transferred to production, and the device is manufactured. In practice, feedback paths would be required between each phase of the process and previous phases, representing the iterative nature of product development. However, this detail has been omitted from the figure to make the influence of the design controls on the design process more distinct. . . .

. . . Although the waterfall model is a useful tool for introducing design controls, its usefulness in practice is limited. The model does apply to the development of some simpler devices. However, for more complex devices, a concurrent engineering model is more representative of the design processes in use in the industry.

In a traditional waterfall development scenario, the engineering department completes the product design and formally transfers the design to production. Subsequently, other departments or organizations develop processes to manufacture and service the product. Historically, there has frequently been a divergence between the intent of the designer and the reality of the factory floor, resulting in such undesirable outcomes as low manufacturing yields, rework or redesign of the product, or unexpectedly high cost to service the product.

One benefit of concurrent engineering is the involvement of production and service personnel throughout the design process, assuring the mutual optimization of the characteristics of a device and its related processes. While the primary motivations of concurrent engineering are shorter development time and reduced production cost, the practical result is often improved product quality.

Concurrent engineering encompasses a range of practices and techniques. . . . various components of a design may enter production before the design as a whole has been approved. Thus, concurrent engineering and other more complex models of development usually require a comprehensive matrix of reviews and approvals to ensure that each component and process design is validated prior to entering production, and the product as a whole is validated prior to design release. . . .

. . . In addition to procedures and work instructions necessary for the implementation of design controls, policies and procedures may also be needed for other determinants of device quality that should be considered during the design process. The need for policies and procedures for these factors is dependent upon the types of devices manufactured by a company and the risks associated with their use. Management with executive responsibility has the responsibility for determining what is needed.

Examples of topics for which policies and procedures may be appropriate are:

- risk management
- device reliability
- device durability
- device maintainability
- device serviceability
- human factors engineering
- software engineering
- use of standards
- configuration management
- compliance with regulatory requirements
- device evaluation (which may include third party product certification or approval)
- clinical evaluations
- document controls
- use of consultants
- use of subcontractors
- use of company historical data

. . . The context within which product design is to be carried out should be set by the manufacturer's senior management. It is their responsibility to establish a design and development plan which sets the targets to be met. This plan defines the constraints within which the design is to be implemented.

The quality system requirements do not dictate the types of design process that a manufacturer must use. Manufacturers should use processes best suited to their needs. However, whatever the processes may be, it is important that the design controls are applied in an appropriate manner. This guidance document contains examples of how this might be achieved in a variety of situations.

. . . Senior management needs to decide how the design function is to be managed and by whom. Senior management should also ensure that internal policies are established for design issues such as:

- assessing new product ideas
- training and retraining of design managers and design staff
- use of consultants
- evaluation of the design process
- product evaluation, including third party product certification and approvals
- patenting or other means of design protection

It is for senior management to ensure that adequate resources are available to carry out the design in the required time. This may involve reinforcing the skills and equipment available internally and/or obtaining external resources.

Quality System Information for Certain Premarket Application Reviews; Guidance for Industry and FDA Staff, Issued on 3 February, 2003

This guidance document can be found at http://www.fda.gov/cdrh/comp/guidance/1140.pdf.

This guidance has been prepared by the Center for Devices and Radiological Health (CDRH), in coordination with the Center for Biologics Evaluation and Research (CBER), to assist medical device manufacturers in preparing and maintaining the QS information required in premarket submissions.

This guidance document requests that you provide copies of written procedures or lists of items related to the QS regulation. In most cases, these procedures or lists are explicitly required under provisions of the QS regulation. In the case where the information is not explicitly required under statute or regulation (e.g., production flow diagram, list of any standards used, process validation master plan), we believe the information is the type you are likely to create and maintain as part of your Quality System. Your submission of such information as part of the application process may reduce or eliminate the need for us to request additional information to determine your compliance with the QS regulation under 21 CFR 820. In addition, we believe your submission of this information can help us focus the preapproval inspection process and limit the amount of time our field staff will need to spend in your facility.

A manufacturer who chooses to meet application requirements for the QS information in an alternative way may wish to consult with the appropriate office within the Center prior to the submission. The FDA staff can help identify areas that might raise particular concerns for Center reviewers or investigators.

The guidance document describes the various kinds of quality system documents that would be part of such a submission. Generally, the listing follows organization of 21 CFR 820 and includes documents associated with the various stages of design and development, production and process control, process validation, acceptance activities, handling of nonconforming product, corrective and preventive actions, handling of complaints, and servicing (if applicable).

FDA Quality System Regulation—1996

§ 820.30(b) ***Design and development planning.*** Each manufacturer shall establish and maintain plans that describe or reference the design and development activities and define responsibility for implementation. The plans shall identify and describe the interfaces with different groups or activities that provide, or result in, input to the design and development process. The plans shall be reviewed, updated, and approved as design and development evolves.

AAMI/ANSI/ISO 13485:2003

Reference § 7.3.1 Design and development planning

The design and development requirements in the Standard are essentially the same as in the QSReg. The Standard explicitly requires documentation of the design and development plans; that requirement is only implied in the QSReg requirements.

There is a note in the Standard that clarifies that as part of the design transfer activities, design outputs are verified as being appropriate for manufacturing the resulting medical device.

FDA Guidance

QSReg Preamble

Comment group 62. . . . The design control requirements are not intended to apply to the development of concepts and feasibility studies. However, once it is decided that a design will be developed, a plan must be established to determine the adequacy of the design requirements and to ensure that the design that will eventually be released to production meets the approved requirements.

Comment group 69. . . . Sec. 820.30(b) [has been revised] to require the plan to describe or reference the activities, rather than requiring that the plan identify each person responsible for carrying out each activity. In making this change, FDA notes that Sec. 820.20(b)(1) requires manufacturers to establish the appropriate responsibility for activities affecting quality, and emphasizes that the assignment of specific responsibility is important to the success of the design control program and to achieving compliance with the regulation. Also, the design and development activities should be assigned to qualified personnel equipped with adequate resources as required under Sec. 820.20(b)(2).

[The design plan should be updated and regularly reviewed.] Therefore, the approval [or the plan] . . . would not be unduly burdensome since the FDA does not dictate how or by whom the plan must be approved. The regulation gives the manufacturer the necessary flexibility to have the same person(s) who is responsible for the review also be responsible for the approval of the plan if appropriate.

Comment group 70. . . . the [design] plan shall identify and describe the interfaces with different groups or activities that provide, or result in, input to the design process. Many organization functions, both inside and outside the design group, may contribute to the design process. For example, interfaces with marketing, purchasing, regulatory affairs, manufacturing, service groups, or information systems may be necessary during the design/development phase. To function effectively, the design plan must establish the roles of these groups in the design process and describe the information that should be received and transmitted.

Comment group 71. . . . Section 820.30(b) does not require manufacturers to complete design and testing criteria before the design process begins. This section has been revised to state that "plans shall be reviewed, updated, and approved as design and development evolves," indicating that changes to the design plan are expected. A design plan typically includes at least proposed quality practices, assessment methodology, recordkeeping and documentation requirements, and resources, as well as a sequence of events related to a particular design or design category. These may be modified and refined as the design evolves. However, the design process can become a lengthy and costly process if the design activity is not properly defined and planned. The more specifically the activities are defined up front, the less need there will be for changes as the design evolves.

Design Control Guidance for Medical Device Manufacturers, Issued 11 March, 1997

This guidance document can be found at http://www.fda.gov/cdrh/comp/designgd.html.

The context within which product design is to be carried out should be set by the manufacturer's senior management. It is their responsibility to establish a design and development plan which sets the targets to be met. This plan defines the constraints within which the design is to be implemented.

Design and development planning is needed to ensure that the design process is appropriately controlled and that device quality objectives are met. . . . The following elements would typically be addressed in the design and development plan or plans:

- Description of the goals and objectives of the design and development program; i.e., what is to be developed;
- Delineation of organizational responsibilities with respect to assuring quality during the design and development phase, to include interface with any contractors;
- Identification of the major tasks to be undertaken, deliverables for each task, and individual or organizational responsibilities (staff and resources) for completing each task;
- Scheduling of major tasks to meet overall program time constraints;
- Identification of major reviews and decision points;
- Selection of reviewers, the composition of review teams, and procedures to be followed by reviewers;
- Controls for design documentation;
- Notification activities.

. . . The extent of design and development planning is dependent on the size of the developing organization and the size and complexity of the product to be developed. Some manufacturers may have documented policies and procedures which apply to all design and development activities. For each specific development program, such manufacturers may also prepare a plan which spells out the project-dependent elements in detail, and incorporates the general policies and procedures by reference. Other manufacturers may develop a comprehensive design and development plan which is specifically tailored to each individual project.

. . . The following paragraphs discuss the key elements of design and development planning.

Organizational Responsibilities. . . . The importance of defining responsibilities with clarity and without ambiguity should be recognized. When input to the design is from a variety of sources, their interrelationships and interfaces (as well as the pertinent responsibilities and authorities) should be defined, documented, coordinated, and controlled.

Task Breakdown. The plan establishes, to the extent possible:

- The major tasks required to develop the product
- The time involved for each major task
- The resources and personnel required
- The allocation of responsibilities for completing each major task
- The prerequisite information necessary to start each major task and the interrelationship between tasks
- The form of each task output or deliverable
- Constraints, such as applicable codes, standards, and regulations

Tasks for all significant design activities, including verification and validation tasks, should be included in the design and development plan. . . .

For complex projects, rough estimates may be provided initially, with the details left for the responsible organizations to develop. As development proceeds, the plan should evolve to incorporate more and better information.

The relationships between tasks should be presented in such a way that they are easily understood. It should be clear which tasks depend on others, and which tasks need to be performed concurrently. Planning should reflect the degree of perceived development risk; for example, tasks involving new technology or processes should be spelled out in greater detail, and perhaps be subjected to more reviews and checks, than tasks which are perceived as routine or straightforward.

The design and development plan may include a schedule showing starting and completion dates for each major task, project milestone, or key decision points. . . .

Unless a manufacturer has experience with the same type of device, the plan will initially be limited in scope and detail. As work proceeds, the plan is refined. . . .

It is important that the schedule be updated to reflect current knowledge. At all times, the plan should be specified at a level of detail enabling management to make informed decisions, and provide confidence in meeting overall schedule and performance objectives. This is important because scheduling pressures have historically been a contributing factor in many design defects which caused injury. . . .

However, no amount of planning can eliminate all development risk. There is inherent conflict between the desire to maximize performance and the need to meet business objectives, including development deadlines. In some corporate cultures, impending deadlines create enormous pressure to cut corners. Planning helps to combat this dilemma by ensuring management awareness of pressure points.

AAMI/ANSI/ISO TR 14969:2004

Reference § 7.3.1 Design and development planning

The objectives of design and development planning as described in this TR are essentially the same as in the QSReg. The TR contains a detailed list of the planning elements of a design and development plan. In addition to the elements outlined in the QSReg and its guidance, the TR recommends that the planning address the goals and objectives of the design and development program, the markets for which the medical device is intended, and the anticipated suppliers that will be involved in providing goods and services to the design and development activities. It recommends that the plan include the normal contents of a plan, that is, a listing of the major tasks to be performed, the individuals responsible for performing them, and a schedule of when the tasks will be performed. The plan should also include tasks associated with the development of any monitoring and measuring equipment that will be needed to ensure that the resulting medical device meets its specification. The plan should also address risk management activities.

The size and complexity of the design and development plan depend on the size and complexity of the medical device being developed. The plan may be a combination of general design and development planning requirements and project-specific requirements.

Design and manufacturing experts should be involved throughout the design and development planning process in order to ensure that a combination of design specifications and manufacturing control capabilities results in the commercial devices consistently meeting requirements. This cooperative participation is especially required during the transfer of the design to manufacturing.

Authors' Notes

It is important that the organization not confuse the requirement for design and development planning with the requirement for the design and development process to be documented. The design and development plan pertains to the particular activities that will be performed during a specific design and development project. It should contain the key elements of any plan: what will be done, who will do it, and when it will be completed.

FDA Quality System Regulation—1996

§ 820.30(c) ***Design input.*** Each manufacturer shall establish and maintain procedures to ensure that the design requirements relating to a device are appropriate and address the intended use of the device, including the needs of the user and patient. The procedures shall include a mechanism for addressing incomplete, ambiguous, or conflicting requirements. The design input requirements shall be documented and shall be reviewed and approved by a designated individual(s). The approval, including the date and signature of the individual(s) approving the requirements, shall be documented.

AAMI/ANSI/ISO 13485:2003

Reference § 7.3.2 Design and development inputs

The Standard includes a list of sources of design input not explicitly called out in the QSReg, including statutory and regulatory requirements, the output of risk assessment, and knowledge gained from similar devices.

FDA Guidance

QSReg Preamble

Comment group 72. . . . FDA recognizes that the provision [that the input requirements completely address the intended use of the device] could be interpreted to impose a burden that may not always be possible to meet and has deleted the word "completely." FDA did not intend the provision to suggest that a manufacturer must foresee every possible event.

FDA emphasizes, however, that the section requires the manufacturer to ensure that the design input requirements are appropriate so the device will perform to meet its intended use and the needs of the user. In doing this, the manufacturer must define the performance characteristics, safety and reliability requirements, environmental requirements and limitations, physical characteristics, applicable standards and regulatory requirements, and labeling and packaging requirements, among other things, and refine the design requirements as verification and validation results are established. For example, when designing a device, the manufacturer should conduct appropriate human factors studies, analyses, and tests from the early stages of the design process until that point in development at which the interfaces with the medical professional and the patient are fixed. The human interface includes both the hardware and software characteristics that affect device use, and good design is crucial to logical, straightforward, and safe device operation. The human factors methods used (for instance, task/function analyses, user studies, prototype tests, mock-up reviews, etc.) should ensure that the characteristics of the user population and operating environment are considered. In addition, the compatibility of system components should be assessed. Finally, labeling (e.g., instructions for use) should be tested for usability.

. . . It is important that incomplete, ambiguous, or conflicting requirements be resolved with those responsible for imposing these requirements. Therefore, FDA has added the requirement that the procedures shall include a mechanism for addressing incomplete, ambiguous, or conflicting requirements. FDA notes that this must be done to "ensure that the design requirements are appropriate and address the intended use of the device," as required under Sec. 820.30(c).

Comment group 73. . . . FDA does not dictate how or by whom the design input requirements must be approved, thus giving the manufacturer the necessary flexibility to have the same person(s) who is responsible for the "review for adequacy" also be responsible for the approval, if appropriate. Further, it is important that the design input be assessed as early as possible in the development process, making this an ideal time in the device's design development to have a design review to "approve" the design input.

Comment group 74. . . . FDA endorses the team approach and believes that designs should be reviewed and evaluated by all disciplines necessary to ensure the design input requirements are appropriate.

Comment group 75. . . . the manufacturer must establish and maintain procedures to ensure that the design requirements are properly addressed. . . . It should be emphasized that the input itself must also be appropriate; the requirement is for the procedures to be defined, documented, and implemented. Thus, if the input requirements related to a device fail to address the intended use of the device, for example, the manufacturer has failed to comply with the provision.

FDA . . . believes that identifying and establishing the environmental limits for safe and effective device operation is inherent in the requirements for ensuring that a device is appropriate for its intended use. Some factors that must be considered when establishing inputs include, where applicable, a determination of energy (e.g., electrical, heat, and electromagnetic fields), biological effects (e.g., toxicity and biocompatibility) and environmental effects (e.g., electromagnetic interference and electrostatic discharge).

Design Control Guidance for Medical Device Manufacturers, Issued 11 March, 1997

This guidance document can be found at http://www.fda.gov/cdrh/comp/designgd.html.

Design input is the starting point for product design. The requirements which form the design input establish a basis for performing subsequent design tasks and validating the design. Therefore, development of a solid foundation of requirements is the single most important design control activity.

. . . If essential requirements are not identified until validation, expensive redesign and rework may be necessary before a design can be released to production.

. . . the development of requirements for a medical device of even moderate complexity is a formidable, time-consuming task. They accept the investment in time and resources required to develop the requirements because they know the advantages to be gained in the long run. . . .

Concept Documents Versus Design Input. In some cases, the marketing staff, who maintain close contact with customers and users, determine a need for a new product, or enhancements to an existing product. Alternatively, the idea for a new product may evolve out of a research or clinical activity. In any case, the result is a concept document specifying some of the desired characteristics of the new product.

Some members of the medical device community view these marketing memoranda, or the equivalent, as the design input. However, that is not the intent of the quality system requirements. Such concept documents are rarely comprehensive, and should not be expected to be so. Rather, the intent of the quality system requirements is that the product conceptual description be elaborated, expanded, and transformed into a complete set of design input requirements which are written to an engineering level of detail.

This is an important concept. The use of qualitative terms in a concept document is both appropriate and practical. This is often not the case for a document to be used as a basis for design. Even the simplest of terms can have enormous design implications. For example, the term "must be portable" in a concept document raises questions in the minds of product developers about issues such as size and weight limitations, resistance to shock and vibration, the need for protection from moisture and corrosion, the capability of operating over a wide temperature range, and many others. Thus, a concept document may be the starting point for development, but it is not the design input requirement. . . .

Research and Development. Some manufacturers have difficulty in determining where research ends and development begins. Research activities may be undertaken in an effort to determine new business opportunities or basic characteristics for a new product. It may be reasonable to develop a rapid prototype to explore the feasibility of an idea or design approach, for example, prior to developing design input requirements. But manufacturers should avoid falling into the trap of equating the prototype design with a finished product design. . . .

Responsibility for Design Input Development. . . . a second key principle is that the product developer(s) ultimately bear responsibility for translating user and/or patient needs into a set of requirements which can be validated prior to implementation. While this is primarily an engineering function, the support or full participation of production and service personnel, key suppliers, etc., may be required to assure that the design input requirements are complete.

. . . the product conceptual description may be expressed in medical terms. Medical terminology is appropriate in requirements when the developers and reviewers are familiar with the language, but it is often preferable to translate the concepts into engineering terms at the requirements stage to minimize miscommunication with the development staff.

. . . both product developers and those representing the user must take responsibility for critically examining proposed requirements, exploring stated and implied assumptions, and uncovering problems.

. . . A basic principle is that design input requirements should specify what the design is intended to do while carefully avoiding specific design solutions at this stage. . . .

There are occasions when it may be appropriate to specify part of the design solution in the design input requirements. For example, a manufacturer may want to share components or manufacturing processes across a family of products in order to realize economies of scale, or simply to help establish a corporate identity. . . . However, it is important to realize that every such design constraint reduces implementation flexibility and should therefore be documented and identified as a possible conflicting requirement for subsequent resolution.

Scope and Level of Detail. Design input requirements must be comprehensive. . . . design input requirements fall into three categories. Virtually every product will have requirements of all three types.

- Functional requirements specify what the device does, focusing on the operational capabilities of the device and processing of inputs and the resultant outputs.
- Performance requirements specify how much or how well the device must perform, addressing issues such as speed, strength, response times, accuracy, limits of operation, etc. This includes a quantitative characterization of the use environment, including, for example, temperature, humidity, shock, vibration, and electromagnetic compatibility. Requirements concerning device reliability and safety also fit into this category.
- Interface requirements specify characteristics of the device which are critical to compatibility with external systems; specifically, those characteristics which are mandated by external systems and outside the control of the developers. One interface which is important in every case is the user and/or patient interface.

. . . the scope of the design input requirements development . . . is dependent upon the complexity of a device and the risk associated with its use. For most medical devices, numerous requirements encompassing functions, performance, safety, and regulatory concerns are implied by the application. These implied requirements should be explicitly stated, in engineering terms, in the design input requirements.

Determining the appropriate level of detail requires experience. However, some general guidance is possible. . . . Some insight as to what is necessary is provided by examining the requirements for a very common external interface. For the power requirements for AC-powered equipment, it is not sufficient to simply say that a unit shall be AC-powered. It is better to say that the unit shall be operable from AC power in North America, Europe, and Japan, but that is still insufficient detail to implement or validate the design. If one considers the situation just in North America, where the line voltage is typically 120 volts, many systems are specified to operate over the range of 108 to 132 volts. However, to account for the possibility of brown-out, critical devices may be specified to operate from 95 to 132 volts or even wider ranges. Based on the intended use of the device, the manufacturer must choose appropriate performance limits.

There are many cases when it is impractical to establish every functional and performance characteristic at the design input stage. But in most cases, the form of the requirement can be determined, and the requirement can be stated with a to-be-determined (TBD) numerical value or a range of possible values. This makes it possible for reviewers to assess whether the requirements completely characterize the intended use of the device, judge the impact of omissions, and track incomplete requirements to ensure resolution.

For complex designs, it is not uncommon for the design input stage to consume as much as thirty percent of the total project time. . . . They fail to realize that building a solid foundation saves time during the implementation. Part of the solution is to structure the requirements documents and reviews such that tangible measures of progress are provided.

At the other extreme, many medical devices have very simple requirements. . . . In such cases, there is no need to recreate the detailed design input requirements of the item. It is acceptable to simply cite the predecessor product documentation, add any new product information, and establish the unique packaging and labeling requirements.

Assessing Design Input Requirements for Adequacy. Eventually, the design input must be reviewed for adequacy. After review and approval, the design input becomes a controlled document. All future changes will be subject to the change control procedures. . . .

Any assessment of design input requirements boils down to a matter of judgment. . . . it is important for the review team to be multidisciplinary and to have the appropriate authority. A number of criteria may be employed by the review team.

- Design input requirements should be unambiguous. That is, each requirement should be able to be verified by an objective method of analysis, inspection, or testing. . . .
- Quantitative limits should be expressed with a measurement tolerance. . . .
- The set of design input requirements for a product should be self-consistent. It is not unusual for requirements to conflict with one another or with a referenced industry standard due to a simple oversight. Such conflicts should be resolved early in the development process.
- The environment in which the product is intended to be used should be properly characterized. . . .
- When industry standards are cited, the citations should be reviewed for completeness and relevance. . . .

Evolution of the Design Input Requirements. Large development projects often are implemented in stages. When this occurs, the design input requirements at each stage should be developed and reviewed following the principles set forth in this section. Fortunately, the initial set of requirements, covering the overall product, is by far the most difficult to develop. As the design proceeds, the output from the early stages forms the basis for the subsequent stages, and the information available to designers is inherently more extensive and detailed.

It is almost inevitable that verification activities will uncover discrepancies which result in changes to the design input requirements. There are two points to be made about this. One is that the change control process for design input requirements must be carefully managed. Often, a design change to correct one problem may create a new problem which must be addressed. Throughout the development process, it is important that any changes are documented and communicated to developers so that the total impact of the change can be determined. The change control process is crucial to device quality.

The second point is that extensive rework of the design input requirements suggests that the design input requirements may not be elaborated to a suitable level of detail, or insufficient resources are being devoted to defining and reviewing the requirements. . . .

AAMI/ANSI/ISO TR 14969:2004

Reference § 7.3.2 Design and development inputs

The TR provides a detailed list of design input requirement sources. It emphasizes that design input requirements are subject to change during the course of a design and development process, and they should be documented in a way that facilitates and controls these changes, identifies who is responsible for the change(s), and determines who needs to be notified of the change(s). The TR indicates that design input changes can be the result of design reviews conducted during the design and development process.

The TR points out that design input requirements, including the requirements related to process validation, should reflect the needs of the manufacturing organization that will produce the commercial version of the medical device. Among the other design input considerations are the design requirements related to device packaging and labeling. The TR refers to ISO 11607, related to sterile packaging, and ISO 15223 and EN 980, related to the use of symbols in device labeling. It cautions that before symbols are used in labeling, the organization should ensure that such symbols are accepted by the regulatory agencies in the countries in which the device will be marketed.

Authors' Notes

Many medical device firms construct a traceability matrix that relates design inputs to design outputs. Detailed traceability matrices include notations related to the sources of design input requirements (for example, regulatory requirement, output of risk management (risk control measure(s))). The traceability matrix is a useful tool in meeting the regulatory requirement that design outputs address design inputs and the requirement for design verification.

FDA Quality System Regulation—1996

§ 820.30 (d) ***Design output.*** Each manufacturer shall establish and maintain procedures for defining and documenting design output in terms that allow an adequate evaluation of conformance to design input requirements. Design output procedures shall contain or make reference to acceptance criteria and shall ensure that those design outputs that are essential for the proper functioning of the device are identified. Design output shall be documented, reviewed, and approved before release. The approval, including the date and signature of the individual(s) approving the output, shall be documented.

AAMI/ANSI/ISO 13485:2003

Reference § 7.3.3 Design and development outputs

The design output requirements in the Standard are essentially the same as those in the QSReg, with the added requirement that the design outputs provide information that facilitates "purchasing, production, and service provision." The Standard also contains a note that lists a number of forms the design outputs can take (for example, specifications, manufacturing prototypes, and engineering drawings).

FDA Guidance

QSReg Preamble

> **Comment group 76.** . . . Design output are the design specifications which should meet design input requirements, as confirmed during design verification and validation and ensured during design review. The output includes the device, its labeling and packaging, associated specifications and drawings, and production and quality assurance specifications and procedures.

These documents are the basis for the DMR. The total finished design output consists of the device, its labeling and packaging, and the DMR.

Comment group 77. . . . the design output must be documented and expressed in terms that can be verified against the design input requirements.

Design output can be "released" or transferred to the next design phase at various stages in the design process, as defined in the design and development plan. The design output is reviewed and approved before release or transfer to the next design phase or production. The design output requirements are intended to apply to all such stages of the design process.

Design Control Guidance for Medical Device Manufacturers, Issued 11 March, 1997

This guidance document can be found at http://www.fda.gov/cdrh/comp/designgd.html.

The quality system requirements for design output can be separated into two elements: Design output should be expressed in terms that allow adequate assessment of conformance to design input requirements and should identify the characteristics of the design that are crucial to the safety and proper functioning of the device. This raises two fundamental issues for developers:

- What constitutes design output?
- Are the form and content of the design output suitable?

. . . As a general rule, an item is design output if it is a work product, or deliverable item, of a design task listed in the design and development plan, and the item defines, describes, or elaborates an element of the design implementation. Examples include block diagrams, flow charts, software high-level code, and system or subsystem design specifications. The design output in one stage is often part of the design input in subsequent stages.

Design output includes production specifications as well as descriptive materials which define and characterize the design.

Production Specifications. Production specifications include drawings and documents used to procure components, fabricate, test, inspect, install, maintain, and service the device, . . .

. . . production specifications may take on other forms. For example, some manufacturers produce assembly instructions on videotapes rather than written instructions. Similarly, a program diskette, used by a computer-aided milling machine to fabricate a part, would be considered a production specification. The videotape and the software on the program diskette are part of the device master record.

Other Descriptive Materials. Other design output items might be produced which are necessary to establish conformance to design input requirements, but are not used in its production. For example, for each part which is fabricated by computer-aided machine, there should be an assembly drawing which specifies the dimensions and characteristics of the part. It is a part of the design output because it establishes the basis for the machine tool program used to fabricate the part. Other examples of design output include the following:

- the results of risk analysis
- software source code
- results of verification activities
- biocompatibility test results
- bioburden test results

Form and Content. Manufacturers must take steps to assure that the design output characterizes all important aspects of the design and is expressed in terms which allow adequate verification and validation. Two basic mechanisms are available to manufacturers to accomplish these objectives.

- First, the manufacturer proactively can specify the form and content of design output at the planning stage. . . .
- Second, form and content can be reviewed retroactively as a part of the design verification process. . . .

DESIGN CONTROLS

"Guideline for the Manufacture of In Vitro Diagnostic Products," January 10, 1994

This guidance document addresses the issue of design output in a section describing product specifications. The guidance document is supported by the FDA Office of IVD Devices Evaluation and Safety. While it was issued in 1994, there is no indication that it has been amended or withdrawn. A copy of this guidance document may be found at http://www.fda.gov/cdrh/comp/918.pdf.

AAMI/ANSI/ISO TR 14969:2004

Reference § 7.3.3 Design and development

The TR contains a more comprehensive list of the various types of design outputs than is contained in the QSReg.

Authors' Notes

See "Authors' Notes" related to design input.

FDA Quality System Regulation—1996

§ 820.30(e) ***Design review.*** Each manufacturer shall establish and maintain procedures to ensure that formal documented reviews of the design results are planned and conducted at appropriate stages of the device's design development. The procedures shall ensure that participants at each design review include representatives of all functions concerned with the design stage being reviewed and an individual(s) who does not have direct responsibility for the design stage being reviewed, as well as any specialists needed. The results of a design review, including identification of the design, the date, and the individual(s) performing the review, shall be documented in the design history file (the DHF).

AAMI/ANSI/ISO 13485:2003

Reference § 7.3.4 Design and development review

There are no additional design review requirements in the Standard beyond those already in the QSReg.

FDA Guidance

QSReg Preamble

> **Comment group 78.** . . . The purpose of conducting design reviews during the design phase is to ensure that the design satisfies the design input requirements for the intended use of the device and the needs of the user. Design review includes the review of design verification data to determine whether the design outputs meet functional and operational requirements, the design is compatible with components and other accessories, the safety requirements are achieved, the reliability and maintenance requirements are met, the labeling and other regulatory requirements are met, and the manufacturing, installation, and servicing requirements are compatible with the design specifications. Design reviews should be conducted at major decision points during the design phase.

For a large manufacturer, design review provides an opportunity for all those who may have an impact on the quality of the device to provide input, including manufacturing, quality assurance, purchasing, sales, and servicing divisions. While small manufacturers may not have the broad range of disciplines found in a large company, and the need to coordinate and control technical interfaces may be lessened, the principles of design review still apply. The requirements under Sec. 820.30(e) allow small manufacturers to tailor a design review that is appropriate to their individual needs.

Comment group 79. . . . design reviews must be conducted at appropriate stages of design development, which must be defined in the established design and development plan. The number of design reviews will depend on the plan and the complexity of the device. . . . the results of a design review [must] include identification of the design, the date, and the individual(s) performing the review. Thus, multiple reviews can occur and the manufacturer must document what is being reviewed, when, and by whom. FDA never intended to mandate that an individual without design responsibility conduct the design reviews and, to clarify its position, . . . and states that the procedures shall ensure that each design review includes an individual(s) who does not have direct responsibility for the design stage being reviewed. This requirement will provide an "objective view" from someone not working directly on that particular part of the design project, to ensure that the requirements are met. In making this change, FDA also notes that it was not FDA's intention to prohibit those directly responsible for the design from participating in the design review.

Design Control Guidance for Medical Device Manufacturers, Issued 11 March, 1997

This guidance document can be found at http://www.fda.gov/cdrh/comp/designgd.html.

In general, formal design reviews are intended to:

- provide a systematic assessment of design results, including the device design and the associated designs for production and support processes;
- provide feedback to designers on existing or emerging problems;
- assess project progress; and/or
- provide confirmation that the project is ready to move on to the next stage of development.

Many types of reviews occur during the course of developing a product. Reviews may have both an internal and external focus. The internal focus is on the feasibility of the design and the produceability of the design with respect to manufacturing and support capabilities. The external focus is on the user requirements; that is, the device design is viewed from the perspective of the user.

The nature of reviews changes as the design progresses. During the initial stages, issues related to design input requirements will predominate. Next, the main function of the reviews may be to evaluate or confirm the choice of solutions being offered by the design team. Then, issues such as the choice of materials and the methods of manufacture become more important. During the final stages, issues related to the verification, validation, and production may predominate.

The term "review" is commonly used by manufacturers to describe a variety of design assessment activities. Most, but not all, of these activities meet the definition of formal design reviews. The following exceptions may help to clarify the distinguishing characteristics of design reviews.

- Each design document which constitutes the formal output, or deliverable, of a design task is normally subject to evaluation activities, sometimes referred to as informal peer review, supervisory review, or technical assessment. These activities, while they may be called reviews, are often better described as verification activities, because they are not intended to be comprehensive, definitive, and multidisciplinary in their scope. . . .
- Developers may conduct routine or ad hoc meetings to discuss an issue, coordinate activities, or assess development progress. Decisions from such meetings may not require formal documentation; however, if a significant issue is resolved, this should be documented. If the outcome results in change to an approved design document, then applicable change control procedures should be followed, . . .

Control of the design review process is achieved by developing and implementing a formal design review program consistent with quality system requirements. The following issues should be addressed and documented in the design and development plan(s).

Number and Type of Reviews. . . . formal design reviews should be planned to detect problems early. A corollary is that planners should presume that problems will be detected, and allocate a reasonable amount of time to implement corrective actions. Typically, formal reviews are conducted at the end of each phase and at important milestones in the design process.

. . . it is beneficial in almost every case to conduct a formal review of the design input requirements early in the development process. The number of reviews depends upon the complexity of the device.

- For a simple design, or a minor upgrade to an existing product, it might be appropriate to conduct a single review at the conclusion of the design process.
- For a product involving multiple subsystems, an early design task is to allocate the design input requirements among the various subsystems. . . . In cases like these, a formal design review is a prudent step

to ensure that all such system-level requirements have been allocated satisfactorily prior to engaging in detailed design of each subsystem.

- For complex systems, additional reviews are often built into the development plan. For example, engineering sketches may be developed for prototyping purposes prior to development of production drawings. Evaluation of the prototype would typically culminate in a formal design review. Similarly, software development commonly includes a high-level design phase, during which requirements are elaborated to a greater level of detail and algorithms are developed to implement key functions. A formal design review would typically be conducted to review this work prior to beginning detailed coding.

There are a number of approaches to conducting formal design reviews at the end of the design process. In some organizations, engineering essentially completes the design, tests an engineering prototype, and conducts a formal design review prior to turning the design over to manufacturing. In such cases, an additional review will be needed after the design has been validated using production devices.

In some instances, components having long lead times may enter production prior to completion of the overall device design. The primary motivation for early production is to reduce time to market. The manufacturer runs the business risk that the design review at the end of the design process will uncover a defect that must be corrected in production devices before any devices are distributed.

All of these approaches to scheduling formal design reviews are valid. What is important is that the manufacturer establish a reasonable rationale for the number and type of reviews, based on sound judgment.

Selection of Reviewers. In determining who should participate in a formal design review, planners should consider the qualifications of reviewers, the types of expertise required to make an adequate assessment, and the independence of the reviewers. Each of these concerns is discussed briefly in the following paragraphs.

Qualifications. Formal design reviews should be conducted by person(s) having technical competence and experience at least comparable to the developers. For a small manufacturer, this may require that an outside consultant be retained to participate in the evaluation of the design.

A manufacturer will often employ one or more specialists to conduct certain types of specialized assessments which are beyond the capabilities of the designers. . . . Such specialists may be assigned to participate in the formal design review. Alternatively, they may be assigned to make an independent assessment and submit observations and recommendations to the reviewers. Either approach is valid.

Types of expertise required. Many medical device designs involve a number of technologies, such as electronics, mechanics, software, materials science, or pneumatics. In addition, a variety of clinical and manufacturing issues may influence the design. Manufacturers should carefully consider which interests should be represented at formal design reviews. Subtle distinctions in reviewer perspective may have dramatic impact on device quality. . . .

Independence. The formal design review should include at least one individual who does not have direct responsibility for the design stage under review. In a small company, complete independence is very difficult to obtain. . . . reviewers will often be from the same organization as the developers, but they should not have been significantly involved in the activities under review. . . .

Design Review Procedures. The manufacturer should have documented formal design review procedures addressing the following:

- Evaluation of the design (including identification of concerns, i.e., issues and potential problems with the design)
- Resolution of concerns
- Implementation of corrective actions

Evaluation of the design. Many formal design reviews take the form of a meeting. At this meeting, the designer(s) may make presentations to explain the design implementation, and persons responsible for verification activities may present their findings to the reviewers. Reviewers may ask for clarification or additional information on any topic, and add their concerns to any raised by the presenters. This portion of the review is focused on finding problems, not resolving them.

There are many approaches to conducting design review meetings. In simple cases, the technical assessor and reviewer may be the same person, often a project manager or engineering supervisor, and the review meeting is a simple affair in the manager's office. For more elaborate reviews, detailed written procedures are desirable to ensure that all pertinent topics are discussed, conclusions accurately recorded, and action items documented and tracked.

There is a dangerous tendency for design review meetings to become adversarial affairs. . . .

These difficulties can be avoided by stating the goals and ground rules for conducting the formal design review clearly at the outset. While the designers are in the best position to explain the best features of the design, they are also most likely to be aware of the design's weaknesses. If the designers and reviewers are encouraged to work together to systematically explore problems and find solutions, the resultant design will be improved and all parties will benefit from the process. Participants must be encouraged to ask questions, avoid making assumptions, and think critically. . . .

Not all formal design reviews involve meetings. For extremely simple designs or design changes, it may be appropriate to specify a procedure in which review materials are distributed or circulated among the reviewers for independent assessment and approval. However, such a procedure negates the benefits of synergy and teamwork, and should be considered only in cases where the design issues are limited in scope and well defined.

Resolution of concerns. . . . There is wide variation in the way companies implement decision-making processes. In some cases, the reviewers play an advisory role to the engineering manager or other company official, who directs the formal design review and ultimately selects a course of action. In other cases, the reviewers are given limited or broad authority to make decisions and commit resources to resolve problems. The approach used should be documented.

In the real world, reviews often leave unresolved issues. Therefore, review procedures should include a process for resolving differences, and provide reviewers with enough leeway to make practical decisions while protecting the integrity of the process.

Implementation of corrective actions. Not all identified concerns result in corrective actions. The reviewers may decide that the issue is erroneous or immaterial. In most cases, however, resolution involves a design change, a requirements change, or a combination of the two. If the solution is evident, the reviewers may specify the appropriate corrective action; otherwise, an action item will be assigned to study the problem further. In any case, action items and corrective actions are normally tracked under the manufacturer's change control procedures.

Relationship of Design Review to Verification and Validation. In practice, design review, verification, and validation overlap one another, and the relationship among them may be confusing. As a general rule, the sequence is: verification, review, validation, review.

In most cases, verification activities are completed prior to the design review, and the verification results are submitted to the reviewers along with the other design output to be reviewed. Alternatively, some verification activities may be treated as components of the design review, particularly if the verification activity is complex and requires multidisciplinary review.

Similarly, validation typically involves a variety of activities, including a determination that the appropriate verifications and reviews have been completed. Thus, at the conclusion of the validation effort, a review is usually warranted to assure that the validation is complete and adequate.

AAMI/ANSI/ISO TR 14969:2004

Reference § 7.3.4 Design and development review

The TR contains a comprehensive list of items that could be included as subject matter for design reviews. The TR also recognizes that some regulatory bodies may require at a design review the presence of "an individual(s) who does not have direct responsibility for the design and development stage being reviewed. . . ."

Authors' Notes

We recommend that the organization keep a record of the design review results even if they are negative and require further design effort before the next design review or if they cause the organization to terminate the design and development effort. All such results must be kept in the DHF. It is possible that the results of a negative design review may be accessed in a future design and development effort or as part of a product problem investigation.

FDA Quality System Regulation—1996

§ 820.30(f) ***Design verification.*** Each manufacturer shall establish and maintain procedures for verifying the device design. Design verification shall confirm that the design output meets the design input requirements. The results of the design verification, including identification of the design, method(s), the date, and the individual(s) performing the verification, shall be documented in the DHF.

AAMI/ANSI/ISO 13485:2003

Reference § 7.3.5 Design and development verification

There are no additional design verification requirements in the Standard beyond those already in the QSReg.

FDA Guidance

QSReg Preamble

> **Comment group 82.** . . . Revised Sec. 820.30(f), "Design verification," and Sec. 820.30(g), "Design validation," require verification and validation of the design output. Section 820.30(d), "Design output," requires that the output be documented in a fashion that will allow for verification and validation. These sections thus contain different requirements that are basic to establishing that the design output meets the approved design requirements or inputs, including user needs and intended uses. All the requirements are

essential to assuring the safety and effectiveness of devices. FDA does not believe that these requirements place undue burden on designers or require additional documentation with no value added. These basic requirements are necessary to assure the proper device performance, and, therefore, the production of safe and effective devices, and are acknowledged and accepted as such throughout the world.

Design Control Guidance for Medical Device Manufacturers, Issued 11 March, 1997

This guidance document can be found at http://www.fda.gov/cdrh/comp/designgd.html.

Verification and validation are associated concepts with very important differences. Various organizations have different definitions for these terms. Medical device manufacturers are encouraged to use the terminology of the quality system requirements in their internal procedures.

. . . Verification is the process of checking at each stage whether the output conforms to requirements for that stage. For example: does the air conditioning system deliver the specified cooling capacity to each room? Is the roof rated to withstand so many newtons per square meter of wind loading? Is a fire alarm located within 50 meters of each location in the building?

At the same time, the architect has to keep in mind the broader question of whether the results are consistent with the ultimate user requirements. . . . Those broader concerns are the essence of validation.

In the initial stages of design, verification is a key quality assurance technique. As the design effort progresses, verification activities become progressively more comprehensive. . . .

Validation follows successful verification, and ensures that each requirement for a particular use is fulfilled. . . .

Types of Verification Activities. Verification activities are conducted at all stages and levels of device design. The basis of verification is a three-pronged approach involving tests, inspections, and analyses. Any approach which establishes conformance with a design input requirement is an acceptable means of verifying the design with respect to that requirement. . . .

Complex designs require more and different types of verification activities. The nature of verification activities varies according to the type of design output. . . . the manufacturer should select and apply appropriate verification techniques based on the generally accepted practices for the technologies employed in their products. Many of these practices are an integral part of the development process, and are routinely performed by developers. The objective of design controls is to ensure adequate oversight by making verification activities explicit and measuring the thoroughness of their execution.

Following are a few examples of verification methods and activities.

- Worst case analysis of an assembly to verify that components are derated properly and not subject to overstress during handling and use.
- Thermal analysis of an assembly to assure that internal or surface temperatures do not exceed specified limits.
- Fault tree analysis of a process or design.
- Failure modes and effects analysis.
- Package integrity tests.
- Biocompatibility testing of materials.
- Bioburden testing of products to be sterilized.
- Comparison of a design to a previous product having an established history of successful use.

For some technologies, verification methods may be highly standardized. In other cases, the manufacturer may choose from a variety of applicable methods. In a few cases, the manufacturer must be creative in devising ways to verify a particular aspect of a design.

Some manufacturers erroneously equate production testing with verification. Whereas verification testing establishes conformance of design output with design input, the aim of production testing is to determine whether the unit under test has been correctly manufactured. . . . production testing is rarely, if ever, comprehensive enough to verify the design. For example, a leakage test may be used during production to ensure that a hermetically-sealed enclosure was properly assembled. However, the leakage test may not be sensitive enough to detect long-term diffusion of gas through the packaging material. Permeability of the packaging material is an intrinsic property of the material rather than an assembly issue, and would likely be verified using a more specialized test than is used during production.

Documentation of Verification Activities. Some verification methods result in a document by their nature. For example, a failure modes and effects analysis produces a table listing each system component, its postulated failure modes, and the effect of such failures on system operation.

Another self-documenting verification method is the traceability matrix. This method is particularly useful when the design input and output are both documents; it also has great utility in software development. In the most common form of the traceability matrix, the input requirements are enumerated in a table, and references are provided to each section in the output documents (or software modules) which address or satisfy each input requirement. The matrix can also be constructed "backwards," listing each feature in the design output and tracing which input requirement bears on that feature. This reverse approach is especially useful for detecting hidden assumptions. . . .

However, many verification activities are simply some sort of structured assessment of the design output relative to the design input. When this is the case, manufacturers may document completion of verification activities by linking these activities with the signoff procedures for documents. This may be accomplished by establishing a procedure whereby each design output document must be verified and signed by designated persons. The presence of the reviewers' signatures on the document signifies that the design output has been verified in accordance with the signoff procedure.

AAMI/ANSI/ISO TR 14969:2004

Reference § 7.3.5 Design and development verification

The TR recommends that any tests or demonstrations used to verify that the design output meets the design input requirements be conducted under conditions that challenge the full range of the intended use of the medical device.

In addition, the TR recommends that any alternative calculations or comparisons conducted as part of the design verification be reviewed to ensure that they are scientifically appropriate and valid.

Authors' Notes

See "Authors' Notes" related to design and development inputs.

FDA Quality System Regulation—1996

§ 820.30(g) ***Design validation.*** Each manufacturer shall establish and maintain procedures for validating the device design. Design validation shall be performed under defined operating conditions on initial production units, lots, or batches, or their equivalents. Design validation shall ensure that devices conform to defined user needs and intended uses and shall include testing of production units under actual or simulated use conditions. Design validation shall include software validation and risk analysis, where appropriate. The results of the design validation, including identification of the design, method(s), the date, and the individual(s) performing the validation, shall be documented in the DHF.

AAMI/ANSI/ISO 13485:2003

Reference § 7.3.6 Design and development validation

The Standard requires that design validation be completed before the commercial delivery or implementation of the medical device. It indicates that for large medical devices assembled for the first time at a customer location, design validation may be completed at that location, and delivery for the purpose of that design validation is not considered to be a commercial delivery.

The Standard also recognizes that clinical evaluations may be part of the design validation of the medical device as required by national regulatory bodies.

FDA Guidance

QSReg Preamble

Comment group 80. . . . FDA regulations do not prohibit the shipment of prototypes for clinical or other studies. Prototypes used in clinical studies involving humans may be shipped in accordance with the IDE provisions in part 812 (21 CFR part 812).

FDA understands that it is not always practical to conduct clinical studies on finished production units and, therefore, the use of prototypes in clinical studies is acceptable. When prototype devices are used on humans they must be verified as safe to the maximum extent feasible. Final design validation, however, cannot be done on prototypes because the actual devices produced and distributed are seldom the same as the research and development prototypes. The final verification and validation, therefore, must include the testing of actual production devices under actual or simulated use conditions.

Comment group 81. . . . the design must be verified and validated. It is important to note that design validation follows successful design verification. Certain aspects of design validation can be accomplished during the design verification, but design verification is not a substitute for design validation. Design validation should be performed under defined operating conditions and on the initial production units, lots, or batches, or their equivalents to ensure proper overall design control and proper design transfer. When equivalent devices are used in the final design validation, the manufacturer must document in detail how the device was manufactured and how the manufacturing is similar to and possibly different from initial production. Where there are differences, the manufacturer must justify why design validation results are valid for the production units, lots, or batches. Manufacturers should not use prototypes developed in the laboratory or machine shop as test units to meet these requirements. Prototypes may differ from the finished production devices. During research and development, conditions for building prototypes are typically better controlled and personnel more knowledgeable about what needs to be done and how to do it than are regular production personnel. When going from laboratory to scale-up production, standards, methods, and procedures may not be properly transferred, or additional manufacturing processes may be added. Often, changes not reflected in the prototype are made in the device to facilitate the manufacturing process, and these may adversely affect device functioning and user interface characteristics. Proper testing of devices that are produced using the same methods and procedures as those to be used in routine production will prevent the distribution and subsequent recall of many unacceptable medical devices.

In addition, finished devices must be tested for performance under actual conditions of use or simulated use conditions in the actual or simulated environment in which the device is expected to be used. The simulated use testing provision no longer requires that the testing be performed on the first three production runs. However, samples must be taken from units, lots, or batches that were produced using the same specifications, production and quality system methods, procedures, and equipment that will be used for routine production. FDA considers this a critical element of the design validation. . . . Manufacturers must also conduct such tests when they make changes in the device design or the manufacturing process that could affect safety or effectiveness. . . . The extent of testing conducted should be governed by the risk(s) the device will present if it fails. FDA considers these activities essential for ensuring that the manufacturing process does not adversely affect the device.

Design validation may also be necessary in earlier stages, prior to product completion, and multiple validations may need to be performed if there are different intended uses. Proper design validation cannot occur without following all the requirements set forth in the design control section of the regulation.

Comment group 82. . . . Revised Sec. 820.30(f), "Design verification," and Sec. 820.30(g), "Design validation," require verification and validation of the design output. Section 820.30(d), "Design output," requires that the output be documented in a fashion that will allow for verification and validation. These sections thus contain different requirements that are basic to establishing that the design output meets the approved design requirements or inputs, including user needs and intended uses. All the requirements are essential to assuring the safety and effectiveness of devices. FDA does not believe that these requirements place undue burden on designers or require additional documentation with no value added. These basic requirements are necessary to assure the proper device performance, and, therefore, the production of safe and effective devices, and are acknowledged and accepted as such throughout the world.

Comment group 83. . . . [FDA has included in this section the requirement for risk analysis.] . . . When conducting a risk analysis, manufacturers are expected to identify possible hazards associated with the design in both normal and fault conditions. The risks associated with the hazards, including those resulting from user error, should then be calculated in both normal and fault conditions. If any risk is judged unacceptable, it should be reduced to acceptable levels by the appropriate means, for example, by redesign or warnings. An important part of risk analysis is ensuring that changes made to eliminate or minimize hazards do not introduce new hazards. Tools for conducting such analyses include Failure Mode Effect Analysis and Fault Tree Analysis, among others.

. . . Software must be validated when it is a part of the finished device. FDA believes that this control is always needed, given the unique nature of software, to assure that software will perform as intended and will not impede safe operation by the user. Risk analysis must be conducted for the majority of devices subject to design controls and is considered to be an essential requirement for medical devices under this regulation, as well as under ISO/CD 13485 and EN 46001. FDA has replaced the phrase "where applicable" with "where appropriate" for consistency with the rest of the regulation.

Comment group 84. . . . The . . . language of Sec. 820.30(f) will permit the use of data from prior experimentation when applicable. When using data from previous experimentation, manufacturers must ensure that it is adequate for the current application.

Design Control Guidance for Medical Device Manufacturers, Issued 11 March, 1997

This guidance document can be found at http://www.fda.gov/cdrh/comp/designgd.html.

. . . design validation is a cumulative summation of all efforts to assure that the design will conform to user needs and intended use(s), given expected variations in components, materials, manufacturing processes, and the use environment.

Validation Planning. Planning for validation should begin early in the design process. The performance characteristics that are to be assessed should be identified, and validation methods and acceptance criteria should be established. For complex designs, a schedule of validation activities and organizational or individual responsibilities will facilitate maintaining control over the process. The validation plan should be reviewed for appropriateness, completeness, and to ensure that user needs and intended uses are addressed.

Validation Review. Validation may expose deficiencies in the original assumptions concerning user needs and intended uses. A formal review process should be used to resolve any such deficiencies. As with verification, the perception of a deficiency might be judged insignificant or erroneous, or a corrective action may be required.

Validation Methods. Many medical devices do not require clinical trials. However, all devices require clinical evaluation and should be tested in the actual or simulated use environment as a part of validation. This testing should involve devices which are manufactured using the same methods and procedures expected to be used for ongoing production. While testing is always a part of validation, additional validation methods are often used in conjunction with testing, including analysis and inspection methods, compilation of relevant scientific literature, provision of historical evidence that similar designs and/or materials are clinically safe, and full clinical investigations or clinical trials.

. . . It may be beneficial to ask the best workers to evaluate and critique the manufacturing process by trying it out, but pilot production should simulate as closely as possible the actual manufacturing conditions.

Validation should also address product packaging and labeling. These components of the design may have significant human factors implications, and may affect product performance in unexpected ways. . . .

Validation should include simulation of the expected environmental conditions, such as temperature, humidity, shock and vibration, corrosive atmospheres, etc. For some classes of device, the environmental stresses encountered during shipment and installation far exceed those encountered during actual use, and should be addressed during validation.

Particular care should be taken to distinguish among customers, users, and patients to ensure that validation addresses the needs of all relevant parties. . . .

Validation Documentation. Validation is a compilation of the results of all validation activities. For a complex design, the detailed results may be contained in a variety of separate documents and summarized in a validation report. Supporting information should be explicitly referenced in the validation report and either included as an appendix or available in the design history file.

Guidance for Industry: Guideline for the Monitoring of Clinical Investigations, Issued November 1998

The guidance document can be found at http://www.fda.gov/ora/compliance_ref/bimo/clinguid.html.

The purpose of this guideline is to present acceptable approaches to monitoring clinical investigations. Existing requirements for sponsors of clinical investigations involving new drugs for human and animal use (including biological products for human use) and medical devices under 21 CFR Parts 312 and 511, and 812 and 813, respectively, require that a sponsor monitor the progress of a clinical investigation. The monitoring functions may be delegated to a contract research organization as defined under 21 CFR 312.3. Proper monitoring is necessary to assure adequate protection of the rights of human subjects and the safety of all subjects involved in clinical investigations and the quality and integrity of the resulting data submitted to the Food and Drug Administration (FDA). . . .

This guideline, issued under 21 CFR 10.90, reflects principles recognized by the scientific community as desirable approaches to monitoring clinical research involving human and animal subjects. These principles are not legal requirements but represent a standard of practice that is acceptable to FDA. . . .

This guidance document contains recommendations related to selection of an investigation monitor, written monitoring procedures, preinvestigation visits, periodic visits, review of subject records, and recording of on-site visits.

Guidance for FDA Staff: Regulating In Vitro Diagnostic Device (IVD) Studies, Issued 17 December, 1999

This guidance document can be found at http://www.fda.gov/cdrh/comp/ivdreg.html.

This document is intended to provide guidance for the Center for Devices and Radiological Health, Office of Compliance, Division of Bioresearch Monitoring, concerning regulation of in vitro diagnostic (IVD) device studies. The guidance explains how the Office of Compliance, Division of Bioresearch Monitoring (DBM), in conjunction with the Office of Device Evaluation (ODE), interprets and enforces the statute and regulations for investigational studies that involve the use of IVD's.

Draft Guidance for Industry and FDA Staff—In Vitro (IVD) Device Studies—Frequently Asked Questions, Distributed for comment purposes only, 25 October, 2007

This guidance document is available at http://www.fda.gov/cdrh/oivd/guidance/1587.html.

This guidance document, written in question and answer format, is intended to assist . . . (the manufacturer, sponsor, applicant, investigator and the IVD device industry in general) in the development of IVD studies, particularly those exempt from most of the requirements of the IDE regulation and to provide you with a broad view of the regulatory framework pertaining to the development phase of IVD devices. The information in this guidance document is also pertinent to investigators who participate in IVD studies and to institutional review boards (IRB) that review and approve such studies. The document is intended to facilitate the movement of new IVD technology from the investigational stage to the marketing stage.

This guidance document outlines FDA regulations applicable to studies for investigational IVD devices, including those regulations related to human subject protection. The guidance also explains data considerations that ultimately will affect the quality of the premarket submission. This document includes a glossary, a reference list with related web addresses, and a quick-reference table. . . .

FDA prepared this comprehensive document as a resource . . . to address issues concerning IVD studies. This guidance document contains information relevant to studies conducted during the development of a new IVD product, as well as other general considerations about applicable requirements and marketing of the new device. It addresses particularly those investigational studies that are exempt from the majority of requirements under 21 CFR Part 812. IVD study investigators and members of IRBs who review and approve such studies may also find it helpful. . . .

Guidance on Informed Consent for In Vitro Diagnostic Device Studies Using Leftover Human Specimens That Are Not Individually Identifiable—Guidance for Sponsor, Institutional Review Boards, Clinical Investigators and FDA Staff, Issued 25 April, 2006

This guidance document can be found at http://www.fda.gov/cdrh/oivd/guidance/1588.html.

FDA is issuing this guidance to inform sponsors, institutional review boards (IRBs), clinical investigators, and agency staff that the FDA intends to exercise enforcement discretion, under certain circumstances, with respect to its current regulations governing the requirement for informed consent when human specimens are used for FDA-regulated in vitro diagnostic (IVD)[6] device investigations. As described below, FDA does not intend to object to the use, without informed consent, of leftover human specimens—remnants of specimens collected for routine clinical care or analysis that would otherwise have been discarded—in investigations that meet the criteria for exemption from the Investigational Device Exemptions (IDE) regulation at 21 CFR 812.2(c)(3), as long as subject privacy is protected by using only specimens that are not individually identifiable. FDA also intends to include in this policy specimens obtained from specimen repositories[7] and specimens that are leftover from specimens previously collected for other unrelated research, as long as these specimens are not individually identifiable.

Under FDA's current regulations governing the conduct of IVD device studies, the definition of human subject includes individuals on whose specimens an investigational device is used [see 21 CFR 812.3(p)]. Because these regulations require informed consent for FDA-regulated human sub-

6. In vitro diagnostic products are those reagents, instruments, and systems intended for use in the diagnosis of disease or other conditions, including a determination of the state of health, in order to cure, mitigate, treat, or prevent disease or its sequelae. Such products are intended for use in the collection, preparation, and examination of specimens taken from the human body. 21 CFR 809.3(a).

7. A specimen repository is a common site for storage of collections of human biological specimens available for study.

ject research, except in limited circumstances specified in the regulations,[8] informed consent is required before specimens can be used in FDA-regulated research [see 21 CFR part 50].

. . . Many clinicians, research hospitals, and companies have viewed the requirement for informed consent for IVD studies using leftover specimens as unnecessary for the protection of human subjects and as overly burdensome and costly. . . .

The confusion regarding the application of informed consent requirements to IVD studies and concerns about unnecessary obstacles to product development have prompted FDA to issue this guidance document. The agency believes this guidance will facilitate product development in a manner consistent with the values of human subject protection. . . .

8. See 21 CFR 50.23(a) and 50.24.

AAMI/ANSI/ISO TR 14969:2004

Reference § 7.3.6 Design and development validation

The TR indicates that a clinical evaluation may consist of a critical review of scientific literature, historical evidence derived from similar devices, and/or a clinical trial(s). The TR refers to ISO 14155-1 for guidance on the conduct of clinical evaluations.

Authors' Notes

For a discussion of risk management, see the chapter "Risk Management" in this book.

FDA Quality System Regulation—1996

§ 820.30(h) ***Design transfer.*** Each manufacturer shall establish and maintain procedures to ensure that the device design is correctly translated into production specifications.

AAMI/ANSI/ISO 13485:2003

There is no Standard section specifically related to design transfer. There are design transfer requirements included in the requirements related to design and development inputs, outputs, and verification.

FDA Guidance

QSReg Preamble

Comment group 85. . . . While FDA believes that three production runs during process validation (process validation may be initiated before or during design transfer) is the accepted standard, FDA recognizes that all processes may not be defined in terms of lots or batches. The number three is, however, currently considered to be the acceptable standard. Therefore, although the number requirement is deleted, FDA expects validation to be carried out properly in accordance with accepted standards, and will inspect for compliance accordingly.

Revised Sec. 820.30(h) now contains a general requirement for the establishment of procedures to ensure that the design basis for the device is correctly translated into production methods and procedures. This is the same requirement that is contained in Sec. 820.100(a) of the original CGMP regulation.

Comment group 86. . . . FDA did not intend the requirements for "Design release" to prohibit manufacturers from beginning the production process until all design activities were completed. The intent of the requirement was to ensure that all design specifications released to production have been approved, verified, and validated before they are implemented as part of the production process. This requirement is now explicitly contained in Sec. 820.30(d).

Design Control Guidance for Medical Device Manufacturers, Issued 11 March, 1997

This guidance document can be found at http://www.fda.gov/cdrh/comp/designgd.html.

Production specifications must ensure that manufactured devices are repeatedly and reliably produced within product and process capabilities. If a manufactured device deviates outside those capabilities, performance may be compromised. Thus, the process of encapsulating knowledge about the device into production specifications is critical to device quality.

The level of detail necessary to accomplish this objective varies widely, based on the type of device, the relationship between the design and manufacturing organizations, and the knowledge, experience, and skills of production workers. . . .

One normally associates the term "production specifications" with written documents, such as assembly drawings, component procurement specifications, workmanship standards, manufacturing instructions, and inspection and test specifications. . . . other equally acceptable means of conveying design information exist, and manufacturers have the flexibility to employ these alternate means of communication as appropriate. For example, each of the following could constitute "production specifications" within the meaning of the quality system requirements:

- documentation (in electronic format as well as paper)
- training materials, . . .
- digital data files, e.g., programmable device files, master EPROM, computer-aided manufacturing (CAM) programming files
- manufacturing jigs and aids, e.g., molds, sample wiring harness to be duplicated

Historically, shortcomings in the production specifications tend to be manifested late in the product life cycle. When the design is new, there is often intensive interaction between the design and production teams, providing ample opportunity for undocumented information flow. Later, as production experience is gained, some decoupling often occurs between design and production teams. In addition, key personnel may leave, and their replacements may lack comparable training, experience, or institutional knowledge.

Particular care should be taken when the product involves new and unproved manufacturing processes, or established processes which are new to the manufacturer. It may not be possible to determine the adequacy of full-scale manufacturing on the basis of successfully building prototypes or models in a laboratory and testing these prototypes or models. The engineering feasibility and production feasibility may be different because the equipment, tools, personnel, operating procedures, supervision and motivation could be different when a manufacturer scales up for routine production.

No design team can anticipate all factors bearing on the success of the design, but procedures for design transfer should address at least the following basic elements.

- First, the design and development procedures should include a qualitative assessment of the completeness and adequacy of the production specifications.
- Second, the procedures should ensure that all documents and articles which constitute the production specifications are reviewed and approved.
- Third, the procedures should ensure that only approved specifications are used to manufacture production devices.

The first item in the preceding list may be addressed during design transfer. The second and third elements are among the basic principles of document control and configuration management. As long as the production specifications are traditional paper documents, there is ample information available to guide manufacturers in implementing suitable procedures. When the production specifications include non-traditional means, flexibility and creativity may be needed to achieve comparable rigor.

AAMI/ANSI/ISO TR 14969:2004

There is no TR section specifically related to design transfer. There are design transfer recommendations included in the TR recommendations related to design and development inputs, outputs, and verification.

Authors' Notes

One of the key functions of the design and development process is to design and develop the manufacturing processes that will be needed to produce the medical device. As part of that process development activity, such processes are validated. Many companies conduct process validation as part of design transfer because the expertise for such validation resides in the manufacturing organization rather than in the design and development organization. Because design transfer is conceived as being at the end of the design and development process, it sometimes is subjected to scheduling constraints that prevent it from being done thoroughly and well. If process validation is part of the design transfer activity, it may be subjected to such pressures that might compromise the quality of the process validation activity. It is better to subject the process design to the same design controls as the product design (that is, planning, input, output, review, verification, and validation).

See further discussion of process validation in § 820.75 of this book.

FDA Quality System Regulation—1996

§ 820.30(i) ***Design changes.*** Each manufacturer shall establish and maintain procedures for the identification, documentation, validation or where appropriate verification, review, and approval of design changes before their implementation.

AAMI/ANSI/ISO 13485:2003

Reference § 7.3.7 Design and development changes

The Standard includes an added requirement that design changes must be reviewed to assess their effect on a product already delivered to customers.

FDA Guidance

QSReg Preamble

Comment group 87. . . . Manufacturers are not expected to maintain records of all changes proposed during the very early stages of the design process. However, all design changes made after the design review that approves the initial design inputs for incorporation into the design, and those changes made to correct design deficiencies once the design has been released to production, must be documented. The records of these changes create a history of the evolution of the design, which can be invaluable for failure investigation and for facilitating the design of future similar products. Such records can prevent the repetition of errors and the development of unsafe or ineffective designs. The evaluation and documentation should be in direct proportion to the significance of the change. Procedures must ensure that after the design requirements are established and approved, changes to the design, both pre-production and post-production are also reviewed, validated (or verified where appropriate), and approved. Otherwise, a device may be rendered unable to properly perform, and unsafe and ineffective. . . .

Note that when a change is made to a specification, method, or procedure, each manufacturer should evaluate the change in accordance with an established procedure to determine if the submission of a premarket notification (510(k)) under Sec. 807.81(a)(3) (21 CFR 807.81(a)(3)), or the submission of a supplement to a PMA under Sec. 814.39(a) (21 CFR 814.39) is required. Records of this evaluation and its results should be maintained.

Comment group 88. . . . The safety and effectiveness of devices cannot be proven by final inspection or testing. Product development is inherently an evolutionary process. While change is a healthy and necessary part of product development, quality can be ensured only if change is controlled and documented in the development process, as well as the production process. Again, manufacturers are not expected to maintain records of changes made during the very early stages of product development; only those design changes made after the approval of the design inputs need be documented. Each manufacturer must establish criteria for evaluating changes to ensure that the changes are appropriate for its designs.

Comment group 89. . . . FDA . . . has amended the requirement to permit verification where appropriate. For example, a change in the sterilization process of a catheter will require validation of the new process, but the addition of more chromium to a stainless steel surgical instrument may only require verification through chemical analysis. Where a design change cannot be verified by subsequent inspection and test, it must be validated.

Design Control Guidance for Medical Device Manufacturers, Issued 11 March, 1997

This guidance document can be found at http://www.fda.gov/cdrh/comp/designgd.html.

There are two principal administrative elements involved in controlling design changes:

- Document control-enumeration of design documents, and tracking their status and revision history. . . .
- Change control-enumeration of deficiencies and corrective actions arising from verification and review of the design, and tracking their resolution prior to design transfer.

For a small development project, an adequate process for managing change involves little more than documenting the design change, performing appropriate verification and validation, and keeping records of reviews. The main objectives are ensuring that:

- corrective actions are tracked to completion;
- changes are implemented in such a manner that the original problem is resolved and no new problems are created; or if new problems are created, they are also tracked to resolution; and
- design documentation is updated to accurately reflect the revised design.

For projects involving more than two persons, coordination and communication of design changes become vitally important. . . .

Document Control. The features of a manufacturing document control system typically include the following:

- Documents should be identified (i.e., named and numbered) in accordance with some logical scheme which links the documents to the product or component they describe or depict and illuminates the drawing hierarchy.
- A master list or index of documents should be maintained . . .
- Approval procedures should be prescribed which govern entry of documents into the document control system.
- A history of document revisions should be maintained.

- Procedures for distributing copies of controlled documents and tracking their location should be prescribed.
- Files of controlled documents should be periodically inventoried to ensure that the contents are up to date.
- A person or persons should be assigned specific responsibility to oversee and carry out these procedures. . . .
- There should be a procedure for removal and deletion of obsolete documents.

Change Control. Manufacturing change control is usually implemented using a set of standardized procedures similar to the following:

- A change request might be originated . . . and identifies a design problem which the requester believes should be corrected. Change requests are typically reviewed following the manufacturer's prescribed review process, and the request might be rejected, deferred, or accepted.
- If a change request is accepted and corrective action is straightforward, a change order might be issued on the spot to implement the change. The change order pertains to an explicitly identified document or group of documents, and specifies the detailed revision of the document content which will fix the identified problem.
- Often, the change request results in an assignment to developers to further study the problem and develop a suitable corrective action. . . .
- Change requests and change orders should be communicated to all persons whose work might be impacted by the change.
- It may not be practical to immediately revise documents affected by a change order. Instead, the common practice is to distribute and attach a copy of the change order to each controlled copy of the original document.
- Change control procedures should incorporate review and assessment of the impact of the design change on the design input requirements and intended uses.
- A mechanism should be established to track all change requests and change orders to ensure proper disposition.
- Change control procedures are usually administered by the document control staff.

Application of Document and Change Controls to Design. . . . It is important that the design change procedures always include re-verifying and re-validating the design. Fortunately, most design changes occur early in the design process, prior to extensive design validation. Thus, for most design changes, a simple inspection is all that is required. The later in the development cycle that the change occurs, the more important the validation review becomes. . . .

AAMI/ANSI/ISO TR 14969:2004

Reference § 7.3.7 Design and development changes

The TR contains a list of factors that might initiate a design change (for example, design review due to risk management activities, safety regulations, or a request from engineering or finance).

The TR emphasizes the need to assess the possibility that a design change may have unexpected negative effects. It provides a list of questions that one should ask to highlight such unanticipated adverse influences and avoid them through redesign, labeling, or other means.

Authors' Notes

An example of the Standard requirement to assess the effect a change may have on an already-delivered product is the situation where a change to a power supply (for example, due to the unavailability of the original power supply) requires a new set of mounting holes. Since the new power supply will be used as a service replacement part, it will be necessary to also provide an adapter mounting plate along with the service replacement power supply.

FDA Quality System Regulation—1996

§ 820.30(j) ***Design history file.*** Each manufacturer shall establish and maintain a DHF for each type of device. The DHF shall contain or reference the records necessary to demonstrate that the design was developed in accordance with the approved design plan and the requirements of this part.

AAMI/ANSI/ISO 13485:2003

There is no Standard section specifically related to the creation of a DHF. Many of the documents and records requirements are the same for the Standard and the QSReg, but the Standard does not require the establishment of a named file called the Design History File.

FDA Guidance

QSReg Preamble

Comment group 90. . . . The DMR contains the documentation necessary to produce a device. The final design output from the design phase, which is maintained or referenced in the DHF, will form the basis or starting point for the DMR. Thus, those outputs must be referred to or placed in the DMR. The total finished design output includes the final device, its labeling and packaging, and the DMR that includes device specifications and drawings, as well as all instructions and procedures for production, installation, maintenance, and servicing.

The DHF, in contrast, contains or references all the records necessary to establish compliance with the design plan and the regulation, including the design control procedures. The DHF illustrates the history of the design, and is necessary so that manufacturers can exercise control over and be accountable for the design process, thereby maximizing the probability that the finished design conforms to the design specifications.

Comment group 91. . . . The intent of the DHF is to document, or reference the documentation of, the activities carried out to meet the design plan and requirements of Sec. 820.30. A DHF is, therefore, necessary for each type of device developed. The DHF must provide documentation showing the actions taken with regard to each type of device designed, not generically link devices together with different design characteristics and give a general overview of how the output was reached.

Comment group 92. . . . The proposed requirement does not state that all records must be contained in the DHF, but that all records necessary to demonstrate that the requirements were met must be contained in the file. FDA has deleted the word "all" but cautions manufacturers that the complete history of the design process should be documented in the DHF. Such records are necessary to ensure that the final design conforms to the design specifications. Depending on the design, that may be relatively few records. Manufacturers who do not document all their efforts may lose the information and experience of those efforts, thereby possibly requiring activities to be duplicated.

Design Control Guidance for Medical Device Manufacturers, Issued 11 March, 1997

This guidance document can be found at http://www.fda.gov/cdrh/comp/designgd.html.

There is no specific requirement in ISO 9001 or ISO 13485 for a design history file. . . .

Other national regulations require some form of documentation and records. Product documentation required by Canada, Europe, and Japan contain certain elements of the U.S. FDA design history file requirements without requiring all the elements to be compiled in a file.

Virtually every section of the design control requirements specifies information which should be recorded. The compilation of these records is sometimes referred to as the design history file. . . .

. . . many . . . cases have been documented in which the manufacturer lacked design information necessary to validate a design and maintain it throughout the product life cycle. This occurs for the most innocent of reasons—contracts expire, companies reorganize, employees move on to new projects or new jobs. Even when the designer is available, he or she may forget why a particular decision was made years, months, or even weeks before. Since design decisions often directly affect the well-being of device users and patients, it is to the manufacturer's benefit to maintain the knowledge base which forms a basis for the product design.

Except for small projects, it is unusual for all design history documents to be filed in a single location. For example, many design engineers maintain laboratory notebooks which are typically retained in the engineers' personal files. In addition, the design history may include memoranda and electronic mail correspondence which are stored at various physical locations. Quality system plans applicable to a development project may reside in the quality assurance department, while the chief engineer may be responsible for maintaining design and development plans. These diverse records need not be consolidated at a single location. The intent is simply that manufacturers have access to the information when it is needed. If a manufacturer has established procedures for multiple filing systems which together satisfy that intent, there is no need to create additional procedures or records.

. . . There are no requirements on the location or organization of the design history file. In some cases, especially for simple designs, the designer will assemble and maintain the entire design history file. For larger projects, a document control system will likely be established for design documents, and these files will likely be maintained in some central location, usually within the product development department.

. . . company policy should state unequivocally that all design history documentation is the property of the manufacturer, not the employee or contractor. Design and development contracts should explicitly specify the manufacturer's right to design information and establish standards for the form and content of design documentation. Finally, certain basic design information may be maintained in a single project file in a specified location. This may include the following:

- Detailed design and development plan specifying design tasks and deliverables.
- Copies of approved design input documents and design output documents.

- Documentation of design reviews.
- Validation documentation.
- When applicable, copies of controlled design documents and change control records.

AAMI/ANSI/ISO TR 14969:2004

There is no TR section specifically related to the establishment of a DHF.

Authors' Notes

The main difference between the QSReg and the Standard is that the former requires two documents (and their attending records), the DHF and the Device Master Record (DMR). The DHF (see 21 CFR § 820.30(j)) describes the design effort for the device, while the DMR (see 21 CFR § 820.181) contains all the information necessary to produce the device. In the case of the Standard, both the aspects of the design and the manufacture of a device are in the documentation and records listed in § 4.2.1 of the Standard and the TR.

SUBPART D

Document Controls

FDA Quality System Regulation—1996

§ 820.40 Document controls

Each manufacturer shall establish and maintain procedures to control all documents that are required by this part. The procedures shall provide for the following: [See § 820.40(a) and § 820.40(b).]

AAMI/ANSI/ISO 13485:2003

Reference § 4 Quality management system
§ 4.2 Documentation requirements
§ 4.2.3 Control of documents

There is no significant difference between the Standard and the QSReg in regard to requirements for document control, except that the Standard requires that the organization define a period for which at least one copy of all obsolete documents is retained. Normally this period is tied to the lifetime of the device, which is also defined by the organization, or to the time required to ensure that relevant documents will be available in order to understand those records that must be retained.

There is a difference in approach, as the QSReg considers a document to be a special form of record subject to regulation under § 820.40 and the Standard considers documents and records to be different forms of objective evidence with their requirements contained in § 4.2.3 and § 4.2.4, respectively.

FDA Guidance

QSReg Preamble

> **Comment group 93.** . . . The verification of document distribution and removal is very important and can directly affect the quality of a product. Section 820.40, which requires that the manufacturer establish and maintain procedures to control all documents, including those that are obsolete and/or to be removed, requires that the removal (or prevention of use) of obsolete documents be verified. . . . The procedures established must, among other things, ensure control of the accuracy and usage of current versions of the documents and the removal or prevention from use of obsolete documents, as well as ensure that the documentation developed is adequate to fulfill its intended purpose or requirement. FDA retained the requirement that the procedures ensure that documents meet the requirements of the regulation because that is the purpose of controlling the documents. . . .

AAMI/ANSI/ISO TR 14969:2004

Reference § 4 Quality management system
§ 4.2 Documentation requirements
§ 4.2.3 Control of documents

The TR includes guidance related to assigning the responsibilities related to the requirement listing in the Standard (for example, use of an implementation date for documents, prompt removal of obsolete documents).

The TR recommends periodic review of documents when certain events occur (for example, facilities, personnel, or organizational changes; introduction of new products or new product lines) to ensure their currency.

The TR recommends that documents have a consistent structure so that they are complete and clear to the persons expected to follow their contents. The TR includes a list of items that should be included in documents.

The TR also discusses the control of electronic documents, warning that there may be national regulations that must be followed for such documentation.

The TR provides a listing of the bases for determining the retention time for documents, including the anticipated commercial lifetime of the device, legal liability considerations, technical reasons for retaining the information contained in the document, and the period of time the product will be supported in the field through the provision of spare parts and/or servicing.

The TR provides further explanation of the Standard's requirement that obsolete documents must be retained. It recommends that in addition to considering any regulatory retention requirement, the organization should retain documents for as long as it is necessary to understand the QMS records that are retained. As a result, the retention of such documents will be tied to the lifetime of the medical device. Also, the TR discusses the need to properly identify obsolete documents as "obsolete" in order to avoid confusion with current approved documentation.

FDA Quality System Regulation—1996

§ 820.40(a) ***Document approval and distribution.*** Each manufacturer shall designate an individual(s) to review for adequacy and approve prior to issuance all documents established to meet the requirements of this part. The approval, including the date and signature of the individual(s) approving the document, shall be documented. Documents established to meet the requirements of this part shall be available at all locations for which they are designated, used, or otherwise necessary, and all obsolete documents shall be promptly removed from all points of use or otherwise prevented from unintended use.

AAMI/ANSI/ISO 13485:2003

Reference § 4 Quality management system
§ 4.2 Documentation requirements
§ 4.2.3 Document control

There is no significant difference between the Standard and the QSReg in regard to the requirements for document approval and distribution.

FDA Guidance

QSReg Preamble

Comment group 94. . . . FDA is aware that many documentation systems are now maintained electronically, and [has] implemented through rulemaking the use of electronic signatures [21 CFR Part 11]. The agency identified several important issues related to the use of such signatures, including how to ensure that the identification is in fact the user's "signature." These issues are discussed in FDA's ANPRM [Advanced Notice of Proposed Rule Making] on the use of electronic signatures, published in the Federal Register on July 21, 1992 (57 FR 32185), and the [regulation]. Therefore, FDA . . . notes that the quality system regulation's use of the term "signature" will permit the use of whatever electronic means the agency determines is the equivalent of a handwritten signature. . . . FDA has not added the term "or stamps" to the regulation; however, stamps could be acceptable if the manufacturer has a formal procedure on how stamps are used in place of handwritten signatures. The procedure would have to address many of the same issues addressed in the electronic signature [regulation], most importantly how the stamps would be controlled and how the manufacturer would ensure that the stamp was in fact the user's "signature."

AAMI/ANSI/ISO TR 14969:2004

Reference § 4 Quality management system
§ 4.2 Documentation requirements
§ 4.2.3 Document control

There is no significant difference between the TR and the QSReg in regard to the guidance for document approval and distribution.

Authors' Notes

Document control plays an important role both in requiring how a product is to be manufactured and in determining how well these instructions have been carried out. Due to the increased complexity of modern medical devices and the proliferation of international trade, such documents become indispensable as a means for investigation of product failure or for product improvement.

The QSReg, the Standard, and the associated guidance documents emphasize that the organization must have a controlled process in place that describes how documentation is created, reviewed, and approved.

Advances in technology have made electronic approvals, rapid dissemination of documents, and electronic storage possible. Guidance documents and the sections of the Standard dealing with these issues agree that any and all uses of technology in this area are permissible if shown to meet the intent of the national or international regulations.

FDA has been silent on the use of an "authority stamp" (popular with some Asian manufacturers). It does permit the use of such stamps as part of the approval procedures, but verifying the stamp user's identity still remains the key issue.

FDA Quality System Regulation—1996

§ 820.40(b) ***Document changes.*** Changes to documents shall be reviewed and approved by an individual(s) in the same function or organization that performed the original review and approval, unless specifically designated otherwise. Approved changes shall be communicated to the appropriate personnel in a timely manner. Each manufacturer shall maintain records of changes to documents. Change records shall include a description of the change, identification of the affected documents, the signature of the approving individual(s), the approval date, and when the change becomes effective.

AAMI/ANSI/ISO 13485:2003

Reference § 4 Quality management system
§ 4.2 Documentation requirements
§ 4.2.3 Control of documents

The requirements of the Standard are essentially the same as those of the QSReg.

FDA Guidance

QSReg Preamble

Comment group 96. . . . FDA has retained the requirement that the approved changes must be communicated in a timely manner to appropriate personnel. FDA has had many experiences where manufacturers made corrections to documents, but the changes were not communicated in a timely manner to the personnel utilizing the documents. The result of these untimely communications was the production of defective devices. . . . FDA [retains the] requirement for changes to be "approved by an individual(s) in the same function or organization that performed the original review and approval, unless specifically designated otherwise." . . . The intent of the requirement is to ensure that those who originally approved the document have an opportunity to review any changes because these individuals typically have the best insight on the impact of the changes. The requirement is flexible, however, because it permits the manufacturer to specifically designate individuals who did not perform the original review and approval to review and approve the changes. To designate such individuals, the manufacturer will need to determine who would be best suited to perform the function, thus ensuring adequate control over the changes. In this way, review and approval will not be haphazard.

AAMI/ANSI/ISO TR 14969:2004

Reference § 4 Quality management system
§ 4.2 Documentation requirements
§ 4.2.3 Control of documents

The guidances in the TR are essentially the same as those in the QSReg.

SUBPART E

Purchasing Controls

FDA Quality System Regulation—1996

§ 820.50 Purchasing controls

Each manufacturer shall establish and maintain procedures to ensure that all purchased or otherwise received product and services conform to specified requirements.

AAMI/ANSI/ISO 13485:2003

Reference § 7.4 Purchasing
§ 7.4.1 Purchasing process

The requirements of the Standard are the same as those of the QSReg.

FDA Guidance

QSReg Preamble

Comment group 99. . . . The failure to implement adequate purchasing controls has resulted in a significant number of recalls due to component failures. Most of these were due to unacceptable components provided by suppliers. Since FDA is not regulating component suppliers, FDA believes that the explicit addition to CGMP requirements of the purchasing controls . . . is necessary to provide the additional assurance that only acceptable components are used. To ensure purchased or otherwise received product or services conform to specifications, purchasing must be carried out under adequate controls, including the assessment and selection of suppliers, contractors, and consultants, the clear and unambiguous specification of requirements, and the performance of suitable acceptance activities. Each manufacturer must establish an appropriate mix of assessment and receiving acceptance to ensure products and services are acceptable for their intended uses. The specifications for the finished device cannot be met unless the individual parts of the finished device meet specifications. The most efficient and least costly approach is to ensure that only acceptable vendors' products and services are received. This means that only suppliers, contractors, and consultants that meet specifications should be used.

The regulation has been written to allow more flexibility in the way manufacturers may ensure the acceptability of products and services. Under the requirements, manufacturers must clearly define in the procedures the type and extent of control they intend to apply to products and services. Thus, a finished device manufacturer may choose to provide greater in-house controls to ensure that products and services meet requirements, or may require the supplier to adopt measures necessary to ensure acceptability, as appropriate. FDA generally believes that an appropriate mix of supplier and manufacturer quality controls is necessary. However, finished device manufacturers who conduct product quality control solely in-house must also assess the capability of suppliers to provide acceptable product. Where audits are not practical, this may be done through, among other means, reviewing historical data, monitoring and trending, and inspection and testing.

. . . manufacturers have flexibility in determining the degree of assessment and evaluation necessary for suppliers, contractors, and consultants. Thus the degree of supplier control necessary to establish compliance may vary with the type and significance of the product or service purchased and the impact of that product or service on the quality of the finished device. In addition, the requirement for manufacturers to establish assessment criteria has been deleted but the evaluation still must include a description how the assessment was made (according to what criteria or objective procedure) and the results must be documented. Each manufacturer must now define the type and extent of control it will exercise over suppliers, contractors, and consultants. . . .

. . . FDA believes that the flexibility of the regulation will allow manufacturers to implement JIT procedures without additional cost. In fact, the new regulation is more conducive to JIT practices by permitting the assessment or evaluation of product or services up front, thereby lessening the degree of in-house control that may be necessary.

Comment group 101. . . . The first sentence of the introductory text of Sec. 820.50 is . . . a general requirement that each manufacturer must establish procedures to ensure that received product and services (purchased or otherwise received) conform to specified requirements. All manufacturers are expected to apply controls to manufacturing materials appropriate to the manufacturing material, the intended use, and the effect of the manufacturing materials on safety and effectiveness. For example, the procedures necessary to ensure that a mold release agent conforms to specified requirements may be less involved than the procedures for controlling latex proteins. The provision allows the manufacturer the flexibility of establishing the procedures to meet its needs and to ensure that the product conforms to specified requirements.

AAMI/ANSI/ISO TR 14969:2004

Reference § 7.4 Purchasing
§ 7.4.1 Purchasing process

The TR provides no additional general guidance related to purchasing control beyond that in the QSReg.

FDA Quality System Regulation—1996

§ 820.50(a) ***Evaluation of suppliers, contractors, and consultants.*** Each manufacturer shall establish and maintain the requirements, including quality requirements that must be met by suppliers, contractors, and consultants. Each manufacturer shall:

(1) Evaluate and select potential suppliers, contractors, and consultants on the basis of their ability to meet specified requirements, including quality requirements. The evaluation shall be documented.

(2) Define the type and extent of control to be exercised over the product, services, suppliers, contractors, and consultants, based on the evaluation results.

(3) Establish and maintain records of acceptable suppliers, contractors, and consultants.

AAMI/ANSI/ISO 13485:2003

Reference § 7.4 Purchasing
§ 7.4.1 Purchasing process

There are no additional requirements in the Standard related to control of suppliers beyond that in the QSReg.

FDA Guidance

QSReg Preamble

Comment group 100. . . . FDA emphasizes that the requirements apply to all product and service received from outside of the finished device manufacturer, whether payment occurs or not. Thus, a manufacturer must comply with these provisions when it receives product or services from its "sister facility" or some other corporate or financial affiliate. "Otherwise received product" would include "customer supplied product" . . . , but would not apply to "returned product" from the customer.

Comment group 102. . . . First, as used in the regulation, "service" means parts of the manufacturing or quality system that are contracted to others, for example, plating of metals, testing, and sterilizing, among others. Second, FDA believes that all suppliers of such services must be assessed and evaluated, just like a supplier of a product. As always, the degree of control necessary is related to the product or service purchased. . . . it is the finished device manufacturer who is responsible for "all" product and services.

Comment group 103. . . . FDA agrees . . . that certification may play a role in evaluating suppliers, but cautions manufacturers against relying solely on certification by third parties as evidence that suppliers have the capability to provide quality products or services. FDA has found during inspections that some manufacturers who have been certified to the ISO standards have not had acceptable problem identification and corrective action programs. Therefore, the initial assessment or evaluation, depending on the type and potential effect on device quality of the product or service, should be a combination of assessment methods, to possibly include third party or product certification. However, third party certification should not be relied on exclusively in initially evaluating a supplier. If a device manufacturer has established confidence in the supplier's ability to provide acceptable products or services, certification with test data may be acceptable.

Comment group 61. . . . Although employing a consultant is a business decision, when a manufacturer hires consultants who do not have appropriate credentials, and manufacturing decisions are made based on erroneous or ill-conceived advice, the public suffers. Of course, the manufacturer is still ultimately responsible for following the CGMP requirements and will bear the consequences of a failure to comply. FDA notes that the use of unqualified consultants has led to regulatory action for the failure to comply with the CGMP regulation in the past. Thus, because of the significant impact a consultant can have on the safety and effectiveness of a device, FDA believes that some degree of control is required in the regulation.

... it is not FDA's goal to dictate whom a manufacturer may use as a consultant, but instead to require that a manufacturer determine what it needs to adequately carry out the requirements of the regulation and to assess whether the consultant can adequately meet those needs. The requirements related to consultants have been added in Sec. 820.50 Purchasing controls because a consultant is a supplier of a service.

Comment group 104. . . . FDA has observed that a surprising number of firms hire consultants who have no particular expertise in the area in which the firm is seeking assistance. Section 820.50 addresses this problem by ensuring that a consultant's capability for the specific tasks for which he or she is retained be assessed and documented. . . .

Comment group 105. . . . Suppliers, contractors, and consultants selected by manufacturers of medical devices should have a demonstrated capability of providing products and services that meet the requirements established by the finished device manufacturer. The capability of the product or service suppliers should be reviewed at intervals consistent with the significance of the product or service provided and the review should demonstrate conformance to specified requirements.

Comment group 106. . . . The intent of Sec. 820.50 is to ensure that device manufacturers select only those suppliers, contractors, and consultants who have the capability to provide quality product and services. As with finished devices, quality cannot be inspected or tested into products or services. Rather, the quality of a [purchased] product or service is established during the design of that product or service, and achieved through proper control of the manufacture of that product or the performance of that service. Section 820.50 thus mandates that products be manufactured and services be performed under appropriate quality assurance procedures. Finished device manufacturers are required under Sec. 820.50 to establish the requirements for, and document the capability of, suppliers, contractors, and consultants to provide quality products and services.

Section 820.80 is specific to a device manufacturer's acceptance program. While finished device manufacturers are required to assess the capability of suppliers, contractors, and consultants to provide quality products and services, inspections and tests, and other verification tools are also an important part of ensuring that components and finished devices conform to approved specifications. The extent of incoming acceptance activities can be based, in part, on the degree to which the supplier has demonstrated a capability to provide quality products or services. An appropriate product and services quality assurance program includes a combination of assessment techniques, including inspection and test.

Comment group 107. . . . auditing a distributor would not meet the intent of Sec. 820.50. Manufacturers should remember that the purpose of assessing the capability of suppliers is to provide quality products and to provide a greater degree of assurance, beyond that provided by receiving inspection and test, that the products received meet the finished device manufacturer's requirements. The agency recognizes that finished device manufacturers may not always be able to audit the supplier of a product. In such cases, the manufacturer must apply other effective means to assure that products are acceptable for use.

Comment group 109. . . . The term "quality requirements" means the quality control and quality assurance procedures, standards, and other requirements necessary to assure that the product or service is adequate for its intended use. FDA does not believe the term is unclear.

AAMI/ANSI/ISO TR 14969:2004

The TR recommends that the nature and extent of the supplier control be based on the risk associated with the product or service being purchased. It suggests that the control exerted over a supplier of logistics services would be different from that exerted over a contract sterilizer, a design and development service, a calibration service, or a supplier of off-the-shelf products.

The organization must be able to demonstrate objective evidence of the controls exerted over the supplier of products and services in order to show that those controls were appropriate and effective.

When relying on third-party certification of a supplier, the organization must be able to show that the basis for the certification is related to the ability of the supplier to meet the organization's needs and specifications.

Authors' Notes

It is the FDA's expectation that purchasing requirements relate to the purchase of distribution services, especially if the distributor is responsible for performing a service that could affect the safety and effectiveness of the medical device. For example, if the manufacturer intends to market its products through distributors, it should assess whether candidate distributors are able to maintain the environmental conditions needed to protect the product against deterioration. The manufacturer should also ensure that the distributor has the intention and the ability to report to the manufacturer all complaints related to malfunctions, serious injuries, and deaths so that the manufacturer can discharge its reporting responsibilities. The FDA expects the manufacturer to include in the contract executed with the distributor all reports of malfunctions, serious injuries, and deaths.

FDA Quality System Regulation—1996

§ 820.50(b) ***Purchasing data.*** Each manufacturer shall establish and maintain data that clearly describe or reference the specified requirements, including quality requirements, for purchased or otherwise received product and services. Purchasing documents shall include, where possible, an agreement that the suppliers, contractors, and consultants agree to notify the manufacturer of changes in the product or service so that manufacturers may determine whether the changes may affect the quality of a finished device. Purchasing data shall be approved in accordance with Sec. 820.40.

AAMI/ANSI/ISO 13485:2003

Reference § 7.4.2 Purchasing information

The Standard includes among the purchasing information the requirements related to the personnel being used by the supplier and other QMS requirements that may be important to ensure that the product or service meets requirements.

FDA Guidance

QSReg Preamble

Comment group 110. . . . Sec. 820.50(b) [does not prohibit] the use of drawings or prints, assuming that the documents contain data clearly describing the product or service ordered, and that the specified requirements are met. However, Sec. 820.50(b) . . . requires manufacturers to establish purchasing "data." This provides manufacturers with the flexibility to use both written and electronic means to establish purchasing information.

Comment group 111. . . . such agreement [that the supplier shall notify the manufacturer of any changes] should be obtained "where possible." FDA still believes that this change information is very important to the manufacturer, and that the manufacturer should obtain information on changes to the product or service. Where a supplier refuses to agree to provide such notification, depending on the product or service being purchased, it may render him an unacceptable supplier. However, where the product is in short supply and must be purchased, the manufacturer will need to heighten control in other ways. . . . manufacturers [have] the flexibility to define in the agreement the types of changes that would require notification.

PURCHASING CONTROLS

Comment group 112. . . . the regulation permits manufacturers to clearly describe or reference requirements. A reference could be to a standard.

Comment group 113. . . . The requirement is for approval of purchasing data or information on the purchasing document used to purchase a product or service. Thus, each manufacturer must review and approve the purchasing data before release of the data. Approval of each purchasing transaction is not required. FDA addressed the use of electronic signatures in response to another comment, and notes that FDA is in the process of developing an agency-wide policy on the use of electronic signatures.

Comment group 114. . . . About 15 percent of the recalls each year are due to unacceptable purchased products. Many of these products are unacceptable because the finished device manufacturer did not properly describe the product. The requirements for purchased products and services must be documented to ensure that the supplier, contractor, and consultant provide a product or service which conforms to specified requirements. This requirement and the goal it seeks to achieve are applicable to both small and large companies.

Comment group 115. . . . the specifications for many manufacturing materials may be so well established that the trade name of the product may be sufficient to describe the material needed. For other materials, specific written specifications may be necessary to ensure that the desired materials are received. The extent of the specification detail necessary to ensure that the product or service purchased meets requirements will be related to the nature of the product or service purchased, taking into account the effect the product or service may have on the safety or effectiveness of the finished device, among other factors. The term . . . "specified requirements" . . . better reflect[s] the intent of the requirement.

AAMI/ANSI/ISO TR 14969:2004

Reference § 7.4.2 Purchasing information

The TR includes a list of examples of requirements and specifications that can be included in purchase agreements between the manufacturer and the supplier (for example, acceptance test descriptions and requirements, environmental requirements, and traceability requirements).

The TR recommends that the specificity of purchasing information relate to the risk associated with the product or service being purchased. It provides an example related to the purchase of cleaning services that may contain information related to the specific cleaning agents and cleaning methods that can be used and the extent of the training to be provided to the cleaning personnel being provided by the supplier.

The responsibility for approval of purchasing information should be specifically assigned to competent personnel to ensure its accuracy.

It may be important to retain information related to the traceability of the purchase information in order to determine the revision level of purchase requirements at which a specific purchased item was made. This information may be needed when doing a failure investigation related to the purchased product.

Authors' Notes

We recommend that the manufacturer consider the following contents in a purchasing contract with the supplier of a product or service. It may not always be possible to get the supplier, especially a sole source supplier, to agree to all of the contents of the contract, but it is worthwhile to try. It is also understood that if the manufacturer can't get these agreements, it must accommodate these needs in some other way that meets the regulations. The following items should be considered in the contract:

- When purchasing a material or subassembly or service, the supplier should include in the contract a requirement for a declaration that the purchase was made or conforms to the proper version of the manufacturer's specification or manufacturer-supplied drawing.
- The contract should contain a prohibition that no changes are to be made by the supplier to the specifications without prior consultation and approval by the purchaser.
- The supplier agrees to inform the organization immediately (orally and in writing) of any manufacturing mishap, especially if the product or service has already been shipped to the manufacturer or the market.
- In case of a product failure that results in a complaint, a CAPA investigation, or an MDR, the supplier agrees to become part of the failure investigation and commits to comply with the manufacturer's timetable for the investigation and to institute corrective action per the corrective and/or preventive action requirements.
- The vendor should immediately inform the manufacturer of any regulatory investigation/audit relating to the manufacturer's products and should provide the manufacturer with copies of any documentation given to the investigator/auditor and any documentation left behind by the inspector/auditor (for example, FDA form 483).

SUBPART F

Identification and Traceability

IDENTIFICATION

FDA Quality System Regulation—1996

§ 820.60 Identification

Each manufacturer shall establish and maintain procedures for identifying product during all stages of receipt, production, distribution, and installation to prevent mix-ups.

AAMI/ANSI/ISO 13485:2003

Reference § 7.5.3 Identification and traceability
§ 7.5.3.1 Identification

The QSReg and the Standard state the same general principle that materials, subassembly, and finished goods be identified as to their status and that the organization have documented policies on this matter (7.5.3.1).

The Standard extends the provision to medical devices that have been returned to the manufacturer for service or repair or as part of a commercial transaction to upgrade the device (see also 6.4.d). The QSReg is silent on this matter, but it is generally understood to include these situations as well.

FDA Guidance

QSReg Preamble

Comment group 117. . . . Sec. 820.60 [is] . . . broad enough to allow the manufacturer the flexibility needed to identify product by whatever means described by the required procedure. The term "critical device" has been deleted, and traceability is addressed solely in Sec. 820.65.

Comment group 118. . . . The purpose of Sec. 820.60 is to ensure that all products, including manufacturing materials used in the manufacture of a finished device, are properly identified. This requirement is intended to help prevent inadvertent use or release of unacceptable product into manufacturing. It is as important that the proper manufacturing materials be used as it is that the proper component be used.

Comment group 119. . . . Section 820.60 only requires that product be identified but says nothing about the acceptance status of that product. Section 820.86 requires that the acceptance status be identified so that inadvertent use of product does not occur. The manufacturer may choose to set up a system by which the identification required by Sec. 820.60 can also show the acceptance status required by Sec. 820.86, but this is up to the manufacturer.

AAMI/ANSI/ISO TR 14969:2004

Reference § 7.5.3 Identification and traceability
§ 7.5.3.1 Identification

The TR cites the various reasons for identifying products used in the manufacture of a medical device (for example, facilitating the control of these products, providing information about where these products were obtained, facilitating tracing of the products, and facilitating fault diagnosis).

The TR also lists a number of ways identification can be accomplished (for example, physical or electronic tagging, marking, and segregating by physical location). Identification can be by serial number or by lot or batch number. The nature and extent of identification can be determined by a number of factors (for example, type of medical device, risk associated with a failure of the device or its components, and the extent of traceability required by regulation).

In addition, the TR warns that any materials used in the identification process should not interfere with the device's ability to meet its performance goals.

FDA Quality System Regulation—1996

§ 820.65 Traceability

Each manufacturer of a device that is intended for surgical implant into the body or to support or sustain life and whose failure to perform when properly used in accordance with instructions for use provided in the labeling can be reasonably expected to result in a significant injury to the user shall establish and maintain procedures for identifying with a control number each unit, lot, or batch of finished devices and where appropriate components. The procedures shall facilitate corrective action. Such identification shall be documented in the DHR.

AAMI/ANSI/ISO 13485:2003

Reference § 7.5.3.2 Traceability
§ 7.5.3.2.1 General

The Standard requires that traceability be considered for all medical devices manufactured by the organization, not just devices intended for surgical implant or devices that could cause significant injury to the user in the course of use. The Standard requires that the extent of the traceability be based on the nature and extent of the risk associated with the use of the medical device.

The Standard notes that configuration management is an effective traceability technique.

Reference § 7.5.3.2.2 Particular requirements for active implantable medical devices and implantable medical devices

The Standard explains in detail that items that must be traced include materials, components, and environmental conditions to the extent that they may affect the safety and effectiveness of the medical device. It explicitly extends the requirement for traceability of active implantable devices to agents and distributors of the manufacturer.

The Standard requires that traceability records include the name and address of the shipping package consignee.

FDA Guidance

QSReg Preamble

Comment group 120. . . . it is imperative that manufacturers use the definition within the requirement of Sec. 820.65 to determine if a particular device needs to be traced; . . . Manufacturers may find it advantageous to provide unit, lot, or batch traceability for devices for which traceability is not a requirement to facilitate control and limit the number of devices that may need to be recalled due to defects or violations of the act.

It is important that the traceability requirements in part 820 are not confused with the Medical Device Tracking regulation in part 821 (21 CFR § 821). The tracking regulation is intended to ensure that tracked devices can be traced from the device manufacturing facility to the person for whom the device is indicated, that is, the patient. Effective tracking of devices from the manufacturing facility, through the distribution network (including distributors, retailers, rental firms and other commercial enterprises, device user facilities, and licensed practitioners) and, ultimately, to any person for whom the device is intended is necessary for the effectiveness of remedies prescribed by the act, such as patient notification (section 518(a) of the act (21 U.S.C. 360h(a)) or device recall (section 518(e)). In contrast, the traceability provision requires that a device that meets the definition of a "critical device" can be traced from the manufacturing facility only to the "initial consignee" as discussed in Sec. 820.160 Distribution.

Comment group 121. . . . the traceability determination should [not] be based solely on economic risk. . . . where traceability is important to prevent the distribution of devices that could seriously injure the user, traceability of components must be maintained so that potential and actual problem components can be traced back to the supplier. The revised requirement mandates traceability of components "where appropriate" as recommended by the GMP Advisory Committee and limited by the discussion in the scope, Sec. 820.1(a)(3). . . . to carry out the requirement of the revised provision, the manufacturer should perform risk analysis first on the finished device, and subsequently on the components of such device, to determine the need for traceability. FDA believes that the extent of traceability for both active and inactive implantable devices should include all components and materials used when such products could cause the medical device not to satisfy its specified requirements. ISO 13485 also requires that the manufacturer's agents or distributors maintain records of distribution of medical devices with regard to traceability and that such records be available for inspection. . . .

While FDA understands that traceability entails additional cost, the agency notes that, if a product recall is necessary, more devices would be subject to recall if units, lots, or batches of specific devices are not traceable, with associated higher recall costs to the manufacturer.

Medical Device Tracking; Guidance for Industry and FDA Staff, Issued 2 November, 2007

This guidance document can be found at http://www.fda.gov/cdrh/comp/guidance/169.html.

The tracking provisions of section 519(e) of the Federal Food, Drug, and Cosmetic Act (the Act), 21 USC 360i(e), were added in 1990 by the Safe Medical Devices Act (SMDA) and amended in 1997 by the Food and Drug Administration Modernization Act (FDAMA). Device tracking is intended to ensure that the Food and Drug Administration (FDA) can require a manufacturer to promptly identify product distribution information and remove a device from the market. The revisions to 519(e) by FDAMA were effective as of February 19, 1998.

Tracking augments FDA's recall authority under section 518(e) of the Act, 21 USC 360h(e), to order a mandatory recall, and FDA's authority, under section 518(a) of the Act, 21 USC 360h(a), to require notification to health professionals and patients regarding unreasonable risk of substantial harm associated with a device.

The tracking provisions enacted by SMDA required mandatory tracking even if FDA did not issue an order. Specifically, section 519(e), as added by SMDA, required manufacturers to track if they were registered with FDA under section 510 of the act and engaged in the manufacture of a device if its failure would be reasonably likely to have serious adverse health consequences, and if that device was either a permanently implantable device or a life-sustaining or life-supporting device used outside a device user facility. Section 519(e)(2) also authorized FDA to "designate" other devices that must be tracked, at the agency's discretion.

FDAMA revised the tracking provisions to make tracking requirements within FDA's discretion. That is, tracking under section 519(e), as revised by FDAMA, applies only when FDA determines that the statutory criteria are met and FDA issues an order. Section 519(e), as revised by FDAMA, states the agency may require tracking for class II or class III devices:

(A) the failure of which would be reasonably likely to have serious adverse health consequences; or

(B) which is intended to be implanted in the human body for more than one year; or

(C) which is a life sustaining or life supporting device used outside a device user facility.

. . . FDA has issued orders to manufacturers who are required to track the following implantable devices:

- Temporomandibular Joint (TMJ) prosthesis
- Glenoid fossa prosthesis
- Mandibular condyle prosthesis
- Implantable pacemaker pulse generator
- Cardiovascular permanent implantable pacemaker electrode

TRACEABILITY

- Replacement heart valve (mechanical only)
- Automatic implantable cardioverter/defibrillator
- Implanted cerebellar stimulator
- Implanted diaphragmatic/phrenic nerve stimulator
- Implantable infusion pumps
- Abdominal aortic aneurysm stent grafts
- Silicone gel-filled breast implants
- Cultured epidermal autografts

FDA has issued orders to manufacturers who are required to track the following devices that are used outside a device user facility:

- Breathing frequency monitors
- Continuous ventilators
- Ventricular bypass (assist) device
- DC-defibrillators and paddles

FDA has discretion on whether to order tracking for devices that meet the statutory requirements or to release devices from tracking based on additional guidance factors and other relevant information that comes to the agency's attention. The following additional guidance factors may be considered to determine whether a tracking order should be issued:

A. likelihood of sudden, catastrophic failure;
B. likelihood of significant adverse clinical outcome; and
C. the need for prompt professional intervention.

. . . The following devices that were subject to tracking orders issued by the agency in February 1998 have received subsequent orders releasing them from mandatory tracking requirements:

- Intraocular Lenses
- Vascular graft prosthesis of less than 6 millimeters diameter
- Vascular graft prosthesis of 6 millimeters and greater diameter
- Interarticular disc prosthesis (interpositional implant)
- Annuloplasty ring
- Tracheal prosthesis
- Arterial stents (used in coronary or peripherial arteries)
- Penile inflatable implant
- Silicone inflatable breast prosthesis
- Testicular prosthesis, silicone gel-filled
- Silicone gel-filled chin prosthesis
- Silicone gel-filled angel chik reflux valve
- Infusion pumps—designated and labeled for use exclusively for fluids with low potential risks, e.g., enteral feeding, anti-infectives
- Electromechanical infusion pumps
- Dura mater

The guidance document contains a list of definitions that are useful when tracking devices. It also includes information related to the following:

- The tracking methods to be used
- The information that must be kept related to the devices that are tracked
- The auditing and FDA inspection of the tracking process
- When tracking may be stopped
- The responsibilities of distributors of tracked devices
- The responsibilities of user facilities

AAMI/ANSI/ISO TR 14969:2004

Reference § 7.5.3.2 Traceability
§ 7.5.3.2.1 General

The TR references ISO 10007 as a source of information on the use of configuration management for the purposes of identification and traceability.

Reference § 7.5.3.2.2 Particular requirements for active implantable medical devices and implantable medical devices

The TR explains that traceability of implantable medical devices forward to the ultimate user is important for minimizing the explantation of such devices by enabling the manufacturer to pinpoint which users actually received devices that are subject to recall.

The TR describes traceability approaches that can be based on the place of manufacture; the specific operator of key manufacturing, distribution, or other functions; changes in raw materials and tooling; machine setups; or other definable criteria. When signatures are used as a traceability tool, they must be clear and understandable.

Authors' Notes

The FDA requirements related to tracking of devices can be found in 21 CFR 821. Under this regulation, manufacturers must establish a tracking mechanism for "devices whose failure would be reasonable likely to have serious, adverse health consequences, or which are intended to be implanted in the human body for more than one year, or are life-sustaining or life-supporting devices used outside of a device user facility." Additional discussion of this issue is found at http://www.fda.gov/cdrh/devadvice/353.html.

SUBPART G

Production and Process Controls

FDA Quality System Regulation—1996

§ 820.70 Production and process controls

§ 820.70(a) *General.* Each manufacturer shall develop, conduct, control, and monitor production processes to ensure that a device conforms to its specifications. Where deviations from device specifications could occur as a result of the manufacturing process, the manufacturer shall establish and maintain process control procedures that describe any process controls necessary to ensure conformance to specifications. Where process controls are needed they shall include:

(1) Documented instructions, standard operating procedures (SOP's), and methods that define and control the manner of production;
(2) Monitoring and control of process parameters and component and device characteristics during production;
(3) Compliance with specified reference standards or codes;
(4) The approval of processes and process equipment; and
(5) Criteria for workmanship which shall be expressed in documented standards or by means of identified and approved representative samples.

AAMI/ANSI/ISO 13485:2003

Reference § 7.5 Production and service provision
§ 7.5.1 Control of production and service provision
§ 7.5.1.1 General requirements

In addition to the process controls listed in the QSReg, § 820.70(a), this section adds controls related to release, delivery and postdelivery activities, labeling, and packaging. These controls are addressed in § 820.80(d) Final acceptance activities, § 820.120 Device labeling, § 820.130 Device packaging, § 820.140 Handling, § 820.150 Storage, § 820.160 Distribution, § 820.170 Installation, and § 820.200 Servicing.

This section introduces the generation of a batch record (equivalent to the requirement for a DHR (§ 820.184)) that facilitates the requirement for traceability (see § 7.5.3) and is verified and approved.

Reference § 7.5.1.3 Particular requirements for sterile medical devices

This section requires the establishment of process parameters for sterilization processes and records traceable to each batch of medical devices subjected to sterilization.

Reference § 7.5.4 Customer property

The Standard requires the organization to protect customer property, including intellectual property and confidential health information, while it is under the organization's control. The organization is required to exercise control over this customer property (for example, identify the property and verify it). The organization must report to the customer any loss of such property and must maintain records of such loss.

Reference § 8.2.3 Monitoring and measurement of processes

The Standard has the same objective(s) as the QSReg. The Standard requires that appropriate correction and corrective action be taken if the monitoring and measurement indicate that the process is not achieving the planned results.

FDA Guidance

QSReg Preamble

Comment group 122. . . . The requirements in Sec. 820.70(a) are intended to ensure that each manufacturer produces devices that conform to their specifications. Thus, where any deviations from specifications could occur during manufacturing, the process control procedures must describe those controls necessary to ensure conformance. Those controls listed in the regulation may not always be relevant; similarly others may be necessary. For example, where deviations from device specifications could occur as a result of the absence of written production methods, procedures, and workmanship criteria, such production controls are required. Thus, FDA has retained the provision, but revised it slightly to conform to the original CGMP requirements in Sec. 820.100(b)(1). As noted, the process control requirements apply when any deviation from specifications could occur. FDA believes that such deviations must be controlled, and that linking the requirements to deviations that directly affect quality is inappropriate and subjective, and that it could lead to the manufacture of potentially dangerous devices through the lack of control of processes known to directly affect a device's specifications. Therefore, the provision has not been restricted in this manner. FDA has, however, revised the requirements to state "Where process controls are needed they shall include:" to make it clear that a manufacturer only has to comply with the requirements stated in Sec. 820.70(a)(1) through (a)(5) if the general criteria described in Sec. 820.70(a) have been met.

Comment group 123. . . . the establishment of procedures is necessary to ensure consistency in manufacture. The procedures may be tailored under the requirement to cover only those controls necessary to ensure that a device meets its specifications. . . . The first sentence in the general requirement also serves to tie the production and process controls to the design and development phase where many of these controls are originally established in order for the device to conform to its design specifications.

In addition to these changes, FDA has added the requirement that production processes be "monitored" because a manufacturer must monitor a controlled process to ensure that the process remains in control.

Comment group 124. FDA deleted the requirement for process controls related to "installation and servicing" from proposed Sec. 820.70(a)(1) and (a)(2) in response to comments. Such control is adequately assured by the requirements in Secs. 820.170 Installation and 820.200 Servicing.

. . . the manufacturer must comply with reference standards or codes which he or she has specified in the DMR.

. . . the "representative samples" [referred to in § 820.70(a)(5)] have to be identified and deemed appropriate before they are used as reference standards.

"Guideline for the Manufacture of In Vitro Diagnostic Products," January 10, 1994

A copy of this guidance document may be found at http://www.fda.gov/cdrh/comp/918.pdf.

This guidance document addresses a number of issues related to production and process control in a section describing process specifications. It also contains a section titled "Production and process control," in which it discusses IVD issues related to sterilization and microbial reduction techniques, lyophilization, filtration, and filling processes.

The guidance document is supported by the FDA Office of IVD Devices Evaluation and Safety. While it was issued in 1994, there is no indication that it has been amended or withdrawn.

Reference § 7.5 Production and service provision
§ 7.5.1 Control of production and service provision
§ 7.5.1.1 General requirements

The TR explains that process control must be exerted when nonconformity can result in an adverse effect on the product performance or when failure to meet a regulatory requirement can result.

The amount of control exerted should be commensurate with the level of risk of the nonconformity as determined by the risk assessment of the process in question.

Reference materials used as part of process control may be physical or visual and should be available to the operator at the site of operation.

Documents used to control processes may be in any useful form (for example, a flowchart or step-by-step instructions with a checklist.

Equipment used in a process should be designed and selected to ensure that production process specifications are met. There should be a record to provide objective evidence that the process equipment will operate within defined process limits.

Reference § 7.5.1.3 Particular requirements for sterile medical devices

The TR references a number of international standards containing parameters for sterilization processes used by medical device organizations (for example, ISO 11134, ISO 11135, ISO 11137, ISO 13863, ISO 14160, and ISO 14937).

Reference § 7.5.4 Customer property

The TR clarifies that the intent of the requirements in this section is to protect the value of such property.

The TR illustrates the various kinds of customer property covered by this subclause (for example, raw materials or components to be incorporated into the medical device, or property that has been supplied so that it can be reworked, repaired, maintained, or further processed and transported to an ultimate customer or a third party). Such property can also be intellectual property required by the organization to fulfill its responsibilities.

Reference § 8.2.3 Monitoring and measurement of processes

The TR contains no additional guidance related to this subject.

Authors' Notes

The QSReg addresses the requirement for a batch record in § 820.184 Device History Record.

The requirements contained in § 820.70 of the QSReg and § 7.5 of the Standard supplement each other. These sections can be read together for a complete picture of the kinds of process controls that must be implemented to ensure consistent production of a product that meets specifications.

FDA Quality System Regulation—1996

§ 820.70(b) ***Production and process changes.*** Each manufacturer shall establish and maintain procedures for changes to a specification, method, process, or procedure. Such changes shall be verified or where appropriate validated according to Sec. 820.75, before implementation and these activities shall be documented. Changes shall be approved in accordance with Sec. 820.40.

AAMI/ANSI/ISO 13485:2003

There is no separate section of the Standard that deals with process changes.

FDA Guidance

QSReg Preamble

> **Comment group 125.** . . . Revised Sec. 820.70(b), "Production and process changes," addresses the requirement for production and process changes to be "verified or where appropriate validated according to Sec. 820.75." This requirement for validation was moved from Sec. 820.40(c), in revised form, to Sec. 820.70. Verification was added to give the manufacturer the flexibility to verify changes that can be tested and inspected because FDA believes that validation is not always necessary. FDA has provided guidance on when changes should be validated in its "Guideline on General Principles of Process Validation." The agency notes that wherever changes may influence a validated process, the process must be revalidated as described in Sec. 820.75. A few examples of processes that must be validated include sterilization, molding, and welding. . . .

AAMI/ANSI/ISO TR 14969:2004

There is no separate section of the TR that deals with process changes.

FDA Quality System Regulation—1996

§ 820.70(c) ***Environmental control.*** Where environmental conditions could reasonably be expected to have an adverse effect on product quality, the manufacturer shall establish and maintain procedures to adequately control these environmental conditions. Environmental control system(s) shall be periodically inspected to verify that the system, including necessary equipment, is adequate and functioning properly. These activities shall be documented and reviewed.

AAMI/ANSI/ISO 13485:2003

Reference § 6.4 Work environment

The Standard calls for "special arrangements" to prevent a potentially contaminated product from contaminating personnel, the work area, or other products.

FDA Guidance

QSReg Preamble

Comment group 126. . . . FDA has amended the requirements now in Sec. 820.70(c) to apply only where environmental conditions could "reasonably be expected to have an adverse effect on product quality." The requirements for procedures to ensure control of conditions, periodic inspection of control systems, and documentation and review of results are similar to the original CGMP requirements. . . . FDA . . . notes that lighting, ventilation, temperature, humidity, air pressure, filtration, airborne contamination, and static electricity are among many conditions that should be considered for control.

FDA reworded the requirement to make it clear that the inspection must be of the control system. FDA also added that the inspection of the control system(s) shall include "any necessary equipment," e.g., pumps, filters, measurement equipment, etc. . . .

Comment group 127. . . . The inspection and review of environmental control systems are routine quality assurance functions that are part of the production quality assurance program. The audits required by Sec. 820.22(a) are audits of the quality system, conducted to ensure the adequacy of and conformance with the quality system requirements. The requirement to conduct a quality audit is in addition to other provisions in the regulation which require that a manufacturer review its specific controls to ensure the requirements are met. FDA may review the activities and results of environmental control system inspections.

Comment group 131. . . . sewage, trash, byproducts, chemical effluvium, and other refuse that could affect a device's safety, effectiveness, or fitness-for-use must be adequately controlled.

"Guideline for the Manufacture of In Vitro Diagnostic Products," January 10, 1994

This guidance document addresses a number of issues related to environmental controls, including airborne and other contamination, air pressure, and filtration. The guidance document is supported by the FDA Office of IVD Devices Evaluation and Safety. While it was issued in 1994, there is no indication that it has been amended or withdrawn. A copy of this guidance document may be found at http://www.fda.gov/cdrh/comp/918.pdf.

AAMI/ANSI/ISO TR 14969:2004

Reference § 6.4 Work environment

The extent to which the work environment needs to be controlled depends on the susceptibility of the product to environmental conditions. The work environment includes the areas in which the product is manufactured, handled, and stored. It includes those periods of time when the product is being manufactured and those times when the product is being held by the manufacturer but is not being "worked" on. The susceptibility of the product can be determined and documented during the risk assessment activities. The elements of environmental control fall into several categories: specifying the controls needed, regulating the environment within those specifications, and monitoring the effectiveness of the regulating activities. The need to control the work environment can affect the design and construction of the facilities, the process equipment used, the operating personnel, and the nature and extent of the documentation required. Work environment control systems should be validated in the same manner as other processes are validated.

The TR contains a note referencing ISO 14644 for information related to clean rooms and associated environments.

The TR lists a number of situations that may require work environment control, for example, when the resulting medical device is intended to be sold "sterile" or "pryrogen-free," when the resulting medical device may have a shelf life that is limited by production or storage conditions, or when the resulting medical device is susceptible to electrostatic discharge or microbial contamination. For medical devices that are susceptible to microbial or particulate contamination and are intended to be cleaned by a validated cleaning process at the end of production, it may still be necessary to control the production process environment to limit the potential contamination to levels that can be controlled by the cleaning process.

The TR lists a number of environmental controls (for example, humidity, airflow, air filtration, air ionization, lighting, pressure differentials among manufacturing areas, noise, vibration, and cleanliness of work surfaces).

The TR recommends that contaminated product that enters the manufacturer's facility should be identified as being potentially contaminated and should be handled, cleaned, and, if necessary, reworked in a controlled manner that does not contaminate the uncontaminated product, work surfaces, and personnel.

FDA Quality System Regulation—1996

§ 820.70(d) ***Personnel.*** Each manufacturer shall establish and maintain requirements for the health, cleanliness, personal practices, and clothing of personnel if contact between such personnel and product or environment could reasonably be expected to have an adverse effect on product quality. The manufacturer shall ensure that maintenance and other personnel who are required to work temporarily under special environmental conditions are appropriately trained or supervised by a trained individual.

AAMI/ANSI/ISO 13485:2003

Reference § 6.2 Human resources
§ 6.2.1 General
§ 6.2.2 Competence, awareness, and training
§ 6.3 Infrastructure
§ 6.4 Work environment

The Standard contains no additional requirements related to personnel beyond those in the QSReg.

FDA Guidance

QSReg Preamble

Comment group 129. . . . FDA has also rewritten the section, now entitled "Personnel," to require procedures to achieve the desired result, rather than dictate the means to achieve the result. The section as rewritten provides the manufacturer with more flexibility. Under this section, a manufacturer's requirements must not permit unclean or inappropriately clothed employees, or employees with medical conditions, to work with devices where such conditions could reasonably be expected to have an adverse effect on product quality. The procedures must also address acceptable clothing, hygiene, and personal practices, if contact between personnel and product or environment could reasonably be expected to have an adverse effect on product quality.

FDA also added the requirement, from ISO 13485, that personnel who are working temporarily (such as maintenance and cleaning personnel) under special environmental conditions (such as a clean room) be appropriately trained and/or supervised by someone trained to work in such an environment.

"Guideline for the Manufacture of In Vitro Diagnostic Products," January 10, 1994

This guidance document addresses a number of issues related to personnel attire, cleaning, and sanitation. The guidance document is supported by the FDA Office of IVD Devices Evaluation and Safety. While it was issued in 1994, there is no indication that it has been amended or withdrawn. A copy of this guidance document may be found at http://www.fda.gov/cdrh/comp/918.pdf.

AAMI/ANSI/ISO TR 14969:2004

Reference § 6.2 Human resources
§ 6.2.1 General
§ 6.2.2 Competence, awareness, and training
§ 6.3 Infrastructure
§ 6.4 Work environment

The TR lists the various kinds of personnel who may temporarily enter environmentally controlled areas (for example, supervisors, managers, material handlers, design and development personnel, quality control personnel, maintenance personnel, customers, and auditors).

The TR cautions that entry of temporary personnel may occur during times other than when the product is being manufactured (for example, evenings, weekends, and holidays).

FDA Quality System Regulation—1996

§ 820.70(e) ***Contamination control.*** Each manufacturer shall establish and maintain procedures to prevent contamination of equipment or product by substances that could reasonably be expected to have an adverse effect on product quality.

AAMI/ANSI/ISO 13485:2003

§ 6.4 Work environment

The Standard contains no additional requirements related to contamination control beyond those in the QSReg.

§ 7.5.1.2.1 Cleanliness of product and contamination control

The Standard outlines a number of situations where the organization must establish documented requirements for product cleanliness (for example, when the organization cleans the product prior to its sterilization and/or its use, when the product is supplied as nonsterile but must be cleaned prior to sterilization or use by another, when its cleanliness is a factor in its safe and effective use, and when there are process agents or manufacturing materials that must be removed during manufacture).

The TR indicates that if the product is cleaned in accordance with the requirements in this section of the Standard, the organization does not have to follow the personnel and work environment cleaning requirements in Section 6.4(a) and (b) of the Standard.

For cleaning of product prior to servicing, see § 820.200.

FDA Guidance

QSReg Preamble

> **Comment group 127.** . . . The inspection and review of environmental control systems are routine quality assurance functions that are part of the production quality assurance program. The audits required by Sec. 820.22(a) are audits of the quality system, conducted to ensure the adequacy of and conformance

with the quality system requirements. The requirement to conduct a quality audit is in addition to other provisions in the regulation which require that a manufacturer review its specific controls to ensure the requirements are met. FDA may review the activities and results of environmental control system inspections.

Comment group 130. . . . The section now contains a broad requirement for the establishment of procedures to prevent contamination of equipment or product by any substance that could reasonably be expected to have an adverse effect on product quality. Again, this revision adds flexibility.

Comment group 131. . . . sewage, trash, byproducts, chemical effluvium, and other refuse that could affect a device's safety, effectiveness, or fitness-for-use must be adequately controlled.

AAMI/ANSI/ISO TR 14969:2004

§ 6.4 Work environment

The TR contains no additional guidance related to contamination control beyond that contained in the QSReg.

§ 7.5.1.2.1 Cleanliness of product and contamination control

The TR recommends that procedures be established to define the product cleanliness requirements, to describe the labeling requirements for manufacturing materials that ensure proper identification and control (for example, cleaning agents, lubricating oils, and mold release agents), and to describe the requirements and process for decontaminating medical devices that will be serviced.

The reader should note that the TR refers to ISO 12891-1 for information related to cleaning procedures.

FDA Quality System Regulation—1996

§ 820.70(f) ***Buildings.*** Buildings shall be of suitable design and contain sufficient space to perform necessary operations, prevent mix-ups, and assure orderly handling.

AAMI/ANSI/ISO 13485:2003

Reference § 6.3 Infrastructure

This section includes the control of buildings, workspaces, utilities, process equipment (including the software associated with it), and associated activities (for example, transportation and communication). It also explicitly requires the establishment of requirements for and recording of maintenance activities.

FDA Guidance

QSReg Preamble

There is no guidance related to buildings in the preamble.

AAMI/ANSI/ISO TR 14969:2004

Reference § 6.3 Infrastructure

The TR recommends that the design of buildings be such that it allows for sufficient space to facilitate the orderly arrangement and spacing of equipment, the cleaning and maintenance of the equipment and the facilities themselves, and other necessary operations. There should also be sufficient space to prevent the mix-up of incoming, in-process, scrapped, reworked, and finished materials.

FDA Quality System Regulation—1996

§ 820.70(g) *Equipment.* Each manufacturer shall ensure that all equipment used in the manufacturing process meets specified requirements and is appropriately designed, constructed, placed, and installed to facilitate maintenance, adjustment, cleaning, and use.

(1) **Maintenance schedule.** Each manufacturer shall establish and maintain schedules for the adjustment, cleaning, and other maintenance of equipment to ensure that manufacturing specifications are met. Maintenance activities, including the date and individual(s) performing the maintenance activities, shall be documented.

(2) **Inspection.** Each manufacturer shall conduct periodic inspections in accordance with established procedures to ensure adherence to applicable equipment maintenance schedules. The inspections, including the date and individual(s) conducting the inspections, shall be documented.

(3) **Adjustment.** Each manufacturer shall ensure that any inherent limitations or allowable tolerances are visibly posted on or near equipment requiring periodic adjustments or are readily available to personnel performing these adjustments.

AAMI/ANSI/ISO 13485:2003

Reference § 6.3 Infrastructure

The Standard contains no additional requirements beyond those in the QSReg.

FDA Guidance

QSReg Preamble

Comment group 132. . . . the equipment must be appropriately designed to facilitate maintenance, adjustment, cleaning, and use. It must also meet the requirements that are necessary to ensure its proper functioning for the manufacture of the device.

Comment group 133. . . . FDA agrees that not all equipment may require maintenance and notes that the general requirement of Sec. 820.70(a) requires process control procedures that describe only those controls which are necessary. . . .

FDA . . . requires that the manufacturer ensure that maintenance is carried out on schedule to comply with the requirement. To satisfactorily meet this requirement, FDA expects that the schedule will be posted on or near the equipment to be maintained, or otherwise made readily available to appropriate personnel . . . [and] . . . permits the manufacturer . . . flexibility in complying with this section.

Comment group 134. . . . FDA believes that to adequately ensure that equipment continues to meet its specifications, and to ensure that inherent limitations and allowable tolerances are known, these requirements are imperative. FDA notes inherent limitations and allowable tolerances must be visibly posted on or near equipment or made readily available to personnel to allow the manufacturer the flexibility to utilize any system to make sure that the limitations or tolerances are readily available to the personnel that need them. . . .

AAMI/ANSI/ISO TR 14969:2004

Reference § 6.3 Infrastructure

The TR contains no additional guidance beyond that contained in the QSReg.

FDA Quality System Regulation—1996

§ 820.70(h) ***Manufacturing material.*** Where a manufacturing material could reasonably be expected to have an adverse effect on product quality, the manufacturer shall establish and maintain procedures for the use and removal of such manufacturing material to ensure that it is removed or limited to an amount that does not adversely affect the device's quality. The removal or reduction of such manufacturing material shall be documented.

AAMI/ANSI/ISO 13485:2003

Reference § 6.3 Infrastructure

The Standard contains no additional requirements beyond those contained in the QSReg.

FDA Guidance

QSReg Preamble

> **Comment group 135.** . . . FDA . . . requires that the fact that manufacturing material was removed or reduced be documented, not how much was removed or how much was lost due to processing. . . . this requirement is necessary "Where a manufacturing material could reasonably be expected to have an adverse effect on product quality." . . . [This requirement is limited to the] removal or reduction to "an amount that does not adversely affect the device's quality."

AAMI/ANSI/ISO TR 14969:2004

Reference § 6.3 Infrastructure

The TR lists a number of manufacturing materials (for example, cleaning agents, mould-release agents, and lubricating oils).

The TR recommends that manufacturing materials be adequately identified and labeled to avoid confusion.

FDA Quality System Regulation—1996

§ 820.70(i) ***Automated processes.*** When computers or automated data processing systems are used as part of production or the quality system, the manufacturer shall validate computer software for its intended use according to an established protocol. All software changes shall be validated before approval and issuance. These validation activities and results shall be documented.

AAMI/ANSI/ISO 13485:2003

Reference § 7.5.2 Validation of processes for production and service provision

The Standard contains no additional requirements beyond those in the QSReg.

FDA Guidance

QSReg Preamble

Comment group 136. . . . FDA . . . [intends] the requirement to mandate validation for the intended use of the software. . . . validation may be performed by those other than the manufacturer. However, whether the manufacturer designates its own personnel or relies on outside assistance to validate software, there must be an established procedure to ensure validation is carried out properly.

FDA . . . believes that it is necessary that software be validated to the extent possible to adequately ensure performance. Where source code and design specifications cannot be obtained, "black box testing" must be performed to confirm that the software meets the user's needs and its intended uses.

FDA emphasizes that manufacturers are responsible for the adequacy of the software used in their devices, and activities used to produce devices. When manufacturers purchase "off-the-shelf" software, they must ensure that it will perform as intended in its chosen application.

. . . Software used in production or the quality system, whether it be in the designing, manufacturing, distributing, or tracing, must be validated.

General Principles of Software Validation; Final Guidance for Industry and FDA Staff, Issued on 11 January, 2002

This guidance document can be found at http://www.fda.gov/cdrh/comp/guidance/938.html.

This guidance outlines general validation principles that the Food and Drug Administration (FDA) considers to be applicable to the validation of medical device software or the validation of software used to design, develop, or manufacture medical devices. . . .

This guidance describes how certain provisions of the medical device Quality System regulation apply to software and the agency's current approach to evaluating a software validation system. For example, this document lists elements that are acceptable to the FDA for the validation of software; however, it does not list all of the activities and tasks that must, in all instances, be used to comply with the law.

The scope of this guidance is somewhat broader than the scope of validation in the strictest definition of that term. Planning, verification, testing, traceability, configuration management, and many other aspects of good software engineering discussed in this guidance are important activities that together help to support a final conclusion that software is validated.

This guidance recommends an integration of software life cycle management and risk management activities. Based on the intended use and the safety risk associated with the software to be developed, the software developer should determine the specific approach, the combination of techniques to be used, and the level of effort to be applied. While this guidance does not recommend any specific life cycle model or any specific technique or method, it does recommend that software validation and verification activities be conducted throughout the entire software life cycle.

Where the software is developed by someone other than the device manufacturer (e.g., off-the-shelf software) the software developer may not be directly responsible for compliance with FDA regulations. In that case, the party with regulatory responsibility (i.e., the device manufacturer) needs to assess the adequacy of the off-the-shelf software developer's activities and determine what additional efforts are needed to establish that the software is validated for the device manufacturer's intended use. . . .

This guidance applies to:

- Software used as a component, part, or accessory of a medical device;
- Software that is itself a medical device (e.g., blood establishment software);
- Software used in the production of a device (e.g., programmable logic controllers in manufacturing equipment); and
- Software used in implementation of the device manufacturer's quality system (e.g., software that records and maintains the device history record).

This document is based on generally recognized software validation principles and, therefore, can be applied to any software. For FDA purposes, this guidance applies to any software related to a regulated medical device, as defined by Section 201(h) of the Federal Food, Drug, and Cosmetic Act (the Act) and by current FDA software and regulatory policy. This document does not specifically identify which software is or is not regulated.

AAMI/ANSI/ISO TR 14969:2004

Reference § 7.5.2 Validation of processes for production and service provision

The TR recommends validation of computer software used in process control, whether it is developed specifically for the control of the manufacturing process or whether it is purchased and used with or without modification.

The TR refers to the Good Automated Manufacturing Practice (GAMP) guidelines for additional guidance with regard to the control of automated processes.

FDA Quality System Regulation—1996

§ 820.72 Inspection, measuring, and test equipment

§ 820.72(a) ***Control of inspection, measuring, and test equipment.*** Each manufacturer shall ensure that all inspection, measuring, and test equipment, including mechanical, automated, or electronic inspection and test equipment, is suitable for its intended purposes and is capable of producing valid results. Each manufacturer shall establish and maintain procedures to ensure that equipment is routinely calibrated, inspected, checked, and maintained. The procedures shall include provisions for handling, preservation, and storage of equipment, so that its accuracy and fitness for use are maintained. These activities shall be documented.

§ 820.72(b) ***Calibration.*** Calibration procedures shall include specific directions and limits for accuracy and precision. When accuracy and precision limits are not met, there shall be provisions for remedial action to reestablish the limits and to evaluate whether there was any adverse effect on the device's quality. These activities shall be documented.

(1) **Calibration standards.** Calibration standards used for inspection, measuring, and test equipment shall be traceable to national or international standards. If national or international standards are not practical or available, the manufacturer shall use an independent reproducible standard. If no applicable standard exists, the manufacturer shall establish and maintain an in-house standard.

(2) **Calibration records.** The equipment identification, calibration dates, the individual performing each calibration, and the next calibration date shall be documented. These records shall be displayed on or near each piece of equipment or shall be readily available to the personnel using such equipment and to the individuals responsible for calibrating the equipment.

AAMI/ANSI/ISO 13485:2003

Reference § 7.6 Control of monitoring and measuring equipment

The Standard lists a number of steps for ensuring that measurement equipment is capable of producing accurate results (for example, periodic calibration or calibration prior to use, adjustment, readjustment, protection from incorrect adjustment, or damage or deterioration that could affect the accuracy of the results).

The Standard specifically requires that software used as part of the calibration process be validated for that use prior to being used.

The Standard refers to ISO 10012 for guidance related to systems for measurement.

Reference § 8 Measurement, analysis, and improvement § 8.1 General

The Standard makes it clear that measurement systems go beyond the measurements related to the product, extending to measurements related to the operation and effectiveness of the QMS. It includes the use of statistical techniques in measurement methods.

The Standard indicates that national and regional regulations can require documented procedures for the implementation and control of statistical techniques.

FDA Guidance

QSReg Preamble

Comment group 137. . . . The requirement is for the equipment to work properly, thereby providing "valid results."

FDA . . . [intends] to make clear that the procedures must also ensure that the equipment is maintained. . . .

Comment group 138. . . . FDA [included] . . . the requirement to . . . clarify this remedial action requirement and its relationship to the requirements in Sec. 820.100 Corrective and preventive action.

Comment group 139. . . . Sec. 820.72(b)(1), "Calibration standards," [allows] the use of international standards. The standards used must be generally accepted by qualified experts as the prevailing standards.

Comment group 140. . . . As long as the required procedures and records are maintained and displayed or readily available as required, the objective of the section, ensuring that calibration is performed and acceptable, will be met. FDA . . . [intends] that equipment is clearly identified in the calibration records even if the records are not displayed on or near the particular piece of equipment.

Comment group 141. . . . FDA . . . [recognizes that] some equipment requires special handling, preservation, and storage. For example, the temperature and humidity of a room may affect the equipment and procedures would need to be established taking those factors into account.

AAMI/ANSI/ISO TR 14969:2004

Reference § 7.6 Control of monitoring and measuring equipment

The TR recommends that the manufacturer view measurement as a process that requires control, including the use of statistics, so that the manufacturer is confident that the results are valid.

The TR recommends that measurement control go beyond the manufacture of product to extend to the operations that occur after manufacturing (for example, handling, storage, distribution, and servicing).

The TR recommends that monitoring and measurement documentation include details related to the type of measurement equipment to be used, its specific identification (for example, model and serial numbers), the location of the equipment, the method and frequency of measurement, and the acceptance criteria.

The TR recognizes that some measurements are not part of the QMS and may not need to be controlled under this section of the Standard. This includes standalone equipment and equipment attached to process equipment used only to give an indication, not intended to control (for example, the pressure gauge on a fire extinguisher), and instruments associated with business administration (for example, the clock on a time card machine).

The TR illustrates measurement equipment that may need to be calibrated only once and not periodically (for example, mercury-in-glass thermometers, steel rulers, and volumetric measurement glassware used in the laboratory under normal environmental conditions).

The TR illustrates a number of different kinds of software related to the control of monitoring and measurement equipment (for example, software that controls the calibration process itself, and software that provides information about the calibration schedule and the status of the measurement equipment).

Reference § 8 Measurement, analysis, and improvement
§ 8.1 General

The TR suggests that the procedures that set out requirements for control of measurement protect the measurement process even when it is performed by individuals who may have a conflict of interest if the results are unsatisfactory (for example, suppliers or production personnel).

For measurement to be of value, it must either provide beneficial guidance to the organization or help it set priorities. Measurement methods should be reviewed as necessary to ensure they are effective.

The use of statistical methods

The TR discusses the value of statistical methods. It can help in deciding what and how much to measure, and it can provide a useful assessment of process capabilities and product conformity to requirements, including customer requirements. The TR lists other areas where statistical techniques are valuable (for example, design and development of products and processes, establishing product and process limits, control of processes, analyzing and solving problems and nonconformities, root cause analysis, and forecasting).

The TR lists a number of statistical methods commonly used by medical device organizations (for example, graphical methods, including Pareto analysis, histograms, sequence charts, and Ishihara cause and effect diagrams; statistical control charts; design of experiments techniques; and regression analysis, analysis of variance (ANOVA), and sampling schemes).

The TR emphasizes that statistical techniques are valuable only if their results are communicated to the groups within the organization that can use the results for making decisions. Results of the use of statistical techniques are quality records that must be controlled as other quality records are.

The TR refers to ISO/TR 10017 as the source of information related to statistical techniques.

FDA Quality System Regulation—1996

§ 820.75 Process validation

§ 820.75(a) Where the results of a process cannot be fully verified by subsequent inspection and test, the process shall be validated with a high degree of assurance and approved according to established procedures. The validation activities and results, including the date and signature of the individual(s) approving the validation and where appropriate the major equipment validated, shall be documented.

§ 820.75(b) Each manufacturer shall establish and maintain procedures for monitoring and control of process parameters for validated processes to ensure that the specified requirements continue to be met.

(1) Each manufacturer shall ensure that validated processes are performed by qualified individual(s).
(2) For validated processes, the monitoring and control methods and data, the date performed, and, where appropriate, the individual(s) performing the process or the major equipment used shall be documented.

§ 820.75(c) When changes or process deviations occur, the manufacturer shall review and evaluate the process and perform revalidation where appropriate. These activities shall be documented.

AAMI/ANSI/ISO 13485:2003

Reference § 7.5.2 Validation of processes for production and service provision
§ 7.5.2.1 General requirements

The Standard and the QSReg state that processes where the output (that is, the product or service) cannot be verified need to be validated to demonstrate that the process can achieve the planned results. The Standard does not use the term "fully verified" as it is used in the QSReg. The intention is that the verification referred to in the Standard applies to all aspects of the output that relate to the output specifications. The Standard also includes those processes where deficiencies become apparent only after the device is in commercial use or the service has been delivered.

As part of the validation process, the organization should address a number of issues (for example, validation acceptance criteria, the qualification of process equipment and operating personnel, validation methods to be used, validation record-keeping requirements, and the conditions that require revalidation).

The Standard also discusses the need for a procedure(s) to describe the validation prior to use of computer software that controls elements of production or service provision, is part of the finished device, or is involved in supporting activities. The validation covers the original software design or changes to it or its application.

Reference § 7.5.2.2 Particular requirements for sterile medical devices

The Standard requires documented validation procedures for sterilization processes before those processes are implemented, with the results of the validation activities retained as controlled records.

FDA Guidance

QSReg Preamble

Comment group 143. . . . The section now requires that when a process "cannot be fully verified by subsequent inspection and test, the process shall be validated with a high degree of assurance. . . ." Examples of such processes include sterilization, aseptic processing, injection molding, and welding, among others. The validation method must ensure that predetermined specifications are consistently met. . . . FDA does not believe this terminology ["fully verified"] is unclear since it has been used in ISO 9001:1987 and 1994 and explained in several guidance documents.

. . . Depending on the process that is validated, it may be necessary to document the person performing the process or the equipment or both in order to have adequate controls on the process.

Comment group 145. . . . Section 820.75(b) applies to the performance of a process after the process has been validated. In contrast, Sec. 820.75(a) relates to the initial validation of the process. FDA . . . concurs that monitoring can be accomplished at a determined interval and frequency depending on the type of validated process being monitored and controlled. FDA notes that the interval and frequency should be periodically evaluated for adequacy, especially during any evaluation or revalidation that occurs in accordance with the requirements in new Sec. 820.75(c).

New Sec. 820.75(b)(1) . . . requires that validated processes be performed by a qualified individual(s). FDA notes that Sec. 820.75(b)(1) is similar to the requirements under Sec. 820.25 Personnel but emphasizes that validated processes must not only be performed by personnel with the necessary education, background, training, and experience for their general jobs but must be performed by personnel qualified for those particular functions. Revised Sec. 820.75(b)(2) . . . contains the amended documentation requirements for validated processes, to include the monitoring and control methods and data. FDA notes that it is always "appropriate" to document the equipment used in the process where the manufacturer uses different equipment on different manufacturing lines. To investigate a problem with the device, the manufacturer will need to know which equipment was used, since the problem could be with the equipment itself. The same holds true for the individual(s) performing the process.

"Guideline for the Manufacture of In Vitro Diagnostic Products," January 10, 1994

This guidance document addresses a number of issues related to process validation, especially for those processes used in the manufacture of IVD reagents (for example, sterilization, lyophilization, filtration, and filling). The guidance document is supported by the FDA Office of IVD Devices Evaluation and Safety. While it was issued in 1994, there is no indication that it has been amended or withdrawn. A copy of this guidance document may be found at http://www.fda.gov/cdrh/comp/918.pdf.

AAMI/ANSI/ISO TR 14969:2004

Reference § 7.5.2 Validation of processes for production and service provision

§ 7.5.2.1 General requirements

The TR explains that each process validation is a planned activity that includes steps that address equipment specifications that have been approved. It also includes qualification of equipment intended to be used in the process, its proper installation, and the proper supply of services and utilities to it (IQ); steps that assess the ability of the process to produce outputs that meet specifications even though the process is operated under worst-case conditions (OQ); and steps that determine the stability of the process over multiple uses (PQ). Process validation planning should consider process equipment variability, the skill and knowledge of process operators, the practicality of process controls, appropriate acceptance criteria to use during the process validation, and the criteria that require revalidation.

The TR lists a number of examples of processes that normally need to be validated (for example, sterilization, environmental control systems, aseptic processing, sealing of sterile packaging, and heat treatment).

The TR also lists a number of examples of processes that do not need to be validated because there are practical methods of fully verifying their output (for example, manual cutting processes; visual inspection of color, turbidity, and other physical or chemical characteristics; and the performance of electrical components and wiring harnesses).

Additionally, the TR lists a number of examples of situations where validation may be needed for certain aspects of processes (for example, cleaning, manual assembly, automated cutting operations, and filling). In these cases a review of the circumstances of the use of these processes and the practicality of controls would need to be considered in order to determine whether validation would be the more practical route.

The TR describes in some detail the focus of validation of cleaning processes, especially those processes intended to remove process agents and contaminants from the product used or that result from the manufacturing processes.

The TR references ISO 11737-1 for information regarding the monitoring of microbial content.

The TR recommends that introduction of new manufacturing and testing methods should prompt an evaluation as to whether process validation is required.

The TR refers to GHTF.SG3.N99-10 as the source of useful information related to process validation.

Statistical methods and tools for process validation

The TR lists a number of statistical tools that are useful in process validations (for example, control charts, capability studies, robust design methods, FMEAs, sampling plans, and mistake-proofing methods).

Computer software used in process control

The TR recommends that process or process control software be validated for its intended use, regardless of whether it was purchased off-the-shelf, purchased and modified by or specifically for the manufacturer, or designed and developed by or specifically for the manufacturer.

The TR references the Good Automated Manufacturing Practice (GAMP) guidelines for useful information about the application of process software.

Reference § 7.5.2.2 Particular requirements for sterile medical devices

The TR warns that while compliance with international sterilization standards as they relate to validation is a good idea, it may still be necessary to validate sterilization processes intended to be effective against certain agents (for example, spongiform encephalopathies like scrapie, BSE, and Creutzfeldt-Jakob disease).

The TR refers to the following for useful information about sterilization in general:

ISO 11134, Sterilization of health care products: Requirements for validation and routine control; Industrial moist heat sterilization (since withdrawn, 2006)

ISO 11135, Medical devices: Validation and routine control of ethylene oxide sterilization

ISO 11137, Sterilization of health care products: Requirements for validation and routine control; Radiation sterilization (since withdrawn, 2006)

ISO 13683, Sterilization of health care products: Requirements for validation and routine control of moist heat sterilization in health care facilities (since withdrawn, 2006)

ISO 14160, Sterilization of single-use medical devices incorporating materials of animal origin: Validation and routine control of sterilization by liquid chemical sterilants

ISO 14937, Sterilization of health care products: General requirements for characterization of a sterilizing agent and the development, validation, and routine control of a sterilization process for medical devices

For useful information about aseptic processes of medical devices, the TR refers to ISO 13408-1: Aseptic processing of health care products, Part 1—General requirements.

The TR recommends that sterilization of the finished product be supplemented by control of the microbiological status of incoming raw materials and the microbiological conditions of the environment in which raw, incoming, and finished materials are stored and processed.

GHTF Guidance

GHTF guidance related to process validation is contained in the second edition of GHTF/SG3/N99-10:2004. This guidance document provides the current regulatory thinking on process validation conducted within a QMS that complies with the requirements of ISO 13485:2003. It addresses the following subjects:

- When process validation is required
- The key activities that make up the process validation process
- How one maintains the state of validation
- Statistical tools that can be used in process validations

Annex A of the Guidance contains brief descriptions of the key tools that are helpful in performing process validations. These tools are intended to accomplish the following:

- Mistake proofing
- Reducing variation in processes
- Understanding and improving the process capabilities
- Challenging the process
- Optimizing sampling plans

Annex B of the Guidance provides an example of a process validation related to a heat-sealing process.

Authors' Notes

It is important that process validation follow a planned and documented protocol. The team that will perform the process validation usually writes the protocol. This team should include representatives from the functional groups that will be affected by or will participate in the process validation. It is a good idea that someone with process validation expertise work directly with the team to develop the protocol, but if that isn't possible, the process validation expert should review the protocol, suggest improvements, and approve it. It is also a good idea for members of the process validation team to be given primer training in process validation if they have not been involved in such a validation previously.

Process validations are very resource-intensive activities. The costs of process validation must be weighed against the costs associated with verification of process outputs, when it is possible to do both.

For organizations that must validate many processes, it can be useful to set priorities for the performance of these validations based on the risks associated with the processes. Processes that can have a direct effect on the safety and effectiveness of the medical device should be validated first.

One of the key functions of process validation involves the handling of discrepant or unexpected results and deviations from the process validation protocol. It is important that these situations be handled objectively. Normally this is accomplished by providing an independent oversight function administered by a team called the validation review board. The board may be made up of management level personnel who understand the organization's product line and the technology(ies) involved and who have expertise in process validation. Many times organizations mistakenly give the responsibility for handling discrepancies and deviations to the individual validation teams, creating a conflict of interest and increasing the likelihood of subjective and inappropriate decisions.

Most manufacturing processes are controlled by software or rely on electronic databases to perform their functions. Such software falls into two basic categories: off-the-shelf software used with or without modification, and specially designed and developed software. In most cases the source code for off-the-shelf software is not available to the medical device manufacturer. This limits the medical device manufacturer's ability to validate the software and confirm that it reproducibly performs the tasks required of it.

In the case of specially designed software, the user is also expected to document the software development process (as in section 820.30, verify the source code and validate that it performs according to its intended use).

SUBPART H

Acceptance Activities

FDA Quality System Regulation—1996

§ 820.80 Receiving, in-process, and finished device acceptance

§ 820.80(a) *General.* Each manufacturer shall establish and maintain procedures for acceptance activities. Acceptance activities include inspections, tests, or other verification activities.

AAMI/ANSI/ISO 13485:2003

Reference § 8.2.4 Monitoring and measurement of product § 8.2.4.1 General requirements

The overall objectives of the Standard are the same as those of the QSReg. The Standard treats the subject of monitoring and acceptance of the product more generally than the QSReg does in that the QSReg outlines specific requirements at the stages of receipt of product, in-process, and final acceptance. The Standard recognizes that acceptance monitoring must be performed at "appropriate stages."

The Standard recognizes generally that the evidence of conformity with acceptance criteria must be recorded; the QSReg has a specific subsection outlining those requirements.

The Standard bases the decision to release a product or service for delivery on whether the arrangements for the product realization process have been completed.

Reference § 8.2.4.2 Particular requirement for active implantable medical devices and implantable medical devices

The Standard requires that the identity of any personnel performing an inspection or testing implantable devices be recorded.

FDA Guidance

QSReg Preamble

> **Comment group 146.** . . . FDA now defines "acceptance activities" to include inspections, test, or other verification activities, such as supplier audits.
>
> **Comment group 147.** . . . FDA believes that the quality system regulation requires the minimum documentation necessary to ensure that safe and effective devices are designed and produced. FDA similarly believes that maintaining records of results of acceptance activities is imperative to ensure that nonconforming product is not inadvertently used or distributed. . . . Further, the regulation does not specify quantitative data but simply requires that the results be recorded. FDA believes that it is essential for the manufacturer to maintain records which provide evidence that the product has gone through the defined acceptance activities. These records must clearly show whether the product has passed or failed the acceptance activities according to the defined acceptance criteria. Where product fails to pass acceptance activities, the procedures for control of nonconforming product must be implemented, to include investigations where defined. If the acceptance records are not clear about how the product failed, then the manufacturer may end up duplicating the acceptance activities in order to perform appropriate investigations.

"Guideline for the Manufacture of In Vitro Diagnostic Products," January 10, 1994

This guidance document may be found at http://www.fda.gov/cdrh/comp/918.pdf.

This guidance document addresses a number of issues related to acceptance of components where deviation from specifications could result in the IVD device being unfit for its intended use. The guidance document discusses several of the ways that water, a key component of IVD reagents, is controlled (for example, control of endotoxins, control of temperature and pressure, and elimination of "dead legs" in water supply systems).

The guidance document is supported by the FDA Office of IVD Devices Evaluation and Safety. While it was issued in 1994, there is no indication that it has been amended or withdrawn.

AAMI/ANSI/ISO TR 14969:2004

Reference § 8.2.4 Monitoring and measurement of product
§ 8.2.4.1 General requirements

The Standard addresses the situation where the medical device is assembled and installed at the user's location (for example, the assembly and installation of large, multicomponent MRI or X-ray equipment). In these cases, the organization must plan and carry out any necessary inspection and testing of the assembled device(s) or must provide sufficient information, including expected results, to allow such inspection and testing to be performed by another party. The QSReg refers to §§ 6.3, 6.4, 7.5.1, 7.5.1.2, and 7.5.2.

The Standard lists a number of things that should be considered when selecting measurement methods, the measurement accuracy required, and the personnel skills required as part of the acceptance process (for example, the product characteristics, the equipment (including software) and tools required, the points at which acceptance testing should be performed, the documentation required and the acceptance criteria, and any regulatory oversight that may be required).

Reference § 8.2.4.2 Particular requirement for active implantable medical devices and implantable medical devices

The TR explains that the recording of the names of personnel performing acceptance testing facilitates any failure investigations or corrective or preventive actions that must be taken.

FDA Quality System Regulation—1996

§ 820.80(b) ***Receiving acceptance activities.*** Each manufacturer shall establish and maintain procedures for acceptance of incoming product. Incoming product shall be inspected, tested, or otherwise verified as conforming to specified requirements. Acceptance or rejection shall be documented.

AAMI/ANSI/ISO 13485:2003

Reference § 7.4.3 Verification of purchased product

In addition to the requirements outlined in the QSReg, the Standard explicitly addresses the situation where verification is performed at the supplier's location. The Standard requires that the documented purchasing information include a description of the verification activities that will be performed at the supplier's location. The organization shall establish and implement the inspection or other activities.

Reference § 8.2.4 Monitoring and measurement of product
§ 8.2.4.1 General requirements

The Standard has no additional requirements beyond those in the QSReg as pertains to the incoming acceptance of materials to be used in a medical device. See the general requirements in the preceding text related to § 820.80(a).

FDA Guidance

QSReg Preamble

> **Comment group 148.** . . . FDA has permitted manufacturers to use incoming items that had not yet been proven acceptable for use, provided that the manufacturer maintained control of the unapproved items and could retrieve the product that contained the unapproved items before distribution. . . . However, FDA emphasizes that while the product can be used in production prior to verification, it cannot be distributed prior to verification. FDA does not permit the distribution of unapproved product through an urgent use provision, because all finished devices must comply with Sec. 820.80(d), "Final acceptance activities," before they are released for distribution.

AAMI/ANSI/ISO TR 14969:2004

Reference § 7.4.3 Verification of purchased product

The TR recommends that if the specifications that must be met are the specifications set out by the supplier, the organization should still inspect and test to make sure the received product meets those specifications.

The TR outlines a number of receiving acceptance activities (for example, certification of suppliers, certificates of conformance, sampling or 100 percent inspection, and skip lot testing). The activity chosen should be consistent with the activities outlined in the QMS documentation.

The TR recommends that the actions taken in the event of nonconformity (for example, identification, segregation, and record keeping) be documented to ensure that consistent timely action is taken.

The nature and extent of the incoming acceptance activities will be influenced by the organization's experience with an individual supplier of the material or product being received and the confidence that the organization has with the individual supplier.

The TR provides additional guidance to that contained in the QSReg when a product is used prior to completion of the incoming acceptance activities. It recommends that only specified personnel be responsible for allowing use of such materials, that the use be based on the potential impact of those materials on the product realization process, and that the product be adequately identified to allow for handling of any nonconformities or corrective actions that may result from its use.

The TR clarifies that controls related to receiving acceptance apply whether or not the materials are paid for.

Reference § 8.2.4 Monitoring and measurement of product § 8.2.4.1 General requirements

The TR clarifies that the Standard considers receiving acceptance activities as part of in-process acceptance of product and materials.

FDA Quality System Regulation—1996

§ 820.80(c) ***In-process acceptance activities.*** Each manufacturer shall establish and maintain acceptance procedures, where appropriate, to ensure that specified requirements for in-process product are met. Such procedures shall ensure that in-process product is controlled until the required inspection and tests or other verification activities have been completed, or necessary approvals are received, and are documented.

AAMI/ANSI/ISO 13485:2003

Reference § 8.2.4 Monitoring and measurement of product § 8.2.4.1 General requirements

This section of the Standard has no additional requirements for in-process materials beyond those applied to acceptance activities in general. See text related to QSReg § 820.80(a).

Reference § 8.2.4.2 Particular requirement for active implantable medical devices and implantable medical devices

This section of the Standard has no additional requirements for in-process materials beyond those applied to acceptance activities in general. See text related to QSReg § 820.80(a).

FDA Guidance

QSReg Preamble

Comment group 149. . . . FDA . . . believes that Sec. 820.80 as now written, with the inclusion of "where appropriate," does not mandate in-process inspection and testing. FDA acknowledges that in-process acceptance activities may not be necessary or possible for every device, for example, medical socks. Further, the requirement states that in-process product must be controlled until the required inspection and test, or other verification activities, have been performed. This will permit manufacturers to use, under defined conditions and procedures, product that has not completed the acceptance activities described in Sec. 820.80(b) and (c). This does not mean that manufacturers can ignore the requirements in Sec. 820.80(b) and (c) because these requirements must be completed in order to comply with Sec. 820.80(d), which must be satisfied before devices are released for distribution.

AAMI/ANSI/ISO TR 14969:2004

Reference § 8.2.4 Monitoring and measurement of product § 8.2.4.1 General requirements

The TR has no additional recommendations for in-process materials beyond those applied to acceptance activities in general. See text related to QSReg § 820.80(a).

Reference § 8.2.4.2 Particular requirement for active implantable medical devices and implantable medical devices

This section of the Standard has no additional recommendations for in-process materials beyond those applied to acceptance activities in general. See text related to QSReg § 820.80(a).

FDA Quality System Regulation—1996

§ 820.80(d) ***Final acceptance activities.*** Each manufacturer shall establish and maintain procedures for finished device acceptance to ensure that each production run, lot, or batch of finished devices meets acceptance criteria. Finished devices shall be held in quarantine or otherwise adequately controlled until released. Finished devices shall not be released for distribution until:

(1) the activities required in the DMR are completed;
(2) the associated data and documentation is reviewed;
(3) the release is authorized by the signature of a designated individual(s); and
(4) the authorization is dated.

AAMI/ANSI/ISO 13485:2003

Reference § 7.5 Production and service provision
§ 7.5.1 Control of production and service provision
§ 7.5.1.1 General requirements

This section of the Standard has no additional requirements related to final acceptance activities beyond those contained in the QSReg.

Reference § 8.2.4 Monitoring and measurement of product
§ 8.2.4.1 General requirements

This section of the Standard has no additional requirements for final acceptance activities beyond those applied to acceptance activities in general. See text related to QSReg § 820.80(a).

§ 8.2.4.2 Particular requirement for active implantable medical devices and implantable medical devices

This section of the TR has no additional requirements for final acceptance activities beyond those that are applied in the QSReg.

There is reference to acceptance activities in general. See text related to QSReg § 820.80(a).

FDA Guidance

QSReg Preamble

Comment group 150. . . . Manufacturers have the flexibility to choose a combination of methods, including finished device inspection and test, provided such methods will accomplish the required result.

FDA believes that it is important for the person responsible for release to have personally documented and dated that release. This can be accomplished through use of an inspection stamp, if the stamp is controlled as discussed above under Sec. 820.40 Document controls. . . .

"Guideline for the Manufacture of In Vitro Diagnostic Products," January 10, 1994

This guidance document may be found at http://www.fda.gov/cdrh/comp/918.pdf.

This guidance document addresses a number of issues related to final acceptance of IVD reagent devices (for example, control of component lots that make up the final reagent product, especially where the component lots cannot be interchanged, and testing for turbidity, sterility, and bioburden). One of the unique aspects of IVD reagent devices is the need to monitor the stability and establish a lot-specific expiration date. Normally the stability of the IVD reagent and the expected expiration period (that is, shelf life) are established during the design and development of the product. The stability is also monitored after the release of selected production lots, in order to confirm the shelf life and to alert the organization to any shifts in shelf life.

The guidance document is supported by the FDA Office of IVD Devices Evaluation and Safety. While it was issued in 1994, there is no indication that it has been amended or withdrawn.

AAMI/ANSI/ISO TR 14969:2004

Reference § 7.5 Production and service provision
§ 7.5.1 Control of production and service provision
§ 7.5.1.1 General requirements

This section of the TR has no additional recommendations related to final acceptance activities beyond those contained in the QSReg.

Reference § 8.2.4 Monitoring and measurement of product § 8.2.4.1 General requirements

The TR introduces the concept that final inspection and testing as part of the final acceptance activities build on the inspection and testing performed at the incoming and in-process stages and use the results of that testing and inspection to the extent that they are relevant to the final medical device.

The TR also recommends that documentation of the final acceptance activities include the acceptance criteria on which the final release is based.

The TR indicates that final acceptance may be based on testing and evaluation that simulate actual use of the product, with that testing and evaluation performed on medical products selected from a lot or batch of the final medical device.

FDA Quality System Regulation—1996

§ 820.80(e) ***Acceptance records.*** Each manufacturer shall document acceptance activities required by this part. These records shall include:

(1) the acceptance activities performed;
(2) the dates acceptance activities are performed;
(3) the results;
(4) the signature of the individual(s) conducting the acceptance activities; and
(5) where appropriate, the equipment used. These records shall be part of the DHR.

AAMI/ANSI/ISO 13485:2003

Reference § 8.2.4 Monitoring and measurement of product § 8.2.4.1 General requirements

This section of the Standard has no additional requirements for final acceptance records beyond those applied to acceptance activities in general. See text related to QSReg § 820.80(a).

Reference § 8.2.4.2 Particular requirement for active implantable medical devices and implantable medical devices

This section of the Standard has no additional requirements for final acceptance records beyond those applied to acceptance activities in general. See text related to QSReg § 820.80(a).

FDA Guidance

QSReg Preamble

Comment group 151. . . . FDA agrees that it may not be necessary to document every piece of equipment used in acceptance activities. The requirement, renamed "Acceptance records," now provides that equipment used shall be documented "where appropriate." For some critical operations and testing, identification of the equipment used will be imperative for proper investigations into nonconforming product.

. . . As discussed above, certain information must be captured on acceptance records for the records to be useful in evaluating nonconformity. Through many years of experience, FDA has determined what it believes to be a minimum requirement for these records. Section 820.80(e) reflects that determination.

AAMI/ANSI/ISO TR 14969:2004

Reference § 8.2.4 Monitoring and measurement of product § 8.2.4.1 General requirements

The TR provides guidance related to the content of acceptance records (for example, identification of the product tested; identification of the inspection and testing procedures used, including the revision level; identification of the test equipment used; the testing data; a reconciliation of the product accepted and rejected, including the disposition of the rejected product and the reason(s) for the rejection; and the signature of the personnel doing the testing).

FDA Quality System Regulation—1996

§ 820.86 Acceptance status

Each manufacturer shall identify by suitable means the acceptance status of product, to indicate the conformance or nonconformity of product with acceptance criteria. The identification of acceptance status shall be maintained throughout manufacturing, packaging, labeling, installation, and servicing of the product to ensure that only product which has passed the required acceptance activities is distributed, used, or installed.

AAMI/ANSI/ISO 13485:2003

Reference § 7.5.3 Identification and traceability
§ 7.5.3.3 Status identification

This section of the Standard contains no additional requirements related to status identification beyond those contained in the QSReg.

FDA Guidance

QSReg Preamble

> **Comment group 152.** . . . FDA agrees that the inspection and test status may be identified by any method that will achieve the result, which might include acceptable computerized identification, markings, etc. . . .

AAMI/ANSI/ISO TR 14969:2004

Reference § 7.5.3 Identification and traceability
§ 7.5.3.3 Status identification

The TR suggests a number of status identification means (for example, marking, storage location, and tagging or signing by physical or electronic means).

The status identification should indicate whether the product has been inspected or tested and what the results of such inspection or testing are (for example, "accepted" for fully meeting requirements, "accepted" with identified nonconformities under concession, "on hold" awaiting further testing or inspection, and "rejected").

The TR warns against using any marking materials that may have a deleterious effect on the medical device or its components.

SUBPART I

Nonconforming Product

FDA Quality System Regulation—1996

§ 820.90 Nonconforming product

§ 820.90(a) ***Control of nonconforming product.*** Each manufacturer shall establish and maintain procedures to control product that does not conform to specified requirements. The procedures shall address the identification, documentation, evaluation, segregation, and disposition of nonconforming product. The evaluation of nonconformity shall include a determination of the need for an investigation and notification of the persons or organizations responsible for the nonconformity. The evaluation and any investigation shall be documented.

AAMI/ANSI/ISO 13485:2003

Reference § 8.3 Control of nonconforming product

The Standard outlines a number of ways of dealing with a nonconforming product, including eliminating the nonconformity, authorizing or releasing the product for use under concession, or changing its original intended use or application. The release under concession is an alternative only if it is allowed by regulation; if it is used, the person(s) authorizing it must be recorded. Records must be kept that relate to the nature of the nonconformity and the steps taken to resolve it.

FDA Guidance

QSReg Preamble

Comment group 155. . . . [FDA] gives the manufacturers the flexibility to define how they are going to "control" products that are nonconforming. . . . the procedures will need to set forth the manufacturer's SOP on when investigations will take place and provisions for trending and/or monitoring the situation in the future . . . [should] include the explanations for not performing investigations and how nonconformities will be trended and/or monitored. . . .

. . . Where some person or organization is responsible for nonconformities, they must be notified to ensure that future nonconformities are prevented. . . .

. . . Therefore the procedures will need to set forth in the manufacturer's SOP describing when an investigation must take place and provision for trending and/or monitoring the situation in the future are required.

. . . Fourth, the FDA added "The evaluation and any investigation shall be documented," which would include the explanation as to why the investigation was not conducted. . . .

AAMI/ANSI/ISO TR 14969:2004

Reference § 8.3 Control of nonconforming product

The TR clarifies that nonconforming product can be incoming, in-process, or finished product delivered or ready for delivery to customers.

The TR recommends that top management provide a documented process for handling product nonconformities, including the empowerment of any person in the organization to report such nonconformities and the review and disposition of such nonconformities.

The procedure for handling nonconformities should include information on how to:

- Distinguish conforming from nonconforming product.
- Identify the nonconforming product (for example, by serial number, lot number, or date of production).
- Characterize the nature and extent of the nonconformity.
- Determine the specific action that will be taken to dispose of the nonconformity, including assessment of any new risks that may be introduced by those actions.
- Determine and evaluate the effectiveness of the disposition of the nonconforming product (for example, segregation, rework, scrapping, and recall). Included in this determination are considerations of safe disposal

and proper identification of the disposed product to prevent it from being reintroduced into manufacturing.

Authors' Notes

Every nonconformity must be identified, and a decision must be made whether to investigate its cause. If the individual making this decision decides not to investigate, his or her name and signature must be affixed to the document. In addition, the reason for the negative decision must be documented. If the individual decides to investigate the cause of the nonconformity and initiate a corrective and/or preventive measure, he or she should document the activities. If the corrective action is rework of the work in progress (WIP), procedures must be in place to show the amount of rework necessary, the effect of the rework on the product, and the testing of the reworked material. On occasion, process revalidation may be necessary. All this must be documented in the DHR.

NONCONFORMING PRODUCT

FDA Quality System Regulation—1996

§ 820.90(b) ***Nonconformity review and disposition.***

(1) Each manufacturer shall establish and maintain procedures that define the responsibility for review and the authority for the disposition of nonconforming product. The procedures shall set forth the review and disposition process. Disposition of nonconforming product shall be documented. Documentation shall include the justification for use of nonconforming product and the signature of the individual(s) authorizing the use.

(2) Each manufacturer shall establish and maintain procedures for rework, to include retesting and reevaluation of the nonconforming product after rework, to ensure that the product meets its current approved specifications. Rework and reevaluation activities, including a determination of any adverse effect from the rework upon the product, shall be documented in the DHR.

AAMI/ANSI/ISO 13485:2003

Reference § 8.3 Control of nonconforming product

If the product is modified or reworked to resolve the nonconformity, the product and its performance must be reverified to ensure that the product continues to meet requirements. The process for modification of the product must be documented, reviewed, and approved, and a risk assessment must also be performed for any modification.

If the nonconformity is detected after delivery of the product, then the organization is required to take appropriate action with regard to delivered and undelivered product. The appropriateness of the action depends on the nature and potential effects of the nonconformity.

FDA Guidance

QSReg Preamble

Comment group 156. FDA . . . [seeks] to make clear that the section requires procedures that define the responsibility for review and authority for disposition of nonconforming product and that set forth the review and disposition process. FDA believes that proper disposition of nonconforming product is essential for ensuring the safety and effectiveness of devices. Manufacturers have made determinations that nonconforming product may be used which have resulted in defective devices being distributed. Thus, although it may be appropriate at times to use nonconforming products, the disposition process must be adequately controlled.

The . . . [regulation] requires that disposition and justification for concessions be documented. FDA believes that the justification should be based on scientific evidence, which a manufacturer should be prepared to provide upon request. Concessions should be closely monitored and not become accepted practice. . . .

Comment group 157. . . . FDA believes that the . . . Sec. 820.90(b)(1) clearly allows for other methods of disposition besides rework. Section 820.90(b)(2) . . . allow[s] manufacturers the flexibility to inspect or use other verification activities. . . .

FDA's intent is that such a determination [of any adverse effect of rework] be made with any rework; given the potential harmful effect rework could have on the product. . . .

AAMI/ANSI/ISO TR 14969:2004

Reference § 8.3 Control of nonconforming product

The TR indicates that the response to a nonconformity can be grouped into three separate categories:

- Correction (that is, action taken to eliminate the nonconformity)
- Corrective action (that is, action taken to eliminate the root cause(s) of the nonconformity to prevent recurrence of the nonconformity)

NONCONFORMING PRODUCT

- Preventive action (that is, action taken to eliminate the root cause(s) of the nonconformity to prevent an occurrence of the nonconformity in product that has not, as yet, experienced the same nonconformity.)

If a nonconforming product is released under concession, the organization must still comply with all regulatory requirements appropriate for the product and any services related to it. The regulation-related deliberations pertaining to the concession must be recorded and signed by the individual(s) authorizing the concession.

Actions that can be taken in regard to a nonconforming product that has been delivered to customers include stopping sale and distribution of the product and recalling the product (that is, provision to customers of alternative instructions for use, safe destruction of the product along with an accounting of the product destroyed, or physical return of the product to the manufacturer). All recalls must comply with the relevant regulatory requirements that cover such actions.

The TR recommends that any product returned to the manufacturer be treated as if it is nonconforming, taking into consideration any contamination that may be introduced by its use in the field. The TR references ISO 12891-1 as a useful source of information related to decontamination.

Authors' Notes

It is not unusual for third-party assessors or regulatory inspectors to audit the methods used to identify, segregate, and dispose of vendor-supplied nonconforming product, and any investigations of the causes of such nonconforming product. If rework is the method chosen to handle nonconforming product and it is decided not to verify the output of the rework, the procedure for rework should be validated.

Nonconformities may arise after the device has changed ownership from the original customer and/or has been repaired or refurbished by persons other than representatives of the manufacturer. In such situations it is difficult for the manufacturer to know when, how, and by whom the device was last repaired and to what specifications. Such information may be crucial for the conduct of an investigation as to the cause. FDA will expect the manufacturer to make sincere attempts to retrieve this information and make the repair. See also comments related to 820.200.

In addition to the methods of disposition of nonconforming products described in the QSReg, the Standard, and the TR, the following dispositions can be used:

- If it is an incoming material or an in-process material, use it in a different product or process where it still meets specifications
- Use it as a teaching aid internally or with customers, with clear labeling that indicates that it is not for patient use
- Donate it to teaching institutions with appropriate labeling that indicates that it is for demonstration or teaching purposes only, and not for patient use
- Break it down for spare parts as long as the parts are within specifications

FDA regulations allow for correction, removal, and recall of nonconforming devices that have reached the user. Requirements related to these actions are not part of the QSReg, but they can be found in 21 CFR § 7, 21 CFR § 810, and 21 CFR § 806. Additional information can be found at http://www.fda.gov/cdrh/devadvice/51.html.

Trends of nonconformities should be referred to the CAPA process.

SUBPART J

Corrective and Preventive Action

FDA Quality System Regulation—1996

§ 820.100 Corrective and preventive action

§ 820.100(a) Each manufacturer shall establish and maintain procedures for implementing corrective and preventive action. The procedures shall include requirements for:

(1) Analyzing processes, work operations, concessions, quality audit reports, quality records, service records, complaints, returned product, and other sources of quality data to identify existing and potential causes of nonconforming product, or other quality problems. Appropriate statistical methodology shall be employed where necessary to detect recurring quality problems;
(2) Investigating the cause of nonconformities relating to product, processes, and the quality system;
(3) Identifying the action(s) needed to correct and prevent recurrence of nonconforming product and other quality problems;
(4) Verifying or validating the corrective and preventive action to ensure that such action is effective and does not adversely affect the finished device;
(5) Implementing and recording changes in methods and procedures needed to correct and prevent identified quality problems;
(6) Ensuring that information related to quality problems or nonconforming product is disseminated to those directly responsible for assuring the quality of such product or the prevention of such problems; and
(7) Submitting relevant information on identified quality problems, as well as corrective and preventive actions, for management review.

§ 820.100(b) All activities required under this section, and their results, shall be documented.

AAMI/ANSI/ISO 13485:2003

Reference § 8.5 Improvement
§ 8.5.1 General

The Standard requires the organization to make improvements to the QMS that ensure that it continues to be effective and operates within its quality policy and quality objectives. The Standard points out that such improvements can be implemented and maintained through the use of QMS processes (for example, internal audits, analysis of data, corrective and preventive actions, and management review).

Reference § 8.5.2 Corrective action

The Standard contains no additional requirements related to corrective action beyond those contained in the QSReg.

Reference § 8.5.3 Preventive action

The Standard contains no additional requirements related to preventive action beyond those contained in the QSReg.

FDA Guidance

QSReg Preamble

Comment group 158. . . . FDA . . . [believes] that it is essential that the manufacturer establish procedures for implementing corrective and preventive action. . . . The procedures must include provisions for the remaining requirements in the section. These procedures must provide for control and action to be taken on devices distributed, and those not yet distributed, that are suspected of having potential nonconformities.

Comment group 159. . . . FDA . . . [believes] that the degree of corrective and preventive action taken to eliminate or minimize actual or potential nonconformities must be appropriate to the magnitude of the problem and commensurate with the risks encountered. FDA cannot dictate in a regulation the degree of action that should be taken because each circumstance will be different, but FDA does expect the manufacturer to develop procedures for assessing the risk, the actions that need to be taken for different levels of risk, and how to correct or prevent the problem from recurring, depending on that risk assessment.

FDA emphasizes that any death, even if the manufacturer attributes it to user error, will be considered relevant by FDA and will have a high risk potentially associated with it. User error is still considered to be a nonconformity because human factors and other similar tools should have been considered during the design phase of the device. FDA acknowledges that a manufacturer cannot possibly foresee every single potential misuse during the design of a device, but when the manufacturer becomes aware of misuse, the corrective and preventive action requirements should be implemented to determine if redesign of the device or labeling changes may be necessary.

Comment group 160. . . . It was not FDA's intent to require that processes unrelated to an existing nonconformity be analyzed. Instead, Sec. 820.100(a)(1) requires an analysis of those items listed that could be related to the problem. . . .

The inclusion of "quality audits" as a valuable feedback mechanism for the manufacturer does not conflict with FDA's policy of not reviewing internal quality audits. Internal audits are valuable and necessary tools for the manufacturer to evaluate the quality system. The audit reports should be used to analyze the entire quality system and provide feedback into the system to close the feedback loop, so that corrective or preventive actions can be taken where necessary. FDA will review the corrective and preventive action procedures and activities performed in conformance with those procedures without reviewing the internal audit reports. FDA wants to make it clear that corrective and preventive actions, including the documentation of these activities, which result from internal audits and management reviews are not covered under Sec. 820.180(c).

. . . there may be other statistical tools available beyond "trend analysis" [for the purposes of performing corrective and preventive actions]. FDA emphasizes that the appropriate statistical tools must be employed when it is necessary to utilize statistical methodology. FDA has seen far too often the misuse of statistics by manufacturers in an effort to minimize instead of address the problem. Such misuse of statistics would be a violation of this section.

FDA has retained the requirement for analysis to identify "potential causes of nonconforming product," however, because FDA believes this is an important aspect of preventive action.

Comment group 161. . . . The requirement in this section is broader than the requirement for investigations under Sec. 820.198, because it requires that nonconforming product discovered before or after distribution be investigated to the degree commensurate with the significance and risk of the nonconformity. At times a very in depth investigation will be necessary, while at other times a simple investigation, followed by trend analysis or other appropriate tools, will be acceptable. In addition, in contrast to Sec. 820.198, the requirement in this section applies to process and quality system nonconformities, as well as product nonconformities. For example, if a molding process with its known capabilities has a normal 5 percent rejection rate and that rate rises to 10 percent, an investigation into the nonconformity of the process must be performed.

Comment group 162. . . . the objective of Sec. 820.100 is to correct and prevent poor practices, not simply bad product. Correction and prevention of unacceptable quality system practices should result in fewer nonconformities related to product. Therefore, this section addresses problems within the quality system itself. For example, it should identify and correct improper personnel training, the failure to follow procedures, and inadequate procedures, among other things.

FDA . . . give[s] the manufacturer the flexibility to use whatever method of analysis is appropriate.

Comment group 163. FDA . . . [believes] that preventive, as well as corrective, action must be verified or validated. . . .

Comment group 165. . . . only certain information need be directed to management. The manufacturer's procedures should clearly define the criteria to be followed to determine what information will be considered "relevant" to the action taken and why. FDA emphasizes that it is always management's responsibility to ensure that all nonconformity issues are handled appropriately. . . .

Comment group 166. . . . information [associated with corrective and preventive actions] is directly relevant to the safety and effectiveness of finished medical devices. FDA has the authority to review such records and the obligation to do so to protect the public health. . . . Manufacturers will be required to make this information readily available to an FDA investigator, so that the investigator may properly assess the manufacturer's compliance with these quality system requirements.

AAMI/ANSI/ISO TR 14969:2004

Reference § 8.5 Improvement
§ 8.5.1 General

The TR emphasizes that one objective of corrective or preventive action is to ensure that the QMS continues to be effective in meeting customer requirements, including regulatory requirements. Any such activities are considered to be "improvements" for the purposes of meeting the requirements of the Standard.

Advisory notices

The TR points out that under national or regional regulations, advisory notices distributed to affected users as part of a corrective action might have to be reported to appropriate regulatory bodies (see 21 CFR 803 and 21 CFR 806). Such advisory notices may contain information that allows a device to be used in a safe and effective manner or may contain instructions for returning the device to the manufacturer for rework or destruction. The regulatory requirements associated with advisory notices must be incorporated into the organization's QMS.

The content of the advisory notice, the actions it calls for, and the need and urgency to report the notice to the regulatory authorities depend on the nature and severity of the harm that could result from the hazard that the medical device presents.

The process for generating and distributing an advisory notice should be documented and should cover situations where alternative personnel will be required to activate it.

The TR lists the recommended content of an advisory notice (for example, a description of the affected medical device(s); the means for identifying the affected medical device(s), for example, serial number, lot number; the reason for the advisory notice; and the recommended course(s) of action by the recipient of the advisory notice to avoid hazard(s) and harm(s)).

If the advisory notice calls for the medical device to be returned to the manufacturer, the organization should monitor the effectiveness of the return process and reconcile the quantities of product affected, reworked, and scrapped.

Reference § 8.5.2 Corrective action

The TR recommends that the organization's corrective action procedures identify corrective action plans with regard to the individual(s) responsible for the corrective action, the timetable for corrective actions, the steps associated with the corrective action, and the manner in which the effectiveness of the corrective action will be verified.

One of the key activities associated with corrective action is to identify the cause(s). The TR outlines many potential causes (for example, problems associated with incoming materials, processes, tools, equipment, or manufacturing and handling equipment and facilities; inadequate or missing procedures or other documentation; failure to follow procedures; inadequate process control; lack of training; and others).

The TR outlines the various sources of information that can contribute to the planning of corrective actions (for example, inspection and testing records, validation study results, nonconformity records, process monitoring records, field service reports, customer complaints, published reports on the same or similar products, and others).

The TR recommends that effective implementation of a corrective action normally include the following:

- Clear and unambiguous identification of the nonconformity to either the process or the product that prompted the corrective action
- Those persons affected by the nonconformance (for example, customers when the nonconformity relates to the product; operational personnel when the nonconformity is related to the process)

- Identification of related products or processes that may also be affected by the nonconformity
- Identification of the root cause of the nonconformity
- Description of the course(s) of action to prevent recurrence of the root cause(s) of the nonconformity
- The approvals necessary to implement and maintain the corrective action(s)
- Objective evidence of the implementation of the corrective action
- Verification/validation records confirming the effectiveness of the corrective action
- Evidence that the corrective action did not introduce any new risks

Reference § 8.5.3 Preventive action

The TR indicates that preventive actions are taken on the basis of the review of information that indicates that a nonconformity could occur if action is not taken. A number of these sources of information include, but are not limited to, incoming, in-process, and final acceptance records, rework records, scrap records, customer complaints or other feedback, warranty claims, audit records, and process control and product field performance trending records.

Authors' Notes

The effectiveness of an organization's CAPA processes is a key indicator of the health of the organization's QMS. In many organizations, CAPA processes are weak and/or in need of significant improvement. Key causes for this weakness include the following:

- Overloading of CAPA processes
- Inadequate resources applied to the processes
- Inadequate follow-up of corrective actions

Overloading of CAPA processes

Many organizations put too many actions into CAPA processes. They fail to understand that not all activities prompted by nonconformities rise to the level of corrective actions. Some of these activities simply represent "corrections" that can be conducted within the QMS process that identified the nonconformity. For example, if an internal audit identifies that a temperature controller record sheet has not been replaced on time, the replacement of the record sheet and possibly the retraining of personnel may be completed and recorded within the audit process. If an out-of-specification part is identified during the testing and inspection process on an assembly line, the manufacturing process can allow for rework of the part and replacement of it in the production line with the correction completed and recorded as part of the manufacturing process. If a number of finished medical devices are returned by customers because they fail to perform as expected, these devices may be corrected, with the corrections recorded, within the complaint handling or servicing processes. Unless the preceding examples are repeated to the extent that there appears to be a systemic QMS problem or an indication that the product involved is unsafe or ineffective, there is no need to refer these problems to the CAPA process.

In summary, the key criteria for determining whether an action should be controlled within the CAPA processes are the following:

- The nonconformity is not randomly occurring
- The nonconformity is indicative of a systemic QMS deficiency
- The nonconformity is indicative of the product being unsafe or ineffective
- The nonconformity can cause the product to be unsafe or ineffective

We have observed situations where a manufacturer has placed a "correction" into the CAPA process only to give it sufficient priority to be addressed. Such a decision tends to overload the CAPA process.

Inadequate resources applied to the processes

In many organizations there are inadequate quality personnel staffing the CAPA processes and the processes that feed into them (for example, internal audit, nonconformity handling, and complaint handling). The inadequacy may take the form of too few personnel or inadequately skilled personnel (for example, personnel without adequate training in root cause analysis and risk management). The inadequacy may reside with suppliers who are made part of the CAPA but fail to address their issues in a timely manner. This leads the personnel in many organizations to decide that, due to understaffing of the feeder processes, a nonconformity will not get addressed unless it is put into the CAPA processes. As a result, too many actions get put into the CAPA processes. When one assesses the CAPA processes, one notes that corrective actions are not completed in a timely manner. Gridlock in CAPA processes can also be caused by not having sufficient skilled personnel available to handle the individual corrective and preventive actions.

Inadequate follow-up of corrective actions

Inadequate follow-up of corrective actions takes two forms: failure to verify the effectiveness of the corrective action and failure to determine if there are additional preventive actions that should be implemented as a result of the nonconformity(ies) that led to the corrective action.

SUBPART K

Labeling and Packaging Control

FDA Quality System Regulation—1996

§ 820.120 Device labeling

Each manufacturer shall establish and maintain procedures to control labeling activities.

§ 820.120(a) ***Label integrity.*** Labels shall be printed and applied so as to remain legible and affixed during the customary conditions of processing, storage, handling, distribution, and, where appropriate, use.

§ 820.120(b) ***Labeling inspection.*** Labeling shall not be released for storage or use until a designated individual(s) has examined the labeling for accuracy including, where applicable, the correct expiration date, control number, storage instructions, handling instructions, and any additional processing instructions. The release, including the date and signature of the individual(s) performing the examination, shall be documented in the DHR.

§ 820.120(c) ***Labeling storage.*** Each manufacturer shall store labeling in a manner that provides proper identification and is designed to prevent mixups.

§ 820.120(d) ***Labeling operations.*** Each manufacturer shall control labeling and packaging operations to prevent labeling mixups. The label and labeling used for each production unit, lot, or batch shall be documented in the DHR.

§ 820.120(e) ***Control number.*** Where a control number is required by Sec. 820.65, that control number shall be on or shall accompany the device through distribution.

AAMI/ANSI/ISO 13485:2003

Reference § 7.5.1.1(g) . . . the implementation of defined operations for labeling and packaging

The Standard treats the subject of control of labeling generally and contains no additional requirements beyond those in the QSReg.

Reference § 7.5.5 Preservation of product

The Standard contains no additional requirements related to control of labeling beyond those in the QSReg.

FDA Guidance

QSReg Preamble

Comment group 167. . . . FDA believes that the degree of detail in this section is necessary because these same requirements have been in place for 18 years, yet numerous recalls every year are the result of labeling errors or mix-ups. FDA, therefore, believes that more, not less, control is necessary. . . .

Comment group 169. . . . A few comments stated that . . . "labeling" inspections should allow automated readers in place of a "designated individual." . . . Several recalls on labeling have been attributed to automated readers not catching errors. The requirement does not preclude manufacturers from using automated readers where that process is followed by human oversight. A "designated individual" must examine, at a minimum, a representative sampling of all labels that have been checked by the automated readers. Further, automated readers are often programmed with only the base label and do not check specifics, such as control numbers and expiration dates, among other things, that are distinct for each label. The regulation requires that labeling be inspected for these items prior to release.

AAMI/ANSI/ISO TR 14969:2004

Reference § 7.3.2 Design and development inputs

The TR refers to regulatory requirements and general and medical device standards as sources for content in the medical device labeling.

The TR recommends that labeling provided in the local language be developed and checked by an individual or individuals with expertise in the technology of the medical device as well as the local language.

The TR recommends that, as much as possible, symbols that have regulatory acceptance and international recognition be used in place of text. The TR suggests that product liability concerns may also affect the decision about the use of symbols. The TR references ISO 15223 and EN 980 as sources of guidance on the use of symbols.

Reference § 7.5 Production and service provision
§ 7.5.1 Control of production and service provision
§ 7.5.1.1 General requirements

The TR notes that labeling and packaging errors can be minimized by a number of means (for example, segregating packaging and labeling operations from other manufacturing operations, avoiding performing operations that use similar packaging and labeling in time and space proximity of each other, clearly identifying packaging and labeling lines, using roll-fed labels, destroying excess batch-identified labels, and establishing and implementing line clearance procedures)

Authors' Notes

ISO Standard 13485 treats labels and labeling as it does any raw material and subassembly that goes into the finished device. FDA, on the other hand, highly emphasizes labeling control. This stems from the evolution of the device regulation based on the predecessor drug regulation, where labeling control was and is essential. Additionally, the similarity between drugs and in vitro diagnostic products, especially during their manufacture, tended to maintain the druglike emphasis as the device regulation evolved. The Standard folds the control of labeling into the control of production materials in general.

FDA Quality System Regulation—1996

§ 820.130 Device packaging

Each manufacturer shall ensure that device packaging and shipping containers are designed and constructed to protect the device from alteration or damage during the customary conditions of processing, storage, handling, and distribution.

AAMI/ANSI/ISO 13485:2003

Reference § 7.5.1.1(g) . . . the implementation of defined operations for labeling and packaging

The Standard treats the subject of control of packaging generally and contains no additional requirements beyond those in the QSReg.

Reference § 7.5.5 Preservation of product

The Standard treats the subject of control of packaging generally and contains no additional requirements beyond those in the QSReg.

FDA Guidance

QSReg Preamble

> **Comment group 172.** FDA believes . . . that any intentional tampering would not be covered because the requirement states "during customary conditions."

AAMI/ANSI/ISO TR 14969:2004

Reference § 7.3.2 Design and development inputs

The TR makes several recommendations for the design and development of packaging materials: the packaging should be compatible with the product, and, if applicable, sterilization processes should be used. Any sterilization and cleanliness requirements should be adhered to. It references ISO 11607 for additional guidance related to packaging of terminally sterilized medical devices.

Reference § 7.5 Production and service provision
§ 7.5.1 Control of production and service provision
§ 7.5.1.1 General requirements

The TR notes that packaging errors can be minimized by a number of means (for example, segregating packaging and labeling operations from other manufacturing operations, avoiding performing operations that use similar packaging and labeling in time and space proximity of each other, and clearly identifying packaging and labeling lines).

Reference § 7.5.5 Preservation of product

The TR notes that packaging materials should protect the product against damage, deterioration, or contamination up to the point of use of the product.

SUBPART L

Handling, Storage, Distribution, and Installation

HANDLING

FDA Quality System Regulation—1996

§ 820.140 Handling

Each manufacturer shall establish and maintain procedures to ensure that mixups, damage, deterioration, contamination, or other adverse effects to product do not occur during handling.

AAMI/ANSI/ISO 13485:2003

Reference § 7.2 Customer-related processes
§ 7.2.1 Determination of requirements related to the product

This section of the Standard addresses the QMS obligation to understand, document, and fulfill the customer requirements surrounding the relationship between the manufacturer and its customer (for example, the contract understanding of specifically what product or service the customer is purchasing, and the delivery and postdelivery activities that the manufacturer is obligated to perform). The handling of the finished product to avoid deterioration, damage, and contamination is one of these requirements. The QSReg addresses similar requirements when describing the purchases of products and services by the manufacturer, but it is silent on the situation where the manufacturer is the supplier to its customers.

The QSReg addresses the QMS obligation to understand and fulfill customer requirements only in the section related to design input.

Reference § 7.2.2 Review of requirements related to the product

The Standard requires the manufacturer to review and agree with its customer about the requirements described in § 7.2.1, and to document those agreements. These requirements are essentially the same as the "contract review" requirements described in ISO 13485:1996. The manufacturer is obligated to ensure that the documents are kept up-to-date and reflect the current agreements.

When the manufacturer sells its products through catalogs or over the Internet, the Standard indicates that the customer order represents the review and acceptance by the customer and the manufacturer of the description of the product and ancillary business services contained in the catalog or Internet information.

Reference § 7.5.5 Preservation of product

HANDLING

The Standard addresses the subject of handling as part of the discussion of the general requirement to preserve the product so that it conforms to its requirements. Preservation includes the functions of identification, handling, packaging, storage, and protection. The QSReg addresses each of the preservation functions individually (see QSReg § 820.140, § 820.150, and § 820.160). The Standard's documentation requirements for preservation are mirrored in the documentation for the individual aspects of preservation in the QSReg.

The Standard requires the manufacturer to establish procedures related to any special storage and handling requirements for products that have limited shelf life or have other special storage limitations. The Standard also requires that fulfillment of these requirements be recorded.

FDA Guidance

QSReg Preamble

Comment group 173. . . . The procedures [for handling] are expected to ensure that mix-ups, damage, deterioration, contamination, or other adverse effects do not occur. . . . The requirement continues to apply to all stages of handling in which a manufacturer is involved, which may in some cases go beyond initial distribution.

The comparable provision in ISO/13485 states, "If appropriate, special provisions shall be established, documented and maintained for the handling of used product in order to prevent contamination of other product, the manufacturing environment and personnel." FDA agrees with this requirement and has therefore added the term "contamination" to Secs. 820.140 Handling and 820.150 Storage.

AAMI/ANSI/ISO TR 14969:2004

Reference § 7.2 Customer-related processes
§ 7.2.1 Determination of requirements related to the product

The TR lists a number of customer-related activities pertaining to preservation of the product (for example, delivery schedules, delivery from one lot of product only, and shipping package size).

Reference § 7.2.2 Review of requirements related to the product

The TR contains no guidance with respect to handling in this section.

Reference § 7.5.5 Preservation of product

The TR lists many methods for safely handling the product (for example, use of antistatic wrist straps, gloves, and protective clothing, and equipment like pallets, conveyors, and rigging used during transportation). Such equipment can help avoid vibration, shock, abrasion, corrosion, temperature variation, and other conditions that can damage or cause deterioration of the product. The manufacturer must also consider maintenance of the handling equipment. Product packaging should also be considered as a means to prevent damage during handling. All these means of protection during handling are identified and documented during the design of the device and the processes for manufacturing and controlling it. . . .

Authors' Notes

The Standard, § 7.5.4 describes the manufacturer's responsibilities for preserving and protecting customer property at the manufacturer's site.

Packaging intended to protect the product during shipping must be validated for that purpose by conducting shipping experiments.

FDA Quality System Regulation—1996

§ 820.150 Storage

(a) Each manufacturer shall establish and maintain procedures for the control of storage areas and stock rooms for product to prevent mixups, damage, deterioration, contamination, or other adverse effects pending use or distribution and to ensure that no obsolete, rejected, or deteriorated product is used or distributed. When the quality of product deteriorates over time, it shall be stored in a manner to facilitate proper stock rotation, and its condition shall be assessed as appropriate.

(b) Each manufacturer shall establish and maintain procedures that describe the methods for authorizing receipt from and dispatch to storage areas and stock rooms.

AAMI/ANSI/ISO 13485:2003

Reference § 7.5.5 Preservation of product

The Standard contains no additional requirements beyond those already found in the QSReg.

FDA Guidance

QSReg Preamble

Comment group 174. . . . FDA understands that a device may no longer be sold, but that parts and subassemblies may still be required for customer support; therefore, those components or subassemblies are not "obsolete." FDA's intent in this requirement is to ensure that only the appropriate product be used or distributed.

. . . a manufacturer must ensure that product can be properly identified.

Comment group 175. . . . FDA . . . believes that strict control over product in storage areas and stock rooms results in decreased distribution of nonconforming product. Thus, even where locked storage rooms are utilized, the procedures should detail, among other things, who is permitted access and what steps should be followed prior to removal.

AAMI/ANSI/ISO TR 14969:2004

Reference § 7.5.5 Preservation of product

The TR suggests that it might be useful to periodically check stored product that is susceptible to deterioration to make sure that it still meets specifications.

The TR lists several measures for preserving the stored product (for example, maintenance of sterile conditions, control of static and dust, monitoring of temperature and humidity, and measures to protect fragile products).

The TR suggests that products with special storage requirements (for example, limited shelf life or special protection needs) be clearly identified. When the limitation is limited shelf life, there must be clear instructions as to the recommended storage conditions and the prohibition of use of the product when its shelf life is exceeded.

Authors' Notes

FDA's main concern in regard to storage controls is that only material and/or products that meet specifications be used in the manufacture and control of medical devices. FDA gives the manufacturer flexibility in deciding which storage protection method(s) to use, as long as those methods and the name of the individual(s) who authorized and approved them are documented.

FDA Quality System Regulation—1996

§ 820.160 Distribution

§ 820.160(a) Each manufacturer shall establish and maintain procedures for control and distribution of finished devices to ensure that only those devices approved for release are distributed and that purchase orders are reviewed to ensure that ambiguities and errors are resolved before devices are released for distribution. Where a device's fitness for use or quality deteriorates over time, the procedures shall ensure that expired devices or devices deteriorated beyond acceptable fitness for use are not distributed.

AAMI/ANSI/ISO 13485:2003

Reference § 7.2 Customer-related processes

§ 7.2.1 Determination of requirements related to the product

See comments in this book related to QSReg § 820.140 related to the manufacturer's obligation to understand and agree to customer requirements related to delivery and postdelivery of the product to the customer.

Reference § 7.2.2 Review of requirements related to the product

See comments in this book related to QSReg § 820.140 related to the manufacturer's obligation to review and agree to customer requirements related to delivery and postdelivery of product to the customer.

Reference § 7.5 Production and service provision
§ 7.5.1 Control of production and service provision
§ 7.5.1.1 General requirements

The Standard contains no additional requirements in this section related to distribution beyond those contained in the QSReg.

Reference § 7.5.5 Preservation of product

See comments in this book related to QSReg § 820.140.

FDA Guidance

QSReg Preamble

There is no guidance with respect to distribution in the preamble.

AAMI/ANSI/ISO TR 14969:2004

Reference § 7.2 Customer-related processes
§ 7.2.1 Determination of requirements related to the product

The TR indicates that the manufacturer is obligated to obtain and understand customer input related to delivery schedules. In regard to distribution, the manufacturer is obligated to identify any customer requirements related to distribution that are not achievable and resolve those issues with the customer. The resolution of any issues related to distribution should be recorded. Any changes to the agreements should also be recorded, and any affected documents should be amended.

Reference § 7.2.2 Review of requirements related to the product

There is no specific medical device guidance beyond the general guidance given in this book related to QSReg § 7.2.1.

Reference § 7.5 Production and service provision
§ 7.5.1 Control of production and service provision
§ 7.5.1.1 General requirements

See comments in this book related to QSReg § 820.150.

Reference § 7.5.5 Preservation of product

The TR recommends that distribution requirements consider any environmental conditions that must be encountered during distribution.

Packaging materials and labeling must protect the product during distribution. See comments in this book related to QSReg §§ 820.140 and 820.150.

FDA Quality System Regulation—1996

§ 820.160(b) Each manufacturer shall maintain distribution records which include or refer to the location of:

(1) The name and address of the initial consignee;
(2) The identification and quantity of devices shipped;
(3) The date shipped; and
(4) Any control number(s) used.

AAMI/ANSI/ISO 13485:2003

Reference § 7.2 Customer-related processes
§ 7.2.1 Determination of requirements related to the product

The Standard contains no additional requirements beyond those in the QSReg.

Reference § 7.2.2 Review of requirements related to the product

The Standard contains no additional requirements beyond those in the QSReg.

Reference § 7.5 Production and service provision
§ 7.5.1 Control of production and service provision
§ 7.5.1.1 General requirements

The Standard contains no additional requirements beyond those in the QSReg.

Reference § 7.5.5 Preservation of product

See comments in this book related to QSReg §§ 820.140 and 820.150.

FDA Guidance

QSReg Preamble

> **Comment group 177.** . . . FDA has retained the word "consignee" and notes that it is a person to whom the goods are delivered.
>
> . . . if the manufacturer is required by Sec. 820.65 to have control numbers, these must be recorded along with any control numbers voluntarily used. Logically, control numbers are used for traceability so they should be recorded in the DHR distribution records. . . .

AAMI/ANSI/ISO TR 14969:2004

Reference § 7.2 Customer-related processes
§ 7.2.1 Determination of requirements related to the product

See comments in this book related to QSReg §§ 820.140 and 820.150.

Reference § 7.2.2 Review of requirements related to the product

There is no additional guidance in this section beyond that contained in the QSReg.

Reference § 7.5 Production and service provision
§ 7.5.1 Control of production and service provision
§ 7.5.1.1 General requirements

See comments in this book related to QSReg § 820.150.

Reference § 7.5.5 Preservation of product

See comments in this book related to QSReg §§ 820.140 and 820.150.

FDA Quality System Regulation—1996

§ 820.170 Installation

§ 820.170(a) Each manufacturer of a device requiring installation shall establish and maintain adequate installation and inspection instructions, and where appropriate test procedures. Instructions and procedures shall include directions for ensuring proper installation so that the device will perform as intended after installation. The manufacturer shall distribute the instructions and procedures with the device or otherwise make them available to the person(s) installing the device.

§ 820.170(b) The person installing the device shall ensure that the installation, inspection, and any required testing are performed in accordance with the manufacturer's instructions and procedures and shall document the inspection and any test results to demonstrate proper installation.

AAMI/ANSI/ISO 13485:2003

Reference § 7.2 Customer-related processes
§ 7.2.1 Determination of requirements related to the product

The Standard contains no additional requirements beyond those in the QSReg.

Reference § 7.2.2 Review of requirements related to the product

The Standard contains no additional requirements beyond those in the QSReg.

Reference § 7.5.1.2.2 Installation activities

The Standard clarifies who is responsible for providing documented requirements for installation and verification, even if the installation is performed by someone other than the manufacturer. The manufacturer is responsible for providing such requirements.

FDA Guidance

QSReg Preamble

Comment group 178. . . . the installation requirements only apply to devices that are capable of being installed. However, to further clarify the requirements in Sec. 820.170, FDA has made clear that the requirement applies to "devices requiring installation." . . .

Comment group 179. . . . Under the . . . requirement in Sec. 820.170(a), the manufacturer establishes installation and inspection instructions, and where appropriate test procedures. The manufacturer distributes the instructions and procedures with the device or makes them available to person(s) installing the device. Section 820.170(b) requires that the person(s) installing the

INSTALLATION

device follow the instructions and procedures described in Sec. 820.170(a) and document the activities described in the procedures and instructions to demonstrate proper installation. . . . Such records will be available for FDA inspection. FDA does not expect the manufacturer of the finished device to maintain records of installation performed by those installers not affiliated with the manufacturer, but does expect the third party installer or the user of the device to maintain such records.

. . . FDA notes . . . that installers are considered to be manufacturers under the original CGMP regulation and that their records are, and will continue to be, subject to FDA inspections when the agency deems it necessary to review such records.

AAMI/ANSI/ISO TR 14969:2004

Reference § 7.2 Customer-related processes
§ 7.2.1 Determination of requirements related to the product

The TR contains no additional guidance beyond that in the QSReg.

Reference § 7.2.2 Review of requirements related to the product

The TR contains no additional guidance beyond that in the QSReg.

Reference § 7.5.1.2.2 Installation activities

The TR clarifies that installation does not cover the process of implantation of a medical device or the process of fitting a medical device to a patient.

The TR also clarifies that if there is some assembly of the medical device required as part of installation, the manufacturer must provide instruction for the assembly and any associated testing, verification, or safety measures to whomever is doing the installation, to confirm the correct operation of the installed medical device.

SUBPART M

Records

FDA Quality System Regulation—1996

§ 820.180 General requirements

All records required by this part shall be maintained at the manufacturing establishment or other location that is reasonably accessible to responsible officials of the manufacturer and to employees of FDA designated to perform inspections. Such records, including those not stored at the inspected establishment, shall be made readily available for review and copying by FDA employee(s). Such records shall be legible and shall be stored to minimize deterioration and to prevent loss. Those records stored in automated data processing systems shall be backed up.

§ 820.180(a) ***Confidentiality.*** Records deemed confidential by the manufacturer may be marked to aid FDA in determining whether information may be disclosed under the public information regulation in part 20 of this chapter.

§ 820.180(b) ***Record retention period.*** All records required by this part shall be retained for a period of time equivalent to the design and expected life of the device, but in no case less than 2 years from the date of release for commercial distribution by the manufacturer.

§ 820.180(c) ***Exceptions.*** This section does not apply to the reports required by Sec. 820.20(c) Management review, Sec. 820.22 Quality audits, and supplier audit reports used to meet the requirements of Sec. 820.50(a) Evaluation of suppliers, contractors, and consultants, but does apply to procedures established under these provisions. Upon request of a designated employee of FDA, an employee in management with executive responsibility shall certify in writing that the management reviews and quality audits required under this part, and supplier audits where applicable, have been performed and documented, the dates on which they were performed, and that any required corrective action has been undertaken.

AAMI/ANSI/ISO 13485:2003

Reference § 4.2.4 Control of records

The Standard requires that there be a procedure describing the control of records. Otherwise there are no additional general requirements related to the control of records in the Standard that are not contained in the QSReg.

FDA Guidance

QSReg Preamble

Comment group 180. . . . FDA . . . notes that records must be kept in a location that is "reasonably accessible" to both the manufacturer and FDA investigators, and that records must be made "readily available." FDA expects that such records will be made available during the course of an inspection. If the foreign manufacturer maintains records at remote locations, such records would be expected to be produced by the next working day or 2, at the latest. FDA has clarified that records can be kept at [locations] other than the inspected establishment, provided that they are made "readily available" for review and copying. This should provide foreign manufacturers and initial distributors the necessary flexibility. . . .

Comment group 181. . . . FDA believes that all records should be retained for a period equivalent to the design and expected life of the device, but in no case less than 2 years, whether the records specifically pertain to a particular device or not. The requirement has been amended to make clear that all records, including quality records, are subject to the requirement. FDA believes this is necessary because manufacturers need all such records when performing any type of investigation. For example, it may be very important to access the wording of a complaint handling procedure at the time a particular complaint came in when investigating a trend or a problem that extends to several products or over an extended period of time. Further, FDA does not believe that allowing the manufacturer to define the retention period will serve the public's best interest with regard to safety concerns and hazard analysis.

. . . FDA will interpret "copying" to include the printing of computerized records, as well as photocopying.

AAMI/ANSI/ISO TR 14969:2004

Reference § 4.2.4 Control of records

The TR clarifies that there are three types of records: those pertaining to the design and development of a particular type of medical device; those pertaining to a specific, individual medical device or lot or batch of medical devices; and those pertaining to the performance of a quality system process(es) or activity(ies) (for example, an internal quality audit report or a calibration record).

The organization must decide how the retention period applies to each of these types of records. It is clear that records pertaining to a particular medical device or batch of devices fall under the "lifetime of the device or two-year" requirement. This requirement also applies to records related to the manufacture and provision of a type of medical device and runs from the date of the last provision of that type of device. It may also be necessary to keep quality system records under the same requirement if they can be helpful in investigating problems with a particular device or type of device (for example, calibration records and environmental control records). For all other records, the organization is required to establish a reasonable retention time period based on risk and regulatory requirements.

The TR recommends that records be safely stored to prevent unauthorized access and alteration.

The TR points out that electronically stored records can be subject to degradation that may compromise their retention time; therefore, they may have to be backed up periodically to meet the required retention period. The TR also reminds the organization that it is necessary to safely retain the equipment and software needed to retrieve electronic records for the entire required retention period.

The TR recommends that any written records be made using indelible media.

Persons accessing controlled records should sign for the access, with the signature or initials followed by the date of access.

The TR lists the characteristics of good recording practices (for example, enter data in a timely manner, do not pre- or postdate entries, do not use another person's name or initials, and complete all relevant data fields when using a data entry form and mark those that are not applicable with "NA" or another indicator). Errors should be corrected in a manner that doesn't obliterate the original entry, and they should be initialed and dated, and contain a reason for the correction.

The TR contains recommendations related to the keeping of electronic records (for example, the automatic generation of an audit trail, the recording of the identities of the originator of the electronic data and any editors of that data, the provision for comments that relate to the data entries, provisions for verification of entered data, and the automated entry of data directly from processes). It recommends that it may be necessary to develop a separate procedure for the control of electronic records.

The TR indicates that there may be national or regional regulation related to the control of electronic records.

Authors' Notes

The Standard and the QSReg differ in their definitions of records and documents. The Standard considers records and documents to be two entirely different items, with controls specific to each. The QSReg considers records to be a more general entity, with documents being a subset of records. We believe the QSReg approach may lead to confusion and therefore recommend that the organization follow the approach taken in the Standard.

The Standard's approach considers "documents" to represent the objective evidence of what the organization intends to do (for example, product specifications, engineering drawings, procedures, training course curricula, and blank forms); "records" would be the objective evidence of what the organization has done (for example, attendance sheets from training programs, completed forms, and inspection and monitoring data).

It would be useful in the case of a supplier audit to leave behind a letter or record, signed by the auditor, that an audit has been performed, without including any of the audit findings. The supplier or the manufacturer can show this record to the FDA as evidence that the audit was performed. It is important to understand that while the FDA has a policy not to request access to records containing the results of management reviews and supplier and quality audits, these records may be subpoenaed if the FDA is contemplating a legal action against the manufacturer.

It is also important to emphasize that FDA has the right to access records related to the requirements of the QSReg. This does not include financial records and some records related to personnel (that is, records not associated with the competency of the personnel.)

Since the publication of the QSReg in 1996, FDA has also promulgated a regulation addressing Electronic Records and Electronic Signatures, 21 CFR Part 11. Enforcement of this regulation is currently in abeyance due to technical difficulties encountered during inspections of such records. The use of such records is still permissible provided the manufacturer utilizes a validated electronic database. In 2003 the FDA published a notice (*Federal Register*, February 25, 2003, pages 8775–6) detailing the agency's intent to revise Part 11 and its thinking regarding the direction such revision will take. The new draft has now been written and has been submitted to FDA upper management for review pending publication in the *Federal Register*. The document will mimic in many respects the current requirements for paper documents, namely, accuracy, change control, signature verification, and document control provisions including version control. The release date (for comments) has not been announced.

FDA Quality System Regulation—1996

§ 820.181 Device master record

Each manufacturer shall maintain device master records (DMR's). Each manufacturer shall ensure that each DMR is prepared and approved in accordance with

Sec. 820.40. The DMR for each type of device shall include, or refer to the location of, the following information:

(a) Device specifications including appropriate drawings, composition, formulation, component specifications, and software specifications;
(b) Production process specifications including the appropriate equipment specifications, production methods, production procedures, and production environment specifications;
(c) Quality assurance procedures and specifications including acceptance criteria and the quality assurance equipment to be used;
(d) Packaging and labeling specifications, including methods and processes used; and
(e) Installation, maintenance, and servicing procedures and methods.

AAMI/ANSI/ISO 13485:2003

Reference § 7.3.3 Design and development outputs

The Standard contains design output requirements that are the same as those contained in the QSReg, but it does not require them to be in a separate named file, "Device Master Record."

Reference § 7.3.7 Design and development changes

The Standard contains design change requirements that are the same as those contained in the QSReg, but it does not require that such design changes be incorporated into a separate named file, "Device Master Record."

Reference § 7.5.1 Control of production and service provision § 7.5.1.1 General requirements

The Standard requires that production and service provision employ controlled procedures and specifications that are the same as those that would be described in the QSReg, but it does not require that these procedures and specifications be contained within a separate named file, "Device Master Record."

FDA Guidance

QSReg Preamble

> **Comment group 183.** . . . FDA . . . [notes] the requirement for the DMR to be prepared, dated, and approved by a qualified individual because the agency believes this is necessary to assure consistency and continuity within the DMR. . . .

Comment group 184. . . . The final software specifications should be transferred into production. Therefore, the final software specification for the particular device or type of device should be located or referenced in the DMR, while any earlier version should be located or referenced in the DHF. FDA believes that it is more important for manufacturers to construct a document structure that is workable and traceable, than to worry about whether something is contained in one file as compared to another. The DMR is set up to contain or reference the procedures and specifications that are current on the manufacturing floor. The DHF is meant to be more of a historical file for utilization during investigations and continued design efforts.

Comment group 185. . . . the quality records required in the DMR relate to the specific current design, not the more general requirements of the quality system, which are addressed under new Sec. 820.186. . . .

There are requirements for validation and verification pertaining to device processing that may be better kept in the DMR instead of the DHF. The documentation of such verification and validation activities relating to processes that are performed for several different devices or types of devices can be placed or referenced in the location that best suits the manufacturer. Again, it is more important that the manufacturer store and retrieve information in a workable manner, than keep such information in particular files.

Comment group 186. . . . FDA emphasizes that the procedures that the manufacturer places in the DMR must clearly define the requirements the manufacturer is following and when particular activities are appropriate. The manufacturer will have failed to comply with the requirements of the section if the procedures simply state that the review or activity occurs at "appropriate stages."

The same principle applies for every section of this regulation, which is written to be flexible enough to cover the manufacture of all types of devices. Manufacturers must adopt quality systems appropriate for their specific products and processes. In establishing these procedures, FDA will expect manufacturers to be able to provide justifications for the decisions reached.

AAMI/ANSI/ISO TR 14969:2004

Reference § 7.3.3 Design and development outputs

The TR contains recommendations related to design and development outputs that are the same as the guidance provided in the QSReg, without requiring that such outputs be contained in a separate named file, "Device Master Record."

Reference § 7.3.7 Design and development changes

The TR contains recommendations related to design and development changes that are the same as the guidance provided in the QSReg, without requiring that such changes be contained in a separate named file, "Device Master Record."

Reference § 7.5.1 Control of production and service provision
§ 7.5.1.1 General requirements

The TR contains recommendations related to the controlled documentation used during production and service provision that are the same as the guidance provided in the QSReg, without requiring that such documentation be contained in a separate named file, "Device Master Record."

Authors' Notes

We recommend that the organization establish and maintain a DMR that complies with the requirements contained in the QSReg.

FDA Quality System Regulation—1996

§ 820.184 Device history record

Each manufacturer shall maintain device history records (DHR's). Each manufacturer shall establish and maintain procedures to ensure that DHR's for each batch, lot, or unit are maintained to demonstrate that the device is manufactured in accordance with the DMR and the requirements of this part. The DHR shall include, or refer to the location of, the following information:

(a) The dates of manufacture;
(b) The quantity manufactured;
(c) The quantity released for distribution;
(d) The acceptance records which demonstrate the device is manufactured in accordance with the DMR;
(e) The primary identification label and labeling used for each production unit; and
(f) Any device identification(s) and control number(s) used.

AAMI/ANSI/ISO 13485:2003

Reference § 7.5 Production and service provision
§ 7.5.1 Control of production and service provision
§ 7.5.1.1 General requirements

The Standard requires the generation of a verified and approved batch record that contains the same contents as the DHR required by the QSReg.

FDA Guidance

QSReg Preamble

Comment group 187. . . . FDA agrees that it may not be necessary to include all labeling used in the DHR. However, FDA continues to believe . . . that increased control over labeling is necessary due to the many labeling errors resulting in recalls. Therefore, FDA has retained a requirement related to labeling in the DHR, but revised it to make it less burdensome. The requirement was amended to "the primary identification label and labeling." . . . FDA believes that the requirement that the DHR contain the primary label and labeling used for each production unit, coupled with the labeling controls in Sec. 820.120, should help to ensure that proper labeling is used and, hopefully, decrease the number of recalls due to improper labeling. . . .

Comment group 188. . . . FDA has also added "device identification" to the requirement under Sec. 820.184(f) because it believes that any identification or control number used should be documented in the DHR to facilitate investigations, as well as corrective and preventive actions. FDA notes that this provision does not add any requirement for identification or traceability not already expressed in Secs. 820.60 and 820.65.

AAMI/ANSI/ISO TR 14969:2004

Reference § 7.5 Production and service provision
§ 7.5.1 Control of production and service provision
§ 7.5.1.1 General requirements

The TR contains recommendations related to the generation and control of a batch record that are the same as the controls related to the DHR contained in the QSReg. The TR indicates that the batch record as described in the Standard and the TR may be called the Device History Record in the organization's QMS.

Authors' Notes

We recommend that the organization establish and maintain a DHR that complies with the requirements contained in the QSReg.

FDA Quality System Regulation—1996

§ 820.186 Quality system record

Each manufacturer shall maintain a quality system record (QSR). The QSR shall include, or refer to the location of, procedures and the documentation of activities required by this part that are not specific to a particular type of device(s), including, but not limited to, the records required by Sec. 820.20. Each manufacturer shall ensure that the QSR is prepared and approved in accordance with Sec. 820.40.

AAMI/ANSI/ISO 13485:2003

Reference § 4 Quality management system
§ 4.2 Documentation requirements
§ 4.2.1 General

The Standard requires the establishment of documentation that describes the organization's QMS and that is the same as the documentation required by the QSReg but does not require that the documentation be contained within a separate named file, Quality System Record.

The Standard provides a more detailed listing of the various types of documentation that describe the QMS than is provided in the QSReg (for example, a Quality Manual).

FDA Guidance

QSReg Preamble

> **Comment group 189.** . . . FDA . . . has developed new Sec. 820.186 Quality system record. This section separates the procedures and documentation of activities that are not specific to a particular type of device from the device specific records.

AAMI/ANSI/ISO TR 14969:2004

Reference § 4 Quality management system
§ 4.2 Documentation requirements
§ 4.2.1 General

The TR contains guidance related to the QMS documentation that is the same as that contained in the QSReg, except that it does not recommend that such documentation be kept in a separate named file, Quality System Record.

Authors' Notes

It is unlikely that an FDA investigator will ask specifically to see an organization's QSR. More likely, the investigator may ask to see individual contents of such a file. It is more important that the organization have these contents because they are indispensable elements of an effective QMS. The organization should also know where to find them so that it can respond to an FDA investigator request in a reasonable amount of time. We recommend that the organization establish and maintain a reference file called the Quality System Record Index.

FDA Quality System Regulation—1996

§ 820.198 Complaint files

§ 820.198(a) Each manufacturer shall maintain complaint files. Each manufacturer shall establish and maintain procedures for receiving, reviewing, and evaluating complaints by a formally designated unit. Such procedures shall ensure that:

(1) All complaints are processed in a uniform and timely manner;
(2) Oral complaints are documented upon receipt; and
(3) Complaints are evaluated to determine whether the complaint represents an event which is required to be reported to FDA under part 803 or 804 of this chapter, Medical Device Reporting.

§ 820.198(b) Each manufacturer shall review and evaluate all complaints to determine whether an investigation is necessary. When no investigation is made, the manufacturer shall maintain a record that includes the reason no investigation was made and the name of the individual responsible for the decision not to investigate.

§ 820.198(c) Any complaint involving the possible failure of a device, labeling, or packaging to meet any of its specifications shall be reviewed, evaluated, and investigated, unless such investigation has already been performed for a similar complaint and another investigation is not necessary.

§ 820.198(d) Any complaint that represents an event which must be reported to FDA under part 803 or 804 of this chapter shall be promptly reviewed, evaluated, and investigated by a designated individual(s) and shall be maintained in a separate portion of the complaint files or otherwise clearly identified. In addition to the information required by Sec. 820.198(e), records of investigation under this paragraph shall include a determination of:

(1) Whether the device failed to meet specifications;
(2) Whether the device was being used for treatment or diagnosis; and
(3) The relationship, if any, of the device to the reported incident or adverse event.

§ 820.198(e) When an investigation is made under this section, a record of the investigation shall be maintained by the formally designated unit identified in paragraph (a) of this section. The record of investigation shall include:

(1) The name of the device;
(2) The date the complaint was received;
(3) Any device identification(s) and control number(s) used;
(4) The name, address, and phone number of the complainant;
(5) The nature and details of the complaint;
(6) The dates and results of the investigation;
(7) Any corrective action taken; and
(8) Any reply to the complainant.

§ 820.198(f) When the manufacturer's formally designated complaint unit is located at a site separate from the manufacturing establishment, the investigated complaint(s) and the record(s) of investigation shall be reasonably accessible to the manufacturing establishment.

§ 820.198(g) If a manufacturer's formally designated complaint unit is located outside of the United States, records required by this section shall be reasonably accessible in the United States at either:

(1) A location in the United States where the manufacturer's records are regularly kept; or
(2) The location of the initial distributor.

AAMI/ANSI/ISO 13485:2003

Reference § 7.2.3 Customer communication

This section of the Standard requires the organization to implement "effective arrangements" for communicating with customers, including, among others, communications related to customer complaints and advisory notices.

Reference § 8.2 Monitoring and measurement
§ 8.2.1 Feedback

This section of the Standard requires the organization to establish a documented process for obtaining customer feedback to provide "early warning of quality problems." Information received through that process can be used in implementing corrective and preventive actions and in meeting any national or regional regulatory requirements to review postproduction product experience.

Reference § 8.5 Improvement
§ 8.5.1 General

This section of the Standard contains the requirement for handling customer complaints, and it recognizes that there may be national or regional reporting requirements associated with the handling of certain complaints. There are no additional requirements for complaint handling beyond those contained in the QSReg.

FDA Guidance

QSReg Preamble

Comment group 190. . . . These requirements are essentially the same as the original CGMP requirements under Sec. 820.198, and 18 years of experience with these requirements shows that many manufacturers still do not understand and properly handle complaints. Therefore, FDA believes that the amount of detail in Sec. 820.198 is appropriate and necessary. . . .

. . . Section 820.198(b) discusses the initial review and evaluation of the complaints in order to determine if complaints are "valid." It is important to note that this evaluation is not the same as a complaint investigation. The evaluation is performed to determine whether the information is truly a complaint or not and to determine whether the complaint needs to be investigated or not. If the evaluation decision is not to investigate, the justification must be recorded.

Section 820.198(c) then describes one subset of complaints that must be investigated, but explains that duplicative investigations are not necessary. In cases where an investigation would be duplicative, a reference to the original investigation is an acceptable justification for not conducting a second investigation.

Section 820.198(d) describes another subset of complaints that must be investigated (those that meet the MDR criteria) and the information that is necessary in the record of investigation of those types of complaints.

Section 820.198(e) sets out the type of information that must be recorded whenever complaints are investigated. The information described in Sec. 820.198(e)(1) through (e)(5) would most likely be attained earlier in order to perform the evaluation in Sec. 820.198(b). This information need not be duplicated in the investigation report as long as the complaint and investigation report can be properly identified and tied together.

Section 820.198(e)(1) through (e)(5) are considered to be basic information essential to any complaint investigation. If there is some reason that the information described in Sec. 820.198(e) cannot be obtained, then the manufacturer should document the situation and explain the efforts made to ascertain the information. This will be considered to be acceptable as long as a reasonable and good faith effort was made. For example, a single phone call to a hospital would not be considered by FDA to be a reasonable, good faith effort to obtain information.

Section 820.198(f) . . . [applies to the situation] where the manufacturing facility is separate or different from that of the formally designated complaint handling unit. In such cases, it is important that the facility involved in the manufacturing of the device receive or have access to complaint and investigation information. In order to give manufacturers the flexibility of using computer or automated data processing systems, the term "reasonably accessible" . . . is used.

Section 820.198(g) is the complaint recordkeeping requirement for distributors. In order to give manufacturers the same flexibility as described in Sec. 820.198(f), FDA has included "reasonably accessible" in Sec. 820.198(g). . . .

Comment group 191. . . . Large corporations may have different complaint handling units for different product types or different manufacturing establishments. However, there should be only one formally designated complaint handling unit for each product type or establishment. If a corporation chooses to operate with different complaint handling units for products and/or establishments, the manufacturer must clearly describe and define its corporate complaint handling procedure to ensure consistency throughout the different complaint handling units. A system that would allow multiple interpretations of handling, evaluating, categorizing, investigating, and following up, would be unacceptable. Each manufacturer should establish in its procedures which one group or unit is ultimately responsible for coordinating all complaint handling functions.

. . . A December 1986 General Accounting Office (GAO) report entitled "Medical Devices; Early Warning of Problems Is Hampered by Severe Underreporting," (Ref. 11) showed that approximately 83 percent of the hospitals report complaints orally. FDA believes that these oral complaints must be captured in the complaint handling process.

Comment group 192. . . . duplicative investigations are not required if the manufacturer can show that the same type of failure or nonconformity has already been investigated.

Comment group 193. . . . FDA . . . [expects] such complaints [pertaining to death, injury, or hazard to health] to be "clearly identified." This will give a manufacturer flexibility in choosing a means of ensuring that these types of complaints can be immediately recognized and segregated for purposes of prioritizing and meeting other requirements.

FDA has substituted the term "promptly" for the term "immediately" to be more consistent with the new MDR regulation timeframes. FDA has also clarified that Sec. 820.198(d)(1) through (d)(3) are in addition to the information that must be recorded in Sec. 820.198(e).

Comment group 194. . . . Where corrective action is not necessary and is not taken, it cannot be documented. . . . As stated in the preamble to the proposal (58 FR 61952 at 61968), the manufacturer's procedures should clearly identify when corrective action will be taken.

Comment group 195. . . . Section 820.198(a) requires that all complaints be evaluated to determine whether they are subject to the requirements of the MDR regulation under part 803 or 804.

Comment group 196. . . . A manufacturer's procedures must ensure that the manufacturing site is alerted to complaints concerning devices produced at that site.

Comment group 197. . . . [FDA] must have access to these [foreign manufacturer] records [associated with evaluation, investigation, and handling of complaints] in the United States.

"Guideline for the Manufacture of In Vitro Diagnostic Products," January 10, 1994

This guidance document addresses the handling of complaints, but it does not contain any additional guidance beyond that provided in the preamble to the QSReg. While it was issued in 1994, there is no indication that it has been amended or withdrawn. A copy of this guidance document may be found at http://www.fda.gov/cdrh/comp/918.pdf.

AAMI/ANSI/ISO TR 14969:2004

Reference § 7.2.3 Customer communication

This section of the TR highlights the subtle differences in the regulations of various countries and regions related to the definitions and responsibilities associated with the handling and reporting of complaints. It is important that the organization understand and accommodate these differences.

Otherwise there is no additional guidance in this section of the TR beyond that contained in the QSReg.

Reference § 8.2 Monitoring and measurement
§ 8.2.1 Feedback

This section of the TR highlights the need for an organization to understand and comply with the various vigilance systems around the world. Otherwise, this section of the TR contains no additional guidance related to complaint handling beyond that contained in the QSReg.

Reference § 8.5 Improvement
§ 8.5.1 General

Customer complaints This section of the TR indicates that if the organization considers other parts of the organization as customers, it can choose to treat complaints from those other parts (internal complaints) in the same way it treats customer complaints.

The TR recognizes that it is possible for a medical device that meets its specifications to cause customer complaints if, in fact, the complaint is pointing out a design flaw. User error complaints may be evidence that instructions for use or user training are inadequate.

The TR suggests that if the organization relies on individuals or external organizations to fulfill some of the complaint handling responsibilities, those responsibilities can be included in contracts between the organization and the others involved.

This section of the TR includes complaint handling responsibilities not explicitly included in the QSReg (for example, the segregating or disposing of the affected product).

The TR points out that customer complaints can prompt review and updating of risk management estimates.

Otherwise this section of the TR contains no additional guidance related to complaint handling beyond that contained in the QSReg.

Authors' Notes

When considering actions related to reporting complaints under the MDR (Medical Device Reporting) regulation, 21 CFR § 803, the manufacturer must understand that it is required to report situations that have caused or could cause a public health problem, serious injuries or deaths that have occurred, and malfunctions that could cause serious injury or death, even if the occurrence was outside the United States.

SUBPART N

Servicing

FDA Quality System Regulation—1996

§ 820.200 Servicing

§ 820.200(a) Where servicing is a specified requirement, each manufacturer shall establish and maintain instructions and procedures for performing and verifying that the servicing meets the specified requirements.

§ 820.200(b) Each manufacturer shall analyze service reports with appropriate statistical methodology in accordance with Sec. 820.100.

§ 820.200(c) Each manufacturer who receives a service report that represents an event which must be reported to FDA under part 803 or 804 of this chapter shall automatically consider the report a complaint and shall process it in accordance with the requirements of Sec. 820.198.

§ 820.200(d) Service reports shall be documented and shall include:

(1) The name of the device serviced;
(2) Any device identification(s) and control number(s) used;
(3) The date of service;
(4) The individual(s) servicing the device;
(5) The service performed; and
(6) The test and inspection data.

AAMI/ANSI/ISO 13485:2003

Reference § 7.5.1.2.3 Servicing activities

The Standard contains no additional requirements beyond those contained in the QSReg.

FDA Guidance

QSReg Preamble

Comment group 199. . . . in this regulation, FDA has chosen to codify only longstanding requirements for servicing performed by original manufacturers and remanufacturers. . . . a separate rulemaking will specify and clarify the requirements for third party service organizations.

Comment group 200. . . . [FDA seeks] to require that the servicing instructions and procedures ensure that the device will meet "specified requirements" for the device's intended use. FDA is aware that with use and age, a device may be serviced to function as intended, but may not meet original specifications. . . .

Comment group 201. . . . Full corrective action may not be required for every service report. However, if the analysis of a service report indicates a high risk to health, or that the frequency of servicing is higher than expected, the remainder of the corrective and preventive action elements are applicable, in accordance with the corrective and preventive action procedures established under Sec. 820.100.

Section 820.200(c) provides that when a service report "represents an event which must be reported to FDA under part 803 or 804 of this chapter," it is automatically considered by FDA to be a complaint that must be handled according to Sec. 820.198. FDA emphasizes that this provision is not intended to limit "complaints" to MDR reportable events.

AAMI/ANSI/ISO TR 14969:2004

Reference § 7.5.1.2.3 Servicing activities

The TR recommends that the manufacturer be responsible for providing information related to the activities that are part of servicing, no matter who performs them (for example, information that clarifies the split of servicing responsibilities among the manufacturer, the distributor, and the user(s); validation of any special purpose tools that may be used during servicing; the use and control of test and measurement equipment; specification of appropriate spare parts; and other servicing-related information).

The TR points out that some medical devices may need to be cleaned or decontaminated prior to servicing using processes that need to be documented. The TR references ISO 12891-1 for guidance on cleaning procedures.

Authors' Notes

In recent years, the FDA has recognized that service activities can represent a major challenge in enforcement of the QSReg.

There are four ways in which service is provided:

- The manufacturer services its own product(s) either with its own personnel or through agents or contractual personnel
- A used device is purchased on the secondary market and serviced by the new owner to restore or maintain the initial performance characteristics
- A used device is purchased on the secondary market, is totally refurbished, and has its performance characteristics upgraded
- A used medical device is serviced by a third party independent of the manufacturer and returned to its original owner

It is clear that servicing provided by the manufacturer must be conducted in compliance with the QSReg. The responsibility for compliance when the servicer is not the manufacturer is a bit more complicated. If the servicer in that case is the owner of the device (for example, when a hospital medical engineering group handles the servicing), the owner is responsible for performing the service according to instructions provided by the manufacturer.

If the servicer is a third party working under contract with the owner to maintain the device's ability to meet its original performance specifications, the responsibility may be shared between the third-party servicer and the owner. For example, if the owner receives servicing instructions by the manufacturer, the owner is responsible for forwarding these instructions to the third-party servicer. The FDA would also like to hold the manufacturer responsible for informing the third-party servicer of the latest instructions for servicing the manufacturer's devices. This responsibility is not so easily handled, since the manufacturer may not be willing to give its competitors free advice or even "paid for" advice on servicing matters. In addition, the manufacturer may not know who is providing the third-party servicing. Many times the third-party servicer has reverse engineered the device and developed its own servicing protocols. It would seem logical that the FDA would hold the third-party servicer responsible for qualifying or validating any changes it makes to the manufacturer's servicing instructions.

Where the third-party servicer has serviced a device in a way that upgrades its performance or changes its applications, the FDA considers the servicer to be a manufacturer and holds the third-party servicer responsible for complying with the premarket notification or premarket approval regulations, whichever is applicable. The effectiveness of FDA's enforcement in this situation is problematic. It is unclear whether the FDA will still hold the original manufacturer liable for meeting the servicing requirements of the QSReg.

Another aspect of servicing is the refurbishing and reuse of single-use devices. In a survey conducted in 2002, the FDA found that almost half of the hospitals surveyed reuse their single-use devices. Following lengthy consultation with the manufacturers of such devices and the user community, the agency published regulations and guidance addressing this issue: Validation Data in Premarket Submission (510(k)) for Reprocessed Single Use Medical Devices. This guidance may be found by reference from the FDA CDRH home page, http://www.fda/cdrh.gov.

Another significant issue related to servicing is the trending of service calls. The FDA believes that service calls should be trended and if a predetermined threshold (that is, seriousness of the service issue or frequency of occurrence of the service issue) has been exceeded, any additional service call of the same type becomes a complaint. The manufacturer should not hide in the service records those service trends that may have safety and effectiveness consequences; they should be handled as complaints. Additionally, the FDA stated that if a service call indicates that a serious injury or death has occurred or a malfunction that could cause a serious injury or death has occurred, the manufacturer must file a Medical Device Report. Such a service call should be handled as a complaint.

Some service issues meet the criteria for being handled within a CAPA process (that is, they reflect a systemic QMS issue, or they are directly related to a product or service safety or effectiveness issue). The agency expects the manufacturers and the service organization (if one was employed) to go through the entire CAPA process outlined in § 820.100.

Special attention must be paid to the subject of decontamination of used medical devices (for example, explanted pacemakers, surgical saws, home-use glucose meters, and endoscopes returned to the manufacturer for servicing or as part of a complaint investigation or recall). Many manufacturers or third-party servicers require the user to decontaminate relevant devices prior to returning them for service. The user must sign a declaration that the device has been either decontaminated or sterilized. This is certainly a step in the right direction, but the service provider cannot rely on such declaration alone and must provide additional protection (in the form of equipment and instruction) to its employees. Several medical device manufacturers will not service such devices if they suspect they have been contaminated. The U.S. Occupational Safety and Health Administration has promulgated rules on the subject (Blood Borne Pathogen Rule, 29 CFR, part 1910, subpart Z) of protection of health care and food-service employees from contaminated products—it was a reaction to the HIV infection scare—and it covers the medical devices industry workers as well. The United States Postal Service and commercial carriers such as FedEx and UPS have internal rules on this subject as well. The potential for infection during service or failure investigation should be part of any risk analysis during the design phase.

SUBPART O

Statistical Techniques

FDA Quality System Regulation—1996

§ 820.250 Statistical techniques

§ 820.250(a) Where appropriate, each manufacturer shall establish and maintain procedures for identifying valid statistical techniques required for establishing, controlling, and verifying the acceptability of process capability and product characteristics.

§ 820.250(b) Sampling plans, when used, shall be written and based on a valid statistical rationale. Each manufacturer shall establish and maintain procedures to ensure that sampling methods are adequate for their intended use and to ensure that when changes occur the sampling plans are reviewed. These activities shall be documented.

AAMI/ANSI/ISO 13485:2003

Reference § 8 Measurement, analysis, and improvement
§ 8.1 General

The Standard makes it clear that measurement systems go beyond the measurements related to the product and extend to measurements related to the operation and effectiveness of the QMS. It includes the use of statistical techniques in measurement methods.

The Standard indicates that national and regional regulations can require documented procedures for the implementation and control of statistical techniques.

Reference § 8.2.3 Monitoring and measurement of processes

The Standard has the same objective(s) as the QSReg. The Standard requires that appropriate corrections and corrective action be taken if the monitoring and measurement indicate that the process is not achieving the planned results.

Reference § 8.2.4 Monitoring and measurement of product
§ 8.2.4.1 General requirements

The Standard contains no additional requirements beyond those in the QSReg.

Reference § 8.2.4.2 Particular requirement for active implantable medical devices and implantable medical devices

The Standard contains no additional requirements beyond those in the QSReg.

Reference § 8.4 Analysis of data

The Standard lists a number of groups that respond to information resulting from the analysis of data (for example, groups responsible for handling customer feedback, groups responsible for the conformity of the product to requirements, groups responding to trends with corrective and/or preventive action, and suppliers).

FDA Guidance

QSReg Preamble

> **Comment group 204.**... FDA's intent was not to require the use of sampling plans, but to require that where they are used, they should be written and valid. ... Sampling plans are not always required, but any time sampling plans are used, they must be based on a valid statistical rationale. Further, FDA acknowledges that the most common use of sampling plans is during receiving acceptance, ...
>
> FDA has also clarified the review requirement by stating "to ensure that when changes occur the sampling plans are reviewed."

"Guideline for the Manufacture of In Vitro Diagnostic Products," January 10, 1994

This guidance document addresses issues associated with trend analysis but does not provide any additional guidance beyond that contained in the preamble to the QSReg. While it was issued in 1994, there is no indication that it has been amended or withdrawn. A copy of this guidance document may be found at http://www.fda.gov/cdrh/comp/918.pdf.

AAMI/ANSI/ISO TR 14969:2004

Reference § 8 Measurement, analysis, and improvement
§ 8.1 General

The TR suggests that the procedures that set out requirements for control of measurement protect the measurement process even when it is performed by persons who may have a conflict of interest if the results are unsatisfactory (for example, suppliers or production personnel).

For measurement to be of value, it must either provide beneficial guidance to the organization or help it set priorities. Measurement methods should be reviewed as necessary to ensure they are effective.

The use of statistical methods

The TR discusses the value of statistical methods. It can help in deciding what to measure and how much to measure, and it can provide useful assessment of process capabilities, product conformity to requirements, and customer requirements. The TR provides a list of other areas where statistical techniques have value (for example, design and development of products and processes, establishing product and process limits, control of processes, analyzing and solving problems and nonconformities, root cause analysis, and forecasting).

The TR lists a number of statistical methods commonly used by medical device organizations (for example, graphical methods including Pareto analysis, histograms, sequence charts, and Ishikawa diagrams; statistical control charts; design of experiments techniques; regression analysis, ANOVA, and sampling schemes).

The TR emphasizes that statistical techniques are valuable only if the results are communicated to the groups within the organization that can use them for making decisions. Results of the use of statistical techniques are quality records that must be controlled as other quality records are.

The TR refers to ISO/TR 10017 as the source of information related to statistical techniques.

Reference § 8.2.3 Monitoring and measurement of processes

The TR contains no additional guidance related to the nature of the statistical approaches to be used in the monitoring and measurement of processes.

Reference § 8.2.4 Monitoring and measurement of product
§ 8.2.4.1 General requirements

The TR lists a number of things the manufacturer should consider when deciding on the methods to be used in measurement of the product (for example, types of product characteristics that need to be measured; available equipment, software, and measurement tools; the manner in which the customer will measure product performance; the appropriate timing for measurements; and the qualification of people who will be making the measurements).

Reference § 8.2.4.2 Particular requirement for active implantable medical devices and implantable medical devices

The TR provides no additional guidance related to statistical techniques beyond that contained in the QSReg.

Reference § 8.4 Analysis of data

The TR provides no additional guidance related to analysis of data beyond that contained in the QSReg.

Risk Management

FDA Quality System Regulation—1996

§ 820.30 Design control

§ 820.30(g) ***Design validation.*** Each manufacturer shall establish and maintain procedures for validating the device design. Design validation shall be performed under defined operating conditions on initial production units, lots, or batches, or their equivalents. Design validation shall ensure that devices conform to defined user needs and intended uses and shall include testing of production units under actual or simulated use conditions. Design validation shall include software validation and risk analysis, where appropriate. The results of the design validation, including identification of the design, method(s), the date, and the individual(s) performing the validation, shall be documented in the DHF.

AAMI/ANSI/ISO 13485:2003

Reference § 7 Product realization
§ 7.1 Planning of product realization

The Standard takes a big step in incorporating risk management into the QMS, especially because ISO 9001, the international standard on which ISO 13485 is originally based, specifically excludes discussion of risk management requirements. The Standard incorporates risk management to the extent that it relates to the medical devices produced by the organization by requiring "the organization to establish documented requirements for risk management throughout product realization" and also by requiring that "records arising from risk management shall be maintained."

The writers of the Standard also realized that risk management should be incorporated into other QMS processes, but they were unwilling to set out requirements in these areas. As a result, they incorporated discussion of how risk management affects these other processes in the TR and the GHTF guidance document.

FDA Guidance

QSReg Preamble

The preamble to the QSReg mentions risk in a number of areas. Text from the following comment groups provides some guidance as to FDA thinking at the time the QSReg was promulgated.

Comment group 4. In fact the [QSReg] is less prescriptive and gives the manufacturer the flexibility to determine the controls that are necessary commensurate with risk. The burden is on the manufacturer, however, to describe the types and degree of controls and how those controls were decided upon. Such determinations are made in accordance with standard operating procedures (SOP's) established by the manufacturer.

Comment group 13. . . . The extent of the documentation necessary to meet the regulatory requirements may vary with the complexity of the design and manufacturing operations, the size of the firm, the importance of a process, and the risk associated with the failure of the device, among other factors. . . .

Comment group 31. . . . Manufacturing materials should be controlled in a manner that is commensurate with their risk. . . .

Comment group 81. . . . The extent of [design validation] testing conducted should be governed by the risk(s) the device will present if it fails. . . .

Comment group 83. FDA has deleted the term "hazard analysis" and replaced it with the term "risk analysis." FDA's involvement with the ISO TC 210 made it clear that "risk analysis" is the comprehensive and appropriate term. [In fact, the proper term is "risk management."] When conducting a risk analysis, manufacturers are expected to identify possible hazards associated with the design in both normal and fault conditions. The risks associated with the hazards, including those resulting from user error, should then be calculated in both normal and fault conditions. If any risk is judged unacceptable, it should be reduced to acceptable levels by the appropriate means, for example, by redesign or warnings. An important part of risk analysis is ensuring that design changes made to eliminate or minimize hazards do not introduce new hazards. Tools for conducting such analyses include Failure Mode Effect Analysis and Fault Tree Analysis, among others.

. . . Risk analysis must be conducted for the majority of devices subject to design controls and is considered to be an essential requirement for medical devices under this regulation, as well as under [AAMI/ANSI/ISO 13485]. . . . Regarding guidance on "risk analysis," manufacturers can reference . . . the work resulting from ISO TC 210 . . . to include AAMI/ANSI/ISO 14971, "Medical Devices—Risk Management—Application of Risk Analysis to Medical Devices."

Comment group 115. . . . FDA agrees that the specifications for many manufacturing materials may be so well established that the trade name of the product may be sufficient to describe the material needed. For other materials, specific written specifications may be necessary to ensure that the desired materials are received. The extent of the specification detail necessary to ensure that the product or service purchased meets requirements will be related to the nature of the product or service purchased, taking into account the effect the product or service may have on the safety or effectiveness of the finished device, among other factors. . . .

Comment group 121. . . . FDA disagrees that the traceability determination should be based solely on economic risk. . . . the manufacturer should perform risk analysis first on the finished device, and subsequently on the components of such device, to determine the need for traceability. FDA believes that the extent of traceability for both active and inactive implantable devices should include all components and materials used when such products could cause the medical device not to satisfy its specified requirements. . . .

Comment group 159. . . . FDA agrees that the degree of corrective and preventive action taken to eliminate or minimize actual or potential nonconformities must be appropriate to the magnitude of the problem and commensurate with the risks encountered. FDA cannot dictate in a regulation the degree of action that should be taken because each circumstance will be different, but FDA does expect the manufacturer to develop procedures for assessing the risk, the actions that need to be taken for different levels of risk, and how to correct or prevent the problem from recurring, depending on that risk assessment.

FDA emphasizes that any death, even if the manufacturer attributes it to user error, will be considered relevant by FDA and will have a high risk potentially associated with it. . . .

Comment group 161. . . . [FDA] requires that nonconforming product discovered before or after distribution be investigated to the degree commensurate with the significance and risk of the nonconformity. At times a very in depth investigation will be necessary, while at other times a simple investigation, followed by trend analysis or other appropriate tools, will be acceptable. In addition, in contrast to Sec. 820.198, the requirement in this section applies to process and quality system nonconformities, as well as product nonconformities. . . .

Comment group 201. . . . Full corrective action may not be required for every service report. However, if the analysis of a service report indicates a high risk to health, or that the frequency of servicing is higher than expected, the remainder of the corrective and preventive action elements are applicable, in accordance with the corrective and preventive action procedures established under Sec. 820.100. . . .

Design Control Guidance for Medical Device Manufacturers, Issued 11 March, 1997

This guidance document can be found at http://www.fda.gov/cdrh/comp/designgd.html.

> . . . Risk management is the systematic application of management policies, procedures, and practices to the tasks of identifying, analyzing, controlling, and monitoring risk. It is intended to be a framework within which experience, insight, and judgment are applied to successfully manage risk. It is included in this guidance because of its effect on the design process.
>
> Risk management begins with the development of the design input requirements. As the design evolves, new risks may become evident. To systematically identify and, when necessary, reduce these risks, the risk management process is integrated into the design process. In this way, unacceptable risks can be identified and managed earlier in the design process when changes are easier to make and less costly. . . .

AAMI/ANSI/ISO 14971:2007

AAMI/ANSI/ISO 14971:2007 (Standard) revises and updates the requirements for a risk management process that is appropriate for organizations providing medical devices. It provides extremely relevant and useful information related to the risk management process itself, the qualifications of personnel managing or otherwise participating directly in the process, key definitions, risk management planning, and the records associated with risk management.

Much effort was expended in agreeing on the definitions included in this Standard, and they are important in clarifying the process and avoiding miscommunication among the professionals responsible for performing risk management.

The Standard breaks down the risk management process into four major activities:

- *Risk analysis*—This activity includes the identification of potential hazards associated with the intended use of the medical device and any reasonably foreseeable misuse of the device. For each of the hazards there is an estimation of the risk of harm (estimate of frequency of occurrence of the harm and the severity of the harm).
- *Risk evaluation*—This activity is made up of a comparison of the estimated risk of harm with risk acceptability criteria established during the planning of the risk management activity.
- *Risk control*—This activity includes an analysis of options available to mitigate the risk, implementation of risk control measures, estimation of the residual risks associated with individual risk and the overall residual risk, determination of the need for additional risk analysis, evaluation, and control.

- *Production and postproduction monitoring*—This activity continues through the commercial lifetime of the medical device, with device performance information being used to assess whether the original estimates of risk and the effectiveness of risk controls measure are still relevant.

The annexes to the Standard provide important information related to the rationale supporting the requirements, a suggested flowchart describing one form of the process, the content of a risk management plan, guidance on risk management for IVD medical devices, and other subjects.

AAMI/ANSI/ISO TR 14969:2004

The TR recognizes that while the Standard contains requirements related to risk management within product realization, the postproduction risk management activities require inputs from the customer feedback and complaint handling, both of which are outside product realization.

The TR lists the key areas of product realization where risk management plays an important part. In addition, it recognizes that a number of areas outside product realization are influenced by and can influence the risk management activities (for example, management review decisions, handling of nonconformities, corrective actions, and preventive actions).

The TR recognizes that effective communication between the manufacturer and the customer will help the manufacturer understand possible and likely misuses of the product by the customer. This will give the manufacturer insight into hazardous situations that must be dealt with in the risk management process.

The TR references ISO 14971 for additional information about the risk management process.

GHTF Guidance

Reference GHTF, SG3/N15/R8: 2005—Implementation of risk management principles and activities within a Quality Management System

The GHTF Guidance is an important document because it describes the agreement among the key regulatory agencies (FDA included) and industry leaders as to the importance of risk management within the QMS. The Guidance presumes a QMS that is compliant with the one described in ISO 13485:2003, but goes beyond the Standard's risk management requirements, which are limited to product realization.

It is clear from the Guidance that risk management plays an important role in top management activities, procurement and outsourcing, acceptance activities, design and development, traceability, production and process control, servicing, analysis of data, corrective actions, and preventive actions.

Authors' Notes

Reference: "The Challenges of Integrating Risk Management into a Compliant Quality Management System," Ed Kimmelman, *The Regulatory Affairs Journal*—Devices, Vol. 14, No. 4, July/August 2006, pg. 207.

Risk management is a very important process within a QMS because it determines to a great extent the following:

- The way the organization performs the other QMS processes (for example, the nature and intensity of acceptance activities for a particular purchased part or service will be tailored based on the risk associated with the part or service. The acceptance of a high-risk part may include inspection and testing at both the vendor location and the organization's manufacturing site. The acceptance of a low-risk part may require only an initial period of inspection and testing followed by acceptance based on a Certificate of Acceptance (C of A) from the supplier).
- The priority the organization gives to many of the QMS activities (for example, the priority given to correcting a nonconformity or dealing with a customer complaint or a corrective action can be determined based on findings of the FMEA performed during the design and development of the product).
- Whether the organization actually performs some of the QMS activities (for example, in a situation where the organization is confronted by an overwhelming process validation load, the findings of the process FMEA can justify a decision that process validation of a process with a low risk level, while required by a literal interpretation of the regulatory requirement, may be given a very low priority or found not to be needed at all).

One of the key responsibilities of top management is to set the tone for the risk management activities to be carried out in the organization. An important piece of objective evidence of this top management mandate is the organization's Risk Management Policy. This policy not only states the objectives for risk management within the organization but also provides guidance related to risk acceptability. The following is an example of a Risk Management Policy:

> It is the policy of XYZ, Inc. to reduce identified risks associated with the provision and use of our medical devices to an acceptable level.
>
> Risk acceptability criteria will be determined on a product by product basis through the use of defendable, documented processes that take into consideration:
>
> - The intended use of the medical device
> - Input from international standards and national or regional regulations
> - Input from technical, legal, and clinical professionals that reflects the current state of the art and science

Risk/benefit determinations will be used in situations where the overall residual risk exceeds the acceptability criteria. Such determinations will employ input from objective and knowledgeable clinical professionals.

Risk management personnel must be qualified. They must have knowledge of the product and the setting(s) for which it is intended and in which it is likely to be used; they must also be able to anticipate reasonable misuse of the product. They must be team players, because risk management is normally a multifunctional activity. And at least one person on the risk management team must be proficient in performing the risk management process.

There must be a documented Risk Management Plan (RMP) that remains "alive" and subject to revision throughout the course of the risk management activity.

All risk management activities must be recorded in a Risk Management File that remains open for additions throughout the lifetime of the medical device. Normally the Risk Management File is evidenced by a written or electronic index that identifies the contents and the actual location of the documents and records that make up the File.

The referenced article:

- Provides a primer on the risk management process
- Outlines top management's risk management responsibilities (for example, establish a risk acceptability policy, provide sufficient human and other resources, participate directly in risk management decisions when appropriate, and monitor the effectiveness of the risk management activities)
- Uses process maps of the inputs and outputs to illustrate how risk management interacts with the key QMS processes

Reference: *The ISO 14971:2007 Essentials: A Practical Handbook for Implementing the ISO 14971 Standard for Medical Devices.*

The ISO 14971:2007 Essentials handbook is part of a series of guidances published by the Canadian Standards Association. A complete listing of these handbooks and Canadian standards relevant to health and safety can be found at http://www.csa.ca/electronic_catalogue/health_and_safety.pdf.

The ISO 14971:2007 handbook is user friendly and contains the following:

- The actual text of the requirements sections of the ISO 14971:2007 standard
- Typical audit questions that might be asked to assess whether an organization complies with requirements
- Guidance that is useful in designing quality system documentation related to risk management

Combination Products

In this chapter we describe the recent regulatory QMS developments related to combination products. We do not discuss any of the other regulatory issues related to this group of medical devices that have a drug component associated with them.

There are two kinds of combination products as follows:

- A single product made up of a drug component and a device component (for example, a drug-containing inhaler) where neither component is a separate product in and of itself
- Two or more independent products packaged together for a specific intended use

The following key questions are addressed in this chapter:

- Under which of the various FDA good manufacturing practices regulations should a particular combination product be manufactured?
- Which of the FDA centers is responsible for investigating the compliance of the manufacturer's QMS and under what rule will the investigation be conducted?

These questions surface during routine inspections of manufacturing sites or during preapproval inspections under the device PMA regulation or the drug regulations.

In September 2004 the FDA published a draft guideline titled "Guidance to Industry on FDA Current Good Manufacturing Practices for Combination Products." On April 24, 2006, it announced its intention to publish in March 2007 a streamlined GMP rule. The notice of proposed rule making contained the following:

1. Recognition that there is considerable overlap among the Quality System Regulation (21 CFR Part 820), the Drug Good Manufacturing Practices (cGMP) (21 CFR Part 210–211), and the Biologics cGMP (21 CFR Part 600–680). FDA recognizes this fact and does not see a need for the manufacturer to employ both the device and the drug quality system in one facility. This is especially true for a combination product where the

finished drug and the device product are fully manufactured in different facilities before being copackaged.

2. Drug yield calculation and product stability determination for a combination product, where CDRH is the lead agency, will be handled as part of the design validation section (820.30(g)).
3. Wherever a CAPA determination is required, the manufacturer should follow the more detailed requirements cited in the device QSReg (820.100), although the drug GMP folded this requirement into the more general Product Record Review section (211.102).
4. A recommendation that manufacturers assess which of the quality systems is best suited to be employed during manufacturing and follow it even when the device and drug are joined. As a rule of thumb, the manufacturer should follow the QMS regulation of the FDA lead center.
5. Identification of the following key sections in the device and drug quality systems:

    a. *Devices*: 820.30 design control; 820.50 purchasing controls; 820.100 CAPA
    b. *Drugs*: 211.84 testing and approval; 211.103 calculation of yield; 211.137 expiration dating determination; 211.165 final release testing; 211.166 stability determination; 211.167 special testing (where required); 211.170 reserve samples (applies to devices as well).

6. A caution that other sections of the QMS regulations may apply to a specific combination product.
7. A recommendation that the FDA offices are willing to consult with manufacturers about how the QMS regulations will be applied in a given instance. The FDA recommends that the manufacturer follow the lead center guidelines for requesting such a meeting. It is advisable to meet with the agency early in the process in order to clarify such issues and inform the agency concerning future plans for such a combination device.

Information on combination products is also available on the Web at http://www.fda.gov/oc/combination and at the e-mail address for correspondence at combination@FDA.gov. The Office of Combination Products is housed in the Office of the Commissioner; the telephone number is 301-427-1934.

Process Interactions within the QMS

	Document control and records management	Management responsibilities	Quality system auditing	Resource management	Design and development	Purchasing and supplier management	Handling of nonconformities	CAPA	Production and process control	Distribution, handling, and storage	Laboratory testing and controls	Corrections and removals	Complaint handling	Acceptance activities	Regulatory submissions and registrations	Servicing and installation	Technical support	Risk management
Risk management																		
Technical support																		129
Servicing and installation																	130	125
Regulatory submissions and registrations																		124
Acceptance activities																		122
Complaint handling																28	126	123
Corrections and removals													18	29	39	42	43	41
Laboratory testing and controls												34	23	83	84		127	85
Distribution, handling, and storage												31	20	57		59		58
Production and process control										91	92	36	25	90	96	99		98
CAPA									10	5	8	3	2	1	13	16	17	15
Handling of nonconformities								7	77	74	75	33	22	73		81	82	80
Purchasing and supplier management							78	11	94	101	102	37	26	100		104		103
Design and development						51	47	4	50	45	48	30	19	44		55	56	54
Resource management					53		79	14	97	117	118	40	27	116	119	121	128	120
Quality system auditing				112	52	110	108	12	95	107	109	38	106	105	111	114	115	113
Management responsibilities			86	88	49		76	9	93			35	24		87			89
Document control and records management		64	67	69	46	66	62	6	65	61	63	32	21	60	68	71	72	70

Figure 2 Process interactions within the QMS.

The number in the matrix cells addresses the rows in Table 2.

Table 1 Legend for Figure 2.

QS process	Includes
Acceptance activities	Acceptance at incoming, in-process, and final stages Testing and inspection at the manufacturer and supplier sites
CAPA	All aspects of corrective and preventive action
Complaint handling/ Corrections/Removals	All aspects of complaint handling/corrections/removals, including: • Recording, communicating, and trending of complaints • Field replacement of equipment and components • Provision of field correction information to customers • Reporting to regulatory agencies of product problem information (i.e., vigilance reporting, MDR)
Design and development	All aspects of design and development
Distribution/Handling/ Storage	All aspects of distribution, handling, and storage of components, subassemblies, and finished product
Document control/ Records management	All aspects of document control, including the validation of any software used to update policies, procedures, or work instructions All aspects of records management
Laboratory testing and controls	All aspects of laboratory testing and controls, including control of: • Appropriate facilities • Development and validation of testing materials and methods
Management responsibilities	All aspects of management responsibilities, including: • Development and communication of the quality policy • Provision of adequate resources • The establishment of an adequate organization with the communication of responsibilities • Effective use of the management review activity
Production/Process control	All aspects of production and process control, including: • Control of monitoring and measuring equipment used in production • Validation of manufacturing processes
Purchasing and supplier management	All aspects of purchasing, including: • Control and communication of purchasing information to suppliers • Management of supplier relations

Continued

Table 1 Legend for Figure 2. *Continued*

QS process	Includes
Regulatory submissions/ Registrations	Activities related to international premarket and compliance-related submissions
Resource management	All aspects of resource management, including: • Infrastructure (e.g., utilities, buildings, and environment) • Human resources (e.g., provision of sufficient qualified resources and training)
Risk management	All aspects of risk management, including: • The initial risk management conducted during design and development • The continuing monitoring of commercial product • The continuing review of the effectiveness of previous risk management activity • The maintenance of compliant records of risk management activity
Servicing/Installation	All aspects of servicing/installation activities, including the communication of information received into the organization (e.g., for design input, complaint handling, corrections/removals, and CAPA purposes)
Technical support	All aspects of technical support, including: • The development of technical information provided to the customer through labeling and one-on-one communication with the customer • The maintenance of records of technical support contact • The communication of technical support information into the organization (e.g., for design input, complaint handling, corrections/removals, and CAPA purposes)

Table 2 Analysis of specific interactions.

Interacting functions	**Specific interactions** *(Interactions include those necessary for the effective operation and control of key QS processes and those data inputs and outputs that are important to use during the practice of the key QS processes)*
1. CAPA/Acceptance activities	Nonconformities identified during the acceptance activities or opportunities for improvement of these activities may be carried out using the controls contained within the documented CAPA process. Imposition or modification of acceptance criteria or the acceptance methods are CAPA approaches.
2. CAPA/Complaint handling	Input from complaint handling that indicates there is a systemic QMS problem, a serious product problem trend, or a problem that directly relates to the safety and effectiveness of a medical device must be entered into the CAPA process. Trending of complaint data, MDR/technical file nonconformances, MDV, MPR and other vigilance reports, and servicing reports may identify significant problems that must be entered into the CAPA process. Output from the CAPA process may provide guidance as to how to handle specific customer complaints or groups of customer complaints. Output of the CAPA process may identify changes that must be made to the complaint handling process in order to increase its effectiveness or to ensure its compliance with quality system and regulatory requirements. The risk assessment process and criteria used for establishing whether an issue needs to be handled through the CAPA system should be consistent with those criteria for establishing priorities and conducting health hazard evaluations for the purposes of regulatory reporting of serious injury and malfunction within the complaint handling system. The risk assessment criteria to determine the level of investigation during complaint handling and the content of the investigation itself shall be consistent with the risk criteria used in setting priorities for corrective and preventive action.

Table 2 Analysis of specific interactions. *Continued*

Interacting functions	**Specific interactions** *(Interactions include those necessary for the effective operation and control of key QS processes and those data inputs and outputs that are important to use during the practice of the key QS processes)*
3. CAPA/Corrections/ Removals	Output of the CAPA process may identify changes that must be made to the corrections and removals process in order to increase its effectiveness or to ensure its compliance with quality system and regulatory requirements. Output from the CAPA process may provide guidance as to how to handle specific corrections and removals situations. Output from the corrections and removals process may lead to the need to eliminate a root cause through the creation of a CAPA item. The risk assessment process and criteria used for establishing whether an issue needs to be handled through the CAPA system should be consistent with those criteria for establishing priorities and conducting health hazard evaluations for the purposes of determining corrections and removals actions. The corrections and removals process should track the progress of the field actions (recalls, corrections, removals, and revision of instructions for use) with such data being used in the CAPA process to determine if improvements are necessary in the corrections and removals process.
4. CAPA/Design and Development	Output of the CAPA process may identify changes that must be made to the design and development processes in order to increase their effectiveness or to ensure their compliance with quality system and regulatory requirements. Output from the CAPA process may result in a design change to the product or the manufacturing process that must be handled through the design and development process. Input from the design and development process that indicates there is a systemic quality management problem or a problem that reflects a significant unsafe condition or significant ineffectiveness with the medical device shall be entered into the CAPA process. The risk assessment process and criteria used for establishing whether a nonconformity identified through any of the quality system processes needs to be handled through the CAPA system should be consistent with those criteria for assessing risk that were first conducted within the design and development process. Design and development efforts can provide inputs to corrections, corrective actions, and preventive actions that result from customer complaints or servicing problems.

Table 2 Analysis of specific interactions. *Continued*

Interacting functions	**Specific interactions** *(Interactions include those necessary for the effective operation and control of key QS processes and those data inputs and outputs that are important to use during the practice of the key QS processes)*
5. CAPA/Distribution/ Handling/Storage	Product performance issues with root cause(s) originating in the distribution, handling, or storage of medical devices may be resolved by employing the documented CAPA process. Output from the CAPA process may result in the imposition of new or changed specifications related to distribution, handling, and/or storage of medical devices.
6. CAPA/Document control/Records management	Output of the CAPA process may identify changes that must be made to document control and records management processes in order to increase their effectiveness or to ensure their compliance with quality system and regulatory requirements. The documents used to control the CAPA process must be controlled within the document control process, and the records generated during the CAPA process must be managed in compliance with the records management requirements.
7. CAPA/Handling of nonconformities	Output of the CAPA process may identify changes that must be made to the nonconformity handling process in order to increase its effectiveness or to ensure its compliance with quality system and regulatory requirements. Individual nonconformities identified by any of the quality system processes (e.g., production and process control, quality system audit, and acceptance testing) may be addressed and corrected through the CAPA process. All information describing the nonconformity must be entered into the CAPA records. Trending of any of the quality system processes may uncover nonconformities that may be required to be handled through the CAPA process. The data management categories for recording nonconformities should be consistent with the CAPA system categories. The risk assessment process and criteria used for establishing whether a nonconformity needs to be handled through the CAPA system should be consistent with those criteria for assessing risk that were first conducted within the design and development process. The correction of nonconformities through the use of the CAPA process shall be verified and validated as appropriate.

Table 2 Analysis of specific interactions. *Continued*

Interacting functions	**Specific interactions** *(Interactions include those necessary for the effective operation and control of key QS processes and those data inputs and outputs that are important to use during the practice of the key QS processes)*
8. CAPA/Laboratory testing and controls	Nonconformities associated with testing performed in the process control labs may be resolved by employing the documented CAPA process. Output from the CAPA process may result in the imposition of new or changed specifications and/or test methods used in the process control and testing labs. The changes can also involve increasing the capabilities of personnel employed by these labs.
9. CAPA/ Management responsibilities	Output of the CAPA process may identify changes that must be made to the manner of discharging management responsibilities (e.g., management review) in order to increase its effectiveness or to ensure its compliance with quality system and regulatory requirements. Significant individual CAPA issues requiring a top management decision or top management action may be discussed at management reviews. Such decisions or action may relate to the effectiveness of quality system processes, including the management review process, or to product issues. Information related to the effectiveness or efficiency of the CAPA process may be discussed at regular intervals at management reviews and may result in management decisions.

Table 2 Analysis of specific interactions. *Continued*

Interacting functions	**Specific interactions** *(Interactions include those necessary for the effective operation and control of key QS processes and those data inputs and outputs that are important to use during the practice of the key QS processes)*
10. CAPA/Production and process control	Significant product or process issues may be identified by other quality system processes (e.g., complaint handling, handling of nonconformities, and quality system audits) resulting in a management review decision to refer the solution of the issue through the CAPA process. The risk assessment process and criteria used for establishing whether a production/process control nonconformity needs to be handled through the CAPA system should be consistent with those criteria for assessing risk that were first conducted within the design and development process. Output of the CAPA process may identify changes that must be made to the process and production control processes in order to increase their effectiveness or to ensure their compliance with the quality system and regulatory requirements. The output may also identify the need for additional process validations. Individual nonconformities related to production and process control may be determined through the process of handling of nonconformities required to be handled through the CAPA process. Process results and process parameters (the limits) as well as long-term process stability should be taken into consideration by the CAPA system. Trending of production nonconformities may identify deficiencies required to be handled through the CAPA process.

Table 2 Analysis of specific interactions. *Continued*

Interacting functions	**Specific interactions** *(Interactions include those necessary for the effective operation and control of key QS processes and those data inputs and outputs that are important to use during the practice of the key QS processes)*
11. CAPA/Purchasing and supplier management	Output from the CAPA process may result in changes to the process for handling purchasing and supplier management in order to ensure the process meets quality system and regulatory requirements.
	Correction of nonconformities identified during the purchasing process (e.g., problems related to the definition of appropriate product, or problems related to servicing requirements and the communication of them to the supplier) may be best handled through the CAPA process.
	Output of the CAPA process may result in a change to the process for managing suppliers (e.g., supplier selection or supplier monitoring).
	Output of the CAPA process may result in a change in the interaction between the manufacturer and individual suppliers and the methods used for acceptance of product or services supplied by an individual supplier.
	Nonconformities identified within the supplier management process may identify deficiencies (e.g., screening, selection, evaluation, continual assessment, and the handling of unsatisfactory supplier performance) that must be handled within the CAPA process.
	The risk assessment process and criteria used for establishing whether a purchase nonconformity needs to be handled through the CAPA system should be consistent with those criteria for assessing risk that were first conducted within the design and development process.
	The complaint handling process may identify information that is useful in evaluating a particular supplier's performance and initiating corrective action with respect to that supplier.

Table 2 Analysis of specific interactions. *Continued*

Interacting functions	**Specific interactions** *(Interactions include those necessary for the effective operation and control of key QS processes and those data inputs and outputs that are important to use during the practice of the key QS processes)*
12. CAPA/Quality system auditing	Routine internal quality system audits of the corrective and preventive action processes may result in corrections, corrective actions, and/or preventive actions. Depending on the risks associated with the audit observations, there may be special follow-up audits or follow-up conducted during the next routine quality system audit. Special quality system audits may be ordered to investigate urgent issues with the CAPA process. Outputs of the CAPA process may identify needed changes that must be made to the quality system audit process in order to increase its effectiveness or to ensure its compliance with the regulatory requirements. Quality system audits may be required to verify the successful implementation of corrective or preventive actions. Quality system audits may identify system deficiencies within the auditing process that are best handled within the CAPA process. Trend data coming from quality system audits and the implementation of remedial activities may be considered during CAPA activities.
13. CAPA/Regulatory submissions/ Registrations	Product or process changes placed into effect through the use of the documented CAPA process may need to be the subject of regulatory submissions.

Table 2 Analysis of specific interactions. *Continued*

Interacting functions	**Specific interactions** *(Interactions include those necessary for the effective operation and control of key QS processes and those data inputs and outputs that are important to use during the practice of the key QS processes)*
14. CAPA/Resource management	Output of the CAPA process may result in changes to the infrastructure, including facilities, equipment, and human resources. Nonconformities identified during the management of resources (e.g., training resources inadequacy, an out-of-specification environmental temperature control, or product mix-up) may result in the identification of deficiencies that must be considered for handling within the CAPA process. The risk assessment process and criteria used for establishing whether a resource management nonconformity needs to be handled through the CAPA system should be consistent with those criteria for assessing risk that were first conducted within the design and development process. Output from the CAPA process may identify changes to the training process needed to ensure training effectiveness and compliance with quality system and regulatory requirements. Output from the CAPA process may identify personnel training and/or competency requirements intended to deal with product and process issues. CAPA management is responsible for identifying the training needs (e.g., training content and frequency) of personnel performing within the CAPA process. The training function sets the administrative requirements related to training of personnel within the various functional groups (including those personnel performing the CAPA process), including how training records are generated and maintained. The training function provides training expertise that can be used by the functional groups to develop effective substantive training programs.
15. CAPA/Risk management	The risk assessment process and criteria used for establishing whether a quality system nonconformity needs to be handled through the CAPA system should be consistent with those criteria for assessing risk that were first conducted within the design and development process.
16. CAPA/Servicing/ Installation	Product performance issues with root cause(s) originating in the servicing or installation of medical devices may be resolved by employing the documented CAPA process. Output from the CAPA process may result in the imposition of new or changed specifications related to servicing or installation of medical devices.

Table 2 Analysis of specific interactions. *Continued*

Interacting functions	**Specific interactions** *(Interactions include those necessary for the effective operation and control of key QS processes and those data inputs and outputs that are important to use during the practice of the key QS processes)*
17. CAPA/Technical support	Output from the CAPA process may result in the information that must be provided by technical support to customers and actions that must be taken by technical support with respect to customers in individual situations. Output of the CAPA process may identify changes that must be made to the technical support process in order to increase its effectiveness or to ensure its compliance with quality system and regulatory requirements. Product performance information derived from technical support activities may identify deficiencies that must be handled within the CAPA process. The risk assessment process and criteria used for establishing whether a technical support nonconformity needs to be handled through the CAPA system should be consistent with those criteria for assessing risk that were first conducted within the design and development process.
18. Complaint handling/ Corrections and removals	The results of the complaint handling process with respect to a given product issue may call for corrections and removals activities. Information generated and recorded that is related to a corrections or removal activity must be communicated to the complaint handling process and appropriately recorded within that process. Such information will be useful in handling identical or similar situations in the future, or it may indicate that alternate actions are required should the complaint reoccur.
19. Complaint handling/Design and development	The output of complaint handling activities often provides design input related to proposed design changes to existing products and design input to new, but similar, products. Design and development efforts can provide inputs to correction, corrective actions, and preventive actions that result from customer complaints or servicing problems.
20. Complaint handling/ Distribution, handling, and storage	Inputs related to the state of distribution and inventory of a product affected by a complaint are provided to the complaint handling group by the distribution, handling, and storage functions. Corrections, corrective actions, and preventive actions that arise from complaint handling situations often involve the distribution, handling, and storage operations to segregate the affected product, to remove the affected product from customer locations, and to make sure the "corrected product" gets into the commercial pipeline.

Table 2 Analysis of specific interactions. *Continued*

Interacting functions	**Specific interactions** *(Interactions include those necessary for the effective operation and control of key QS processes and those data inputs and outputs that are important to use during the practice of the key QS processes)*
21. Complaint handling—Document control/Records management	The documents used to control the complaint handling process must be controlled within the document control process, and the records generated during the complaint handling process must be managed in compliance with the records management requirements.
22. Complaint handling/ Handling of nonconformities	Inputs from the complaint handling function are used by personnel investigating product and process nonconformances, and vice versa. Internal nonconformances that are undetected can result in customer complaints.
23. Complaint handling/ Laboratory control	Laboratory testing is often used as an investigative tool during a complaint investigation.
24. Complaint handling/ Management responsibilities	Significant individual complaint handling issues requiring a top management decision or top management action may be discussed at management reviews. Information related to the effectiveness or efficiency of the complaint handling process may be discussed at regular intervals at management reviews and may result in management decisions that can affect these processes.
25. Complaint handling/ Production and process control	The course of action related to the handling of complaint situations will require input from the production and process control function with regard to the manufacturability of the "corrected" product and the anticipated availability of the replacement product.
26. Complaint handling/ Purchasing and supplier management	Output of the complaint handling process may identify changes that must be made to the purchasing and supplier management process in order to increase its effectiveness or to ensure its compliance with the quality system and regulatory requirements. Output of the complaint investigation process may identify gaps in the process related to the definition, review, and approval of purchasing data in order to guarantee traceability requirements. The complaint handling process may identify information that is useful in evaluating a particular supplier's performance and initiating corrective action with respect to that supplier.

Table 2 Analysis of specific interactions. *Continued*

Interacting functions	**Specific interactions** *(Interactions include those necessary for the effective operation and control of key QS processes and those data inputs and outputs that are important to use during the practice of the key QS processes)*
27. Complaint handling/Resource management	Complaint handling management is responsible for identifying the training needs (e.g., training content and frequency) of personnel performing within the complaint handling process. The training function sets the administrative requirements related to training of personnel within the various functional groups (including those personnel handling complaints), including how training records are generated and maintained. The training function provides training expertise that can be used by the functional groups to develop effective substantive training programs.
28. Complaint handling/Servicing and installation	Servicing and installation contacts with customers may gather information that must be handled as a complaint. The corrections and/or corrective actions resulting from the analysis of a complaint may result in activities to be carried out by the servicing and installation personnel. Servicing reports must be reviewed to determine the need for reporting malfunctions or serious injuries to the regulatory authorities within their vigilance processes. Servicing report trending is required to assess the effectiveness of complaint handling activities.
29. Corrections and removals/ Acceptance activities	The course of action related to the handling of corrections and removals situations will require input from the acceptance function with regard to the anticipated availability of replacement product.
30. Corrections and removals/Design and development	Information from the corrections and removals process enters the design and development process through design inputs and design change requests. Such information is valuable to describe the design requirements and to assess and validate the effectiveness of the design. The criteria for establishing priorities and conducting health hazard evaluations for the purposes of determining corrections and removals actions should be consistent with risk management criteria used in the design and development risk management activities. Design and development output may provide the corrections and removals process with significant guidance related to priorities, traceability, installation, and servicing.
31. Corrections and removals/ Distribution, handling, and storage	The course of action related to the handling of corrections and removals situations will require input from the distribution, handling, and storage functions with regard to the anticipated availability of the replacement product.

Table 2 Analysis of specific interactions. *Continued*

Interacting functions	**Specific interactions** *(Interactions include those necessary for the effective operation and control of key QS processes and those data inputs and outputs that are important to use during the practice of the key QS processes)*
32. Corrections and removals/ Document control and records management	The documents used to control the corrections and removals process must be controlled within the document control process, and the records generated during the corrections and removals process must be managed in compliance with the records management requirements.
33. Corrections and removals/ Handling of nonconformities	Outputs of the process for handling nonconformities may result in the handling of an issue through the corrections and removals process. Information generated within the corrections and removals process should be fed back to the handling of nonconformities process (e.g., effectiveness check data on the correction or removal).
34. Corrections and removals/ Laboratory testing and controls	If a proposed correction requires the customer to perform a testing function, the internal laboratory function may be consulted to develop the customer testing method or to confirm that the customer would be able to perform the testing proposed as the correction.
35. Corrections and removals/ Management responsibilities	Significant individual corrections and removals issues may require a top management decision or top management action due to the business impact of any action taken and may be discussed at a top management review. Information related to the effectiveness or efficiency of the corrections and removals process may be discussed at regular intervals at management reviews and may result in management decisions. Output of the corrections and removals process may provide data that top management will review at management review meetings and use for the analysis of the functional effectiveness of other processes within the QMS and the ability of the QMS to meet objectives.
36. Corrections and removals/ Production and process control	Changes to the design of a medical device that are introduced during the production of the device could trigger corrections and removals activities. Such activities must be conducted in a manner that complies with the documented corrections and removals process. Correction and removal activities may trigger production and process control changes. Such changes must be introduced using a controlled manner that complies with the documented production and process control processes. The course of action related to the handling of corrections and removals situation will require input from the production and process control function with regard to the manufacturability of the "corrected" product and the anticipated availability of the replacement product.

Table 2 Analysis of specific interactions. *Continued*

Interacting functions	**Specific interactions** *(Interactions include those necessary for the effective operation and control of key QS processes and those data inputs and outputs that are important to use during the practice of the key QS processes)*
37. Corrections and removals/ Purchasing and supplier management	The purchasing function will be consulted during the formulation of the strategy and tactics of a corrections and removals situation in order to ensure that any needed purchased product or service can be delivered in sufficient quantities and quality, within the appropriate time frame.
38. Corrections and removals/Quality system auditing	Routine internal quality system audits of the corrections and removals activities may result in corrections, corrective actions, and/or preventive actions. Depending on the risks associated with the audit observations, there may be special follow-up audits or follow-up conducted during the next routine quality system audit. Special quality system audits may be ordered to investigate urgent issues with respect to individual corrections and removals activities.
39. Corrections and removals/ Regulatory submissions and registration	Manufacturers and importers must keep records of corrections and removals activities even if the activities are not required to be reported to regulatory agencies or authorities.
40. Corrections and removals/Resource management	Correction and removal management is responsible for identifying training needs (e.g., training content and frequency) of the personnel performing within the corrections and removals process. The training function sets the administrative requirements related to training of personnel within the various functional groups (including those personnel performing corrections and removals), including how training records are generated and maintained. The training function provides training expertise that can be used by the functional groups to develop effective substantive training programs.
41. Corrections and removals/Risk management	The risk associated with proposed corrections must be assessed prior to their implementation. Once a correction or removal is accomplished, there must be follow-up to assess the effectiveness of the correction. Data generated during this follow-up activity must be fed back into the risk management file in order to update the risk assessment of the product involved.

Table 2 Analysis of specific interactions. *Continued*

Interacting functions	**Specific interactions** *(Interactions include those necessary for the effective operation and control of key QS processes and those data inputs and outputs that are important to use during the practice of the key QS processes)*
42. Corrections and removals/ Servicing and installation	Servicing reports should be analyzed to determine the need for correction or removal activities. Servicing reports should be analyzed to determine if correction or removal actions need to be reported to the regulatory authority or another authority. Servicing and installation personnel may be required to gather information for a comprehensive failure investigation and for the execution of corrections and removals.
43. Corrections and removals/ Technical support	Decisions related to corrections and removals provide input into the content of information that technical support personnel will communicate to customers and the methodology to be used to make that communication. Technical support personnel may be required to gather information for a comprehensive failure investigation and for the execution of corrections and removals. The technical support function provides feedback to the corrections and removals process that enables the analysis of the effectiveness of corrections and removals.
44. Design and development/ Acceptance activities	Any inspection and testing methods required for the acceptance of newly designed and developed products are provided by the design and development function. Changes to the acceptance methods proposed during the commercial lifetime of a medical device may require the input of design and development personnel. Acceptance experience with particular suppliers of products and services can influence the selection of such suppliers by the design and development function.
45. Design and development/ Distribution, handling, and storage	Any distribution, handling, and storage methods required for newly designed and developed products are provided by the design and development function.
46. Design and development/ Document control and records management	The documents and records contained in the DHF must be kept under control within the document control and records management process. Design outputs provide the substantive content of the DMR and must be controlled within the document control process.

Table 2 Analysis of specific interactions. *Continued*

Interacting functions	**Specific interactions** *(Interactions include those necessary for the effective operation and control of key QS processes and those data inputs and outputs that are important to use during the practice of the key QS processes)*
47. Design and development/ Handling of nonconformities	Information generated during the handling of nonconformities provides valuable design input during the design and development of medical devices and the processes for manufacturing them. The risk assessment performed during design and development of a medical device provides important input to the priority and method to be used during the handling of nonconformities.
48. Design and development/ Laboratory testing and controls	Any inspection and testing methods required for the use or acceptance of newly designed and developed products may be developed by the design and development personnel with the input of laboratory testing and controls personnel.
49. Design and development/ Management responsibilities	Top management at periodic management reviews will discuss the effectiveness of the design and development process and may make decisions related to how the process will be conducted. Significant change request issues requiring a top management decision or top management action may be discussed at management reviews. The design and development process may provide a collection of data that the management review will use for the analysis of the functional effectiveness of other processes with the QMS and the ability of the QMS to meet objectives. Management business decisions may provide significant design input to the design and development of a medical device and to the specific design and development activities to be used on a given project.
50. Design and development/ Production and process control	Design outputs provide the substantive content of the DMR used to produce and control production of the medical device. The production and process control activities provide valuable input related to the manufacturability of the proposed device designs. Suppliers of products and services during the design and development of medical devices and the processes for manufacturing them must be evaluated separately with regard to their ability to provide production quantities of these products and services.

Table 2 Analysis of specific interactions. *Continued*

Interacting functions	**Specific interactions** *(Interactions include those necessary for the effective operation and control of key QS processes and those data inputs and outputs that are important to use during the practice of the key QS processes)*
51. Design and development/ Purchasing and supplier management	The DMR provides the input to purchase specifications for parts and services and to the identification of initial and alternate suppliers. Suppliers of products and services during the design and development of medical devices and the processes for manufacturing them must be evaluated separately with regard to their ability to provide production quantities of these products and services.
52. Design and development/ Quality system auditing	Routine internal quality system audits of the design and development processes and activities may result in corrections, corrective actions, and/or preventive actions. Depending on the risks associated with the audit observations, there may be special follow-up audits or follow-up conducted during the next routine quality system audit. Special quality system audits may be ordered to investigate urgent issues with the design and development process. Regulatory submissions input can influence design and development strategy and tactics (e.g., if a particular technical methodology requires extensive regulatory processing, it may prompt the design decision to use a more well-accepted methodology).
53. Design and development/ Resource management	The design and development process provides important specifications with regard to environmental, facilities, and utilities requirements. The risk assessment performed during the design and development process provides input as to the priorities associated with the resource specifications. The resource management function provides important input to the design and development process as to the feasibility of providing the resources required by a given design. Design and development management is responsible for identifying the training needs (e.g., training content and frequency) of the personnel performing within the design and development process. The training function sets the administrative requirements related to training of personnel within the various functional groups (including those personnel performing design and development), including how training records are generated and maintained. The training function provides training expertise that can be used by the functional groups to develop effective substantive training programs.

Table 2 Analysis of specific interactions. *Continued*

Interacting functions	**Specific interactions** *(Interactions include those necessary for the effective operation and control of key QS processes and those data inputs and outputs that are important to use during the practice of the key QS processes)*
54. Design and development/Risk management	Risk management activities (e.g., risk assessment and risk control) are an integral part of the design and development process. There is a constant two-way exchange of information between those personnel doing the design work and those assessing the risks associated with the design. Risk-associated data generated during the commercial lifetime of a medical device can result in redesign and redevelopment of the medical device. Design changes proposed in response to customer complaints or identified nonconformities must be risk assessed in order to determine whether they control the risk satisfactorily or they introduce new risks.
55. Design and development/ Servicing and installation	Information generated during servicing activities provides design inputs to the design and development of a medical device. Installation and servicing procedures and materials are design outputs of the design and development process.
56. Design and development/ Technical support	Input from technical support personnel may be used in the initial design and development of a medical device. Technical support personnel may be directly involved in the development and conduct of field evaluations of new devices (i.e., design validation) or changes to existing devices. Input from design and development personnel is used to develop the information and tools used by technical support in communicating with the customer about the design and use of medical devices.
57. Distribution, handling, and storage/ Acceptance activities	There is communication between the distribution, handling, and storage personnel and the acceptance personnel to ensure continued, timely supply of product to customers. Many times this communication is coordinated through automated materials supply processes.
58. Distribution, handling, and storage/Risk management	Information may be communicated to distribution, handling, and storage personnel from the risk management activity if any of the distribution, handling, or storage practices or conditions present a risk to the safe and effective use of the product (e.g., storage temperature and humidity, temperature and humidity control during shipping, and the need for protective packaging).
59. Distribution, handling, and storage/Servicing and installation	Inventory control must include the needs of the servicing organization for parts.

Table 2 Analysis of specific interactions. *Continued*

Interacting functions	**Specific interactions** *(Interactions include those necessary for the effective operation and control of key QS processes and those data inputs and outputs that are important to use during the practice of the key QS processes)*
60. Document control and records management/ Acceptance activities	Acceptance activities must be proceduralized, with the procedures controlled within the document control process. Records generated during acceptance activities must be controlled within the documented records management process.
61. Document control and records management/ Distribution, handling, and storage	Distribution, handling, and storage activities must be proceduralized, with the procedures controlled within the document control process. Records generated during distribution, handling, and storage activities must be controlled within the documented records management process.
62. Document control and records management/ Handling of nonconformities	Activities associated with the handling of nonconformities must be proceduralized, with the procedures controlled within the document control process. Records generated during nonconformity handling activities must be controlled within the documented records management process.
63. Document control and records management/ Laboratory testing and controls	Laboratory testing and control materials descriptions and testing and control methods must be documented and proceduralized, with the documents and procedures controlled within the document control process. Records generated during laboratory testing and control activities must be controlled within the documented records management process.
64. Document control and records management/ Management responsibilities	Certain top management activities must be proceduralized, with the procedures controlled within the document control process (e.g., management review procedure). Records generated during top management activities must be controlled within the documented records management process (e.g., minutes of management review meetings, quality policy, and overall organizational objectives).
65. Document control and records management/ Production and process control	Activities associated with production and process control must be proceduralized, with the procedures controlled within the document control process. Records generated during production and process control activities must be controlled within the documented records management process.

Table 2 Analysis of specific interactions. *Continued*

Interacting functions	**Specific interactions** *(Interactions include those necessary for the effective operation and control of key QS processes and those data inputs and outputs that are important to use during the practice of the key QS processes)*
66. Document control and records management/ Purchasing and supplier management	Activities associated with purchasing and supplier management must be proceduralized, with the procedures controlled within the document control process. Records generated during purchasing and supplier management activities must be controlled within the documented records management process.
67. Document control and records management/ Quality system auditing	Activities associated with quality system auditing must be proceduralized, with the procedures controlled within the document control process. Records generated during quality system auditing activities must be controlled within the documented records management process. Routine internal quality system audits of the document control and records management processes and activities may result in corrections, corrective actions, and/or preventive actions. Depending on the risks associated with the audit observations, there may be special follow-up audits or follow-up conducted during the next routine quality system audit. Special quality system audits may be ordered to investigate urgent issues with the document control and records management processes.
68. Document control and records management/ Regulatory submissions and registrations	Activities associated with handling of regulatory submissions and registrations must be proceduralized, with the procedures controlled within the document control process. Records generated during regulatory submission and registration activities must be controlled within the documented records management process.

Table 2 Analysis of specific interactions. *Continued*

Interacting functions	**Specific interactions** *(Interactions include those necessary for the effective operation and control of key QS processes and those data inputs and outputs that are important to use during the practice of the key QS processes)*
69. Document control and records management/ Resource management	Activities associated with resource management must be documented and proceduralized, with the documents and procedures controlled within the document control process (e.g., specifications for environmental control, the procedure for determining training needs, and the procedure for personnel performance review). Records generated during resource management activities must be controlled within the documented records management process. Management over the document control and records management processes is responsible for identifying the training needs (e.g., training content and frequency) of the personnel performing within the document control and records management processes. The training function sets the administrative requirements related to training of personnel within the various functional groups (including those personnel performing document control and records management), including how training records are generated and maintained. The training function provides training expertise that can be used by the functional groups to develop effective substantive training programs.
70. Document control and records management/Risk management	Activities associated with risk management must be proceduralized, with the procedures controlled within the document control process. Records generated during risk management activities must be controlled within the documented records management process.
71. Document control and records management/ Servicing and installation	Activities associated with servicing and installation must be proceduralized, with the procedures controlled within the document control process. Records generated during servicing and installation activities must be controlled within the documented records management process.
72. Document control and records management/ Technical support	Activities associated with technical support must be proceduralized, with the procedures controlled within the document control process (e.g., the procedure for filling out technical support reports and the procedure describing technical support corrections and removals responsibilities). Records generated during technical support activities must be controlled within the documented records management process.

Table 2 Analysis of specific interactions. *Continued*

Interacting functions	**Specific interactions** *(Interactions include those necessary for the effective operation and control of key QS processes and those data inputs and outputs that are important to use during the practice of the key QS processes)*
73. Handling of nonconformities/ Acceptance activities	Nonconformities identified during acceptance activities must be handled in a controlled manner (i.e., using a documented nonconformity handling process), with the level of control related to the potential risk associated with the nonconformity. Information generated during the handling of the nonconformity (e.g., information related to the criteria used for acceptance) must be fed back into the acceptance process so it can be used to ensure accurate nonconformity identification in the future.
74. Handling of nonconformities/ Distribution, handling, and storage	Nonconformities associated with the distribution, handling, and storage activities must be handled in a controlled manner (i.e., using a documented nonconformity handling process), with the level of control related to the potential risk associated with the nonconformity. Information generated during the handling of the nonconformity (e.g., information related to the effectiveness of the distribution, handling, and storage activities) must be fed back into the distribution, handling, and storage process so it can be used to prevent nonconformities in the future.
75. Handling of nonconformities/ Laboratory testing and controls	Nonconformities identified during laboratory testing control activities must be handled in a controlled manner (i.e., using a documented nonconformity handling process), with the level of control related to the potential risk associated with the nonconformity. Information generated during the handling of the nonconformity (e.g., information related to the effectiveness of the laboratory testing and control activities) must be fed back into the laboratory testing and control process so it can be used to ensure accurate nonconformity identification in the future.
76. Handling of nonconformities/ Management responsibilities	Information related to the effectiveness or efficiency of the nonconformity handling process may be discussed at regular intervals at management reviews and may result in management decisions that may change this quality management process. Significant individual nonconformity issues requiring a top management decision or top management action may be discussed at management reviews.

Table 2 Analysis of specific interactions. *Continued*

Interacting functions	**Specific interactions** *(Interactions include those necessary for the effective operation and control of key QS processes and those data inputs and outputs that are important to use during the practice of the key QS processes)*
77. Handling of nonconformities/ Production and process control	Every nonconformity related to production and process control must be handled in a controlled manner (i.e., using a documented nonconformity handling process). The level of control must be related to the risk associated with the nonconformity. The level of risk can be estimated by reference to the process FMEA generated during the design and development of the medical device and the processes for manufacturing and controlling it. The nonconformities associated with production and process control relate to the production of the device, the inspections and measurements associated with that production, and the validations performed on these processes. Information generated during the handling of the nonconformity (e.g., information related to the effectiveness of the correction or corrective actions) must be fed back into the production and process control process so it can be used to prevent future nonconformities.
78. Handling of nonconformities/ Purchasing and supplier management	Nonconformities related to the purchasing of products and services and the management of suppliers must be handled in a controlled manner (i.e., using a documented nonconformity handling process), with the level of control related to the potential risk associated with the nonconformity. Information generated during the handling of the nonconformity (e.g., information related to the effectiveness of the correction or corrective actions) must be fed back into the purchasing and supplier management process so it can be used to prevent future nonconformities.

Table 2 Analysis of specific interactions. *Continued*

Interacting functions	**Specific interactions** *(Interactions include those necessary for the effective operation and control of key QS processes and those data inputs and outputs that are important to use during the practice of the key QS processes)*
79. Handling of nonconformities/ Resource management	Nonconformities related to the management of resources must be handled in a controlled manner (i.e., using a documented nonconformity handling process), with the level of control related to the potential risk associated with the nonconformity. Information generated during the handling of the nonconformity (e.g., information related to the effectiveness of the correction or corrective actions) must be fed back into the resource management process so it can be used to prevent future nonconformities. Management over the handling of nonconformities is responsible for the identification of the training needs (e.g., training content and frequency) for personnel performing nonconformity handling activities. The training function sets the administrative requirements related to training of personnel within the various functional groups (including those personnel handling nonconformities), including how training records are generated and maintained. The training function provides training expertise that can be used by the functional groups to develop effective substantive training programs.
80. Handling of nonconformities/ Risk management	Risk assessment performed during design and development of a medical device provides important guidance in the priorities and methods for handling of nonconformities. Every nonconformity related to production and process control must be handled in a controlled manner (i.e., using a documented nonconformity handling process). The level of control must be related to the risk associated with the nonconformity. The level of risk can be estimated by reference to the process FMEA generated during the design and development of the medical device and the processes for manufacturing and controlling it. The nonconformities associated with production and process control relate to the production of the device, the inspections and measurements associated with that production, and the validations performed on these processes. Information generated during the handling of nonconformities must be fed back into the risk assessment process for each medical device.

Table 2 Analysis of specific interactions. *Continued*

Interacting functions	**Specific interactions** *(Interactions include those necessary for the effective operation and control of key QS processes and those data inputs and outputs that are important to use during the practice of the key QS processes)*
81. Handling of nonconformities/ Servicing and installation	Nonconformities related to the servicing and installation of medical devices must be handled in a controlled manner (i.e., using a documented nonconformity handling process), with the level of control related to the potential risk associated with the nonconformity. If the servicing organization is to participate in the handling of a nonconformity, it must receive accurate instructions as part of the nonconformity handling process. Information generated during the handling of the nonconformity (e.g., information related to the effectiveness of the correction or corrective actions) must be fed back into the device servicing and installation process so it can be used to prevent future nonconformities.
82. Handling of nonconformities/ Technical support	Information related to device nonconformities may be provided to customers through the technical support organization. Such information must be developed and communicated in a controlled manner (i.e., using a documented nonconformity handling process).
83. Laboratory testing and controls/ Acceptance activities	There must be communication between laboratory testing and controls personnel and acceptance personnel related to acceptance testing being performed by the laboratory testing and control personnel.
84. Laboratory testing and controls/ Regulatory submissions and registrations	Regulatory submissions personnel should communicate to laboratory testing personnel specific regulatory testing requirements contained in regulatory guidance documents for particular medical devices. There must be communication between laboratory testing and control personnel and regulatory submissions personnel related to regulatory Good Laboratory Practices requirements.
85. Laboratory testing and controls/Risk management	Laboratory testing and controls activities generate information and data that are part of the risk monitoring that continues throughout the commercial lifetime of a medical device. Output of risk management activities may result in risk control measures to be carried out by laboratory testing and controls personnel.

Table 2 Analysis of specific interactions. *Continued*

Interacting functions	**Specific interactions** *(Interactions include those necessary for the effective operation and control of key QS processes and those data inputs and outputs that are important to use during the practice of the key QS processes)*
86. Management responsibilities/ Quality system auditing	Audit results shall be reviewed by management as part of the management review activities. Top management may order special quality system audits in order to assess the state of compliance of the QMS. Routine internal quality system audits of the quality system activities of top management (e.g., organization, management representative, and management review) may result in corrections, corrective actions, and/or preventive actions. Depending on the risks associated with the audit observations, there may be special follow-up audits or follow-up conducted during the next routine quality system audit. Special quality system audits may be ordered to investigate urgent issues with respect to individual quality system management activities.
87. Management responsibilities/ Regulatory submissions and registrations	Information related to the effectiveness or efficiency of the regulatory submissions and registrations process may be discussed at regular intervals at management reviews and may result in management decisions that may change this quality management process. Significant individual regulatory submissions and registrations issues requiring a top management decision or top management action may be discussed at management reviews.
88. Management responsibilities/ Resource management	Significant individual infrastructure and work environment issues (e.g., the need for new resources or resource improvements) requiring a top management decision or top management action may be discussed at management reviews. Management review outputs may include decisions related to the improvements of the QMS resources and to the maintenance of the effectiveness of the infrastructure and work environment to achieve conformity to product requirements. Top management is responsible for identifying the training needs (e.g., training content and frequency) of the personnel with top management responsibilities. The training function sets the administrative requirements related to training of personnel within the various functional groups, including those personnel performing management responsibilities, and including how training records are generated and maintained. The training function provides training expertise that can be used by the functional groups to develop effective substantive training programs.

Table 2 Analysis of specific interactions. *Continued*

Interacting functions	**Specific interactions** *(Interactions include those necessary for the effective operation and control of key QS processes and those data inputs and outputs that are important to use during the practice of the key QS processes)*
89. Management responsibilities/ Risk management	Information related to the effectiveness or efficiency of the risk management process may be discussed at regular intervals at management reviews and may result in management decisions that may change this quality management process. Significant individual risk management issues requiring a top management decision or top management action may be discussed at management reviews.
90. Production and process control/ Acceptance activities	Production and process control personnel and acceptance personnel must be in continual communication to ensure accurate (i.e., products that meet specifications) and sufficient supply of parts and devices. There should be communication of specifications from production and process control to acceptance group for acceptance testing.
91. Production and process control/ Distribution, handling, and storage	Personnel involved with production and process control and personnel involved with distribution, handling, and storage must be in continual communication to ensure accurate (i.e., products that meet specifications) and sufficient supply of parts and devices.
92. Production and process control/ Laboratory testing and controls	There is communication between production and process control personnel related to laboratory testing and control activities required by production and process control and performed by laboratory testing and control personnel (e.g., evaluation of testing materials used by production and process control).
93. Production and process control/ Management responsibilities	Significant individual production and process control issues requiring a top management decision or top management action may be discussed at management reviews. Information related to the effectiveness or efficiency of the production and process control processes may be discussed at regular intervals at management reviews and may result in management decisions that can affect these processes.

Table 2 Analysis of specific interactions. *Continued*

Interacting functions	**Specific interactions** *(Interactions include those necessary for the effective operation and control of key QS processes and those data inputs and outputs that are important to use during the practice of the key QS processes)*
94. Production and process control/ Purchasing and supplier management	Production and process control functions must provide requirements and specifications input to purchasing with regard to products and services to be outsourced. Such input (e.g., process parameters, equipment, and tools) must be documented in detail. Approved changes to specifications must be communicated to the supplier. Suppliers should notify the purchaser when changes are made to the product/service being purchased. The contract with such suppliers must attempt to get agreement from such suppliers to notify the manufacturer of any such changes before they are made. If such an agreement cannot be obtained, then production and process control must provide adequate acceptance activities to identify if such changes are made by the supplier. Production and process control functions may be involved in the evaluation of the capabilities of candidate suppliers of products and services.
95. Production and process control/ Quality system auditing	Routine internal quality system audits of the production and process control processes and activities may result in corrections, corrective actions, and/or preventive actions. Depending on the risks associated with the audit observations, there may be special follow-up audits or follow-up conducted during the next routine quality system audit.
96. Production and process control/ Regulatory submissions and registrations	There is communication among production and process control personnel with regard to quality system requirements associated with the content of technical files and other premarket regulatory requirements (e.g., premarket approval submissions and arrangements for preapproval plant inspections).
97. Production and process control/Resource management	Production and process control management is responsible for identifying the training needs (e.g., training content and frequency) of the personnel performing production and process control activities. Training needs related to changes in the manufacturing and control activities must also be determined. The training function sets the administrative requirements related to training of personnel within the various functional groups (including those personnel performing production and process control activities), including how training records are generated and maintained. The training function provides training expertise that can be used by the functional groups to develop effective substantive training programs.

Table 2 Analysis of specific interactions. *Continued*

Interacting functions	**Specific interactions** *(Interactions include those necessary for the effective operation and control of key QS processes and those data inputs and outputs that are important to use during the practice of the key QS processes)*
98. Production and process control/ Risk management	Every nonconformity related to production and process control must be handled in a controlled manner (i.e., using a documented nonconformity handling process). The level of control must be related to the risk associated with the nonconformity. The level of risk can be estimated by reference to the process FMEA generated during the design and development of the medical device and the processes for manufacturing and controlling it. The nonconformities associated with production and process control relate to the production of the device, the inspections and measurements associated with that production, and the validations performed on these processes.
99. Production and process control/ Servicing and installation	There should be coordination of efforts to build the parts and subassemblies needed as field servicing spare parts.
100. Purchasing and supplier management/ Acceptance activities	Suppliers should notify the purchaser when changes are made to the product/service being purchased. The contract with such suppliers must attempt to get agreement from such suppliers to notify the manufacturer of any such changes before they are made. If such an agreement cannot be obtained, then production and process control must provide adequate acceptance activities to identify if such changes are made by the supplier. The acceptance function may be involved in the evaluation of the capabilities of candidate suppliers of products and services.
101. Purchasing and supplier management/ Distribution, handling, and storage	Personnel involved with purchasing and supplier management and personnel involved with distribution, handling, and storage must be in continual communication to ensure accurate (i.e., products that meet specifications) and sufficient supply of parts and devices to customers.
102. Purchasing and supplier management/ Laboratory testing and controls	There may be communication between purchasing and supplier management and laboratory testing and control personnel when laboratory services are being outsourced.

Table 2 Analysis of specific interactions. *Continued*

Interacting functions	**Specific interactions** *(Interactions include those necessary for the effective operation and control of key QS processes and those data inputs and outputs that are important to use during the practice of the key QS processes)*
103. Purchasing and supplier management/ Risk management	Purchasing and supplier management activities generate information and data that are part of the risk monitoring that continues throughout the commercial lifetime of a medical device. Output of risk management activities may result in risk control measures to be carried out by purchasing and supplier management personnel.
104. Purchasing and supplier management/ Servicing and Installation	Purchasing and supplier management activities must include the needs of the servicing organization for parts.
105. Quality system auditing/ Acceptance activities	Routine internal quality system audits of the acceptance processes may result in corrections, corrective actions, and/or preventive actions. Depending on the risks associated with the audit observations, there may be special follow-up audits or follow-up conducted during the next routine quality system audit. Special quality system audits may be ordered to investigate urgent quality system issues with acceptance activities. Quality system audits at supplier facilities may be part of the product acceptance activities.
106. Quality system auditing/ Complaint handling	Routine internal quality system audits of the complaint handling process may result in corrections, corrective actions, and/or preventive actions. Depending on the risks associated with the audit observations, there may be special follow-up audits or follow-up conducted during the next routine quality system audit. Special quality system audits may be ordered to investigate urgent quality system issues with the complaint handling process.
107. Quality system auditing/ Distribution, handling, and storage	Routine internal quality system audits of the distribution, handling, and storage processes may result in corrections, corrective actions, and/or preventive actions. Depending on the risks associated with the audit observations, there may be special follow-up audits or follow-up conducted during the next routine quality system audit. Special quality system audits may be ordered to investigate urgent quality system issues with distribution, handling, and storage activities.

Table 2 Analysis of specific interactions. *Continued*

Interacting functions	**Specific interactions** *(Interactions include those necessary for the effective operation and control of key QS processes and those data inputs and outputs that are important to use during the practice of the key QS processes)*
108. Quality system auditing/ Handling of nonconformities	Routine internal quality system audits of the handling of nonconformities may result in corrections, corrective actions, and/or preventive actions. Depending on the risks associated with the audit observations, there may be special follow-up audits or follow-up conducted during the next routine quality system audit. Special quality system audits may be ordered to investigate urgent quality system issues with the handling of nonconformities. Special internal quality system audits may be ordered to assess the effectiveness of corrections or corrective actions for nonconformities.
109. Quality system auditing/ Laboratory testing and controls	Routine internal quality system audits of the testing and control laboratories and the associated processes may result in corrections, corrective actions, and/or preventive actions. Depending on the risks associated with the audit observations, there may be special follow-up audits or follow-up conducted during the next routine quality system audit. Special quality system audits may be ordered to investigate urgent quality system issues with control and testing laboratory processes.
110. Quality system auditing/ Purchasing and supplier management	Routine internal quality system audits of the purchasing and supplier management processes may result in corrections, corrective actions, and/or preventive actions. Depending on the risks associated with the audit observations, there may be special follow-up audits or follow-up conducted during the next routine quality system audit. Special quality system audits may be ordered to investigate urgent quality system issues with the purchasing and supplier management processes. Quality system audits at supplier facilities may be part of the product acceptance activities.
111. Quality system auditing/ Regulatory submissions and registrations	Routine internal quality system audits of the regulatory submissions and registrations processes may result in corrections, corrective actions, and/or preventive actions. Depending on the risks associated with the audit observations, there may be special follow-up audits or follow-up conducted during the next routine quality system audit. Special quality system audits may be ordered to investigate urgent quality system issues with the regulatory submissions and registrations processes.

Table 2 Analysis of specific interactions. *Continued*

Interacting functions	**Specific interactions** *(Interactions include those necessary for the effective operation and control of key QS processes and those data inputs and outputs that are important to use during the practice of the key QS processes)*
112. Quality system auditing/ Resource management	Routine internal quality system audits of the various aspects of resource management (e.g., infrastructure, human resources, and training) may result in corrections, corrective actions, and/or preventive actions. Depending on the risks associated with the audit observations, there may be special follow-up audits or follow-up conducted during the next routine quality system audit. Special quality system audits may be ordered to investigate urgent quality system issues with resource management. Quality system audit management is responsible for identifying the training needs (e.g., training content and frequency) of the personnel performing quality system audits. The training function sets the administrative requirements related to training of personnel within the various functional groups (including those personnel performing quality system audits), including how training records are generated and maintained. The training function provides training expertise that can be used by the functional groups to develop effective substantive training programs.
113. Quality system auditing/Risk management	Routine internal quality system audits of the risk management activities may result in corrections, corrective actions, and/or preventive actions. Depending on the risks associated with the audit observations, there may be special follow-up audits or follow-up conducted during the next routine quality system audit. Special quality system audits may be ordered to investigate urgent quality system issues with the risk management processes.
114. Quality system auditing/ Servicing and installation	Routine internal quality system audits of the servicing and installation processes may result in corrections, corrective actions, and/or preventive actions. Depending on the risks associated with the audit observations, there may be special follow-up audits or follow-up conducted during the next routine quality system audit. Special quality system audits may be ordered to investigate urgent quality system issues with the servicing and installation processes.

Table 2 Analysis of specific interactions. *Continued*

Interacting functions	**Specific interactions** *(Interactions include those necessary for the effective operation and control of key QS processes and those data inputs and outputs that are important to use during the practice of the key QS processes)*
115. Quality system auditing/ Technical support	Routine internal quality system audits of the technical support processes and activities may result in corrections, corrective actions, and/or preventive actions. Depending on the risks associated with the audit observations, there may be special follow-up audits or follow-up conducted during the next routine quality system audit. Special quality system audits may be ordered to investigate urgent quality system issues with the technical support activities.
116. Resource management/ Acceptance activities	Management over acceptance activities is responsible for identifying the training needs (e.g., training content and frequency) of the personnel performing acceptance activities. The training function sets the administrative requirements related to training of personnel within the various functional groups (including those personnel performing acceptance activities), including how training records are generated and maintained. The training function provides training expertise that can be used by the functional groups to develop effective substantive training programs.
117. Resource management/ Distribution, handling, and storage	Distribution, handling, and storage management is responsible for identifying the training needs (e.g., training content and frequency) of the personnel performing the distribution, handling, and storage activities. The training function sets the administrative requirements related to training of personnel within the various functional groups (including those personnel performing distribution, handling, and storage), including how training records are generated and maintained. The training function provides training expertise that can be used by the functional groups to develop effective substantive training programs.
118. Resource management/ Laboratory testing and controls	Testing laboratory management is responsible for identifying the training needs (e.g., training content and frequency) for personnel performing laboratory testing activities. The training function sets the administrative requirements related to training of personnel within the various functional groups (including those personnel performing laboratory activities), including how training records are generated and maintained. The training function provides training expertise that can be used by the functional groups to develop effective substantive training programs.

Table 2 Analysis of specific interactions. *Continued*

Interacting functions	**Specific interactions** *(Interactions include those necessary for the effective operation and control of key QS processes and those data inputs and outputs that are important to use during the practice of the key QS processes)*
119. Resource management/ Regulatory submissions and registration	Regulatory submissions and registrations management is responsible for identifying the training needs (e.g., training content and frequency) of the personnel performing regulatory submissions and registrations activities. The training function sets the administrative requirements related to training of personnel within the various functional groups (including those personnel performing regulatory submissions and registration activities), including how training records are generated and maintained. The training function provides training expertise that can be used by the functional groups to develop effective substantive training programs.
120. Resource management/ Risk management	Management over the risk management activities or the risk management process owner is responsible for identifying the training needs (e.g., training content and frequency) of the personnel performing risk management activities. The training function sets the administrative requirements related to training of personnel within the various functional groups (including those personnel performing risk management), including how training records are generated and maintained. The training function provides training expertise that can be used by the functional groups to develop effective substantive training programs.
121. Resource management/ Servicing and installation	Servicing and installation management is responsible for identifying the training needs (e.g., training content and frequency) of the personnel performing servicing and installation activities. The training function sets the administrative requirements related to training of personnel within the various functional groups (including those personnel performing servicing and installation activities), including how training records are generated and maintained. The training function provides training expertise that can be used by the functional groups to develop effective substantive training programs.
122. Risk management/ Acceptance activities	Acceptance activities generate information and data that are part of the risk monitoring that continues throughout the commercial lifetime of a medical device. Output of risk management activities may result in risk control measures to be carried out by acceptance personnel.

Table 2 Analysis of specific interactions. *Continued*

Interacting functions	**Specific interactions** *(Interactions include those necessary for the effective operation and control of key QS processes and those data inputs and outputs that are important to use during the practice of the key QS processes)*
123. Risk management/ Complaint handling	Complaint handling activities generate information and data that are part of the risk monitoring that continues throughout the commercial lifetime of a medical device. Output of risk management activities may result in risk control measures to be carried out by complaint handling personnel.
124. Risk management/ Regulatory submissions and registrations	The output of risk management activities provides information that becomes part of premarket and regulatory compliance submissions.
125. Risk management/ Servicing and installation	Servicing and installation activities generate information and data that are part of the risk monitoring that continues throughout the commercial lifetime of a medical device. Output of risk management activities may result in risk control measures to be carried out by servicing and installation personnel.
126. Technical support/ Complaint handling	Technical support contacts with customers may gather information that must be handled as a complaint. The corrections and/or corrective actions resulting from the analysis of a complaint may result in activities to be carried out by the technical support personnel.
127. Technical support/ Laboratory testing and controls	Laboratory testing and controls personnel may provide assistance to technical support personnel in investigating product performance issues in the field.
128. Technical support/ Resource management	Technical support management is responsible for identifying the training needs (e.g., training content and frequency) of the personnel performing technical support activities. The training function sets the administrative requirements related to training of personnel within the various functional groups, including how training records are generated and maintained. The training function provides training expertise that can be used by the functional groups to develop effective substantive training programs.

Table 2 Analysis of specific interactions. *Continued*

Interacting functions	**Specific interactions** *(Interactions include those necessary for the effective operation and control of key QS processes and those data inputs and outputs that are important to use during the practice of the key QS processes)*
129. Technical support/Risk management	Technical support activities generate information and data that are part of the risk monitoring that continues throughout the commercial lifetime of a medical device. Output of risk management activities may result in risk control measures to be carried out by technical support personnel.
130. Technical support/ Servicing and installation	Communication between technical support and the servicing and installation organization must continue during the lifetime of a medical device in order to ensure they are providing consistent information to customers.

How to Present and Advocate for Your QMS During Inspections and Assessments

Introduction

Establishing and maintaining an organization's QMS is a large, resource-consuming process. It takes enlightened leadership and enormous energy to overcome organizational inertia and move an organization from its old ways to a QMS that is compliant with the U.S. QSReg and the ISO 13485:2003 Standard. And once the QMS is established and compliant, it requires fierce dedication to maintain it in the face of forces that argue for expediency and cost reduction.

Too often organizations expend energy and resources to establish and maintain their QMS but still get into compliance trouble because they do not effectively advocate for their QMS. The settings for this advocacy are inspections by regulatory compliance personnel and assessments by private sector registrars or notified bodies. Unfortunately for many organizations, external inspections and assessments are the beginning of "compliance hell"—a predicament that can be costly, can prevent the organization from competing in the marketplace, and can threaten the organization's existence.

In the United States a medical device manufacturer is subject to unannounced FDA inspections. This uncertainty forces the organization to "be on its toes" throughout the year.

A foreign manufacturing site (that is, one located outside the United States, whether or not it is owned and operated by a U.S. company) will get some advance notice of an inspection, from several weeks to several months. It would be foolish for a foreign manufacturing site to treat an FDA inspection lightly or to wait until it gets notice to prepare for an inspection. A poor inspection can result in a warning letter and possibly an import detention. Such a detention can be imposed with almost no delay from legal or other activities, and it will prevent the manufacturer's products from being imported into the United States.

For the purposes of this chapter we focus our discussion on preparing for a successful regulatory compliance inspection or third-party QMS assessment. Top management must not measure the success of an inspection by the QMS deficiencies that were not identified by the inspector. It is foolish to expect that such deficiencies will escape the findings of an effective inspection.

The reader should note that in this chapter, the authors use the term "inspection" to mean "inspection or assessment" and the term "inspector" to mean "investigator or assessor," unless it is important to distinguish between those terms.

Pick the Right Advocates

A successful inspection is one in which the observations are clearly stated, understood by all parties, and accurate. A successful inspection largely depends on the personnel representing the organization. It can be the kiss of death for an organization that has a compliant and effective QMS to send inexperienced regulatory, operations, and management personnel into the inspection setting.

The executive manager who approaches his organization's QMS as a necessary nuisance and shows his ignorance of even basic QMS requirements in his conversations with the inspector sets a dangerous tone for an inspection. The functional manager who thinks she knows better than the investigator and presents an arrogant image is waving a red cape in front of a bull. The subject matter expert (SME) who is too reticent to answer questions creates the impression that the organization may not be addressing an important QMS issue. The SME who is too forthcoming and answers not only the question but other unasked questions, possibly trying to show off his expertise, can get the organization in trouble by inadvertently or intentionally revealing or misrepresenting a QMS problem area. All personnel participating in the inspection must be carefully coached to avoid these pitfalls or be kept away from the inspection.

The key person is the Inspection Coordinator. A good candidate for this job is the Management Representative or, in a large organization, someone reporting to this person. The Inspection Coordinator should understand that preparing the organization for and then coordinating the inspection is a large part of his or her responsibility and not just another of those responsibilities that aren't part of the "real job." A small company may not have the resources to assign these responsibilities to an employee and may have to seek consultant help on a part-time basis to ensure effective handling of inspections. The Inspection Coordinator should be preparing for the inspection throughout the entire year by:

- Keeping abreast of the regulatory agencies' evolving inspection policies and tactics
- Reviewing public records of inspections being performed throughout the medical device industry to discover the regulatory focuses of attention
- Keeping in touch with the recent activities of the organization's registrars and notified bodies to understand their policies and tactics
- Reviewing internal audit reports to identify QMS areas that may require special attention when planning an inspection
- Training organization personnel to better prepare them for their inspection and assessment roles

Know the Reason for the Assessment or Inspection

The FDA can inspect a manufacturer's facility for a number of reasons, and it may conduct any of the following inspections:

1. A routine QMS inspection. More and more, routine QMS inspections are conducted using the Quality System Inspection Technique (QSIT), which focuses on controls related to management responsibilities, design and development, corrective and preventive actions, and production and process control. FDA Web sites that provide access to useful information on QSIT are http://www.fda.gov/cdrh/gmp/gmp.html and http://www.fda.gov/ora/inspect_ref/igs/qsit/qsitguide.htm.

   Some routine inspections conducted by FDA "old timers" may use an approach that identifies a number of product problems from a review of complaint files and then follows the handling and resolution of such complaints through other QMS processes like complaint handling, nonconformity handling, corrective and preventive action, production and process control, corrections and removals, and so forth.

   The routine QMS inspection of a domestic manufacturer will likely be unannounced, so it will be important for the manufacturer to determine the FDA objective(s) very early in the inspection. This can be done during the opening meeting to ensure that appropriate staff members are available and relevant information is presented in an effective and timely way.

   Additional information related to a current FDA inspection program appears later in this chapter. See "Inspection of Medical Device Manufacturers, Program 7382.845, Issued 15 June, 2006."
2. An inspection to follow up observations made at a previous inspection or to confirm completion of a manufacturer's corrective actions promised in response to an FDA 483 or an FDA warning letter. This type of inspection is made after the manufacturer has submitted comprehensive information to the FDA related to the previous inspection or warning letter observations.
3. A "for cause" inspection related to a product problem that has reached FDA attention (for example, to follow up on an MDR, to follow up on a recall, or to gather information related to a public health concern). This type of inspection focuses on the handling of the product problem and the effectiveness of the manufacturer's QMS processes that handled the problem. This kind of inspection will also likely be unannounced if it is for a domestic manufacturer.
4. A preapproval inspection related to a PMA application for a Class III product.
5. An information-gathering visit as part of an FDA study on a QMS issue or product performance area. For this kind of inspection, the FDA usually publishes its intentions and asks the affected manufacturers to voluntarily participate in the program.

Registrars or notified bodies conduct QMS assessments for two reasons:

1. To preassess the manufacturer's compliance with the regulation(s) or international standard(s) and provide consultation on areas of weakness or deficiencies
2. To assess the state of compliance of the QMS for certification purposes or for the purpose of determining compliance with the essential or regulatory requirements related to regulations in other countries (for example, Canada, Australia, and Japan) or regions (for example, the European Union (EU)).

These assessments are conducted under contract conditions between the manufacturer and the registrar or notified body, so there is ample notice and opportunity for the manufacturer to know the assessment objectives and prepare for the assessment.

Know the State of Compliance of Your QMS

It is important for the Inspection Coordinator to keep abreast of the current state of compliance of the manufacturer's QMS. This knowledge will help executive management assess the organization's inspection vulnerabilities and establish QMS corrective action priorities. It will also help the Inspection Coordinator in selecting for the FDA investigator or the registrar good examples that reflect the state of compliance of the organization. The organization will also be able to plan for likely deficiency findings for weak QMS processes.

Prepare for the Inspection/Assessment

The first step in preparing for inspections is to have a written inspection procedure that does the following:

- Contains a policy that pledges cooperation with regulatory inspectors in accordance with the requirements of the law and regulations and authorized, private sector assessors. The policy should require those personnel involved with such inspections to act on behalf of the organization in a professional manner.
- Identifies the personnel to be involved with inspections and outlines their responsibilities and authorities.
- Establishes the company policies and processes related to the following:
  - —*Communication with line employees*—Generally such communication should be allowed, but it should not be allowed to negatively affect production processes. Normally such line employees should be relieved of duty and replaced by competent personnel before the line employee is allowed to be interviewed by the inspector. It is important that the Inspection Coordinator ensure that questions asked of line employees:
    - Are within the regulatory authority granted to inspectors and any contract limitations placed on assessors
    - Are not misleading

- Are not hypothetical to the point of not being relevant to the objectives of the inspection or assessment

  The Inspection Coordinator should also be careful not to let line employee answers stray from the direct subject of the questions asked.

—*Copying of records*—Such copying is allowed by regulation and should be accommodated. The manufacturer should establish a guideline as to the extent of such copying that will be provided at no cost to the inspector, and the charge to be requested if the guideline is exceeded. Copies of all material copied by the inspector should be retained in the inspection file for future use if necessary.

—*Provision of requested samples*—A similar approach to that for copying of records should be established for charging for samples of product or other materials requested by the inspector. Duplicates of all samples provided to an inspector should be retained by the manufacturer to confirm any test results generated from those samples. The manufacturer should determine what the inspector intends to do with the provided samples and should request copies of any testing results obtained by the agency.

—*Handling of confidential or trade secret information*—Inspectors should be given access to such information if it is relevant to the objectives of the inspection. Regulatory inspectors are bound by law to protect information marked as "confidential" or "trade secret." Assessors are normally bound to protect such information by the terms of the contract between the manufacturer and the assessor organization. It is important, however, that the marking of such information be clear and specifically relevant. FDA will not honor such marking if it does not appear to be specific enough (for example, if all the pages of procedures or records are marked as "confidential").

—*Photography on site*—Normally on-site photography is prohibited, but if the regulatory inspector makes a reasonable request, the manufacturer should offer to take the photographs in a way that doesn't unnecessarily reveal any proprietary information.

- Describes the logistics associated with inspections, including the following:

  —A listing and filing of procedures and records commonly requested during such an inspection (for example, the Quality Manual and QMS level procedures including design and development, CAPA, handling of nonconforming materials, and complaint handling). There should also be a listing of records that may be requested but will not be supplied unless subpoenaed (for example, personnel records other than those related to education and training, company economic data, and internal and supplier quality audit records).

  —Other documentation (for example, business cards of personnel participating in the inspection, copies of the Quality System Regulation and the ISO 13485:2003 Standard, forms used to request documents and records during the inspection, plant layout diagrams, and organization charts).

—Organization and operation of the "war room" that will be set up to deal with documentation and records requests, accommodate any strategic or tactical meetings needed during the inspection, and maintain the records of the inspection.

- Describes the process for keeping the manufacturer management apprised of the inspection progress and findings in a timely manner.

Personnel likely to participate in inspections should be trained or periodically refreshed in regard to the organization's inspection policies and procedures.

It can be useful to include inspection preparedness as one of the organization's processes that is periodically audited.

Conduct the Inspection/Assessment Professionally and Cooperatively

There is a long list of inspection dos and don'ts that can ensure a successful, effective, and efficient inspection.

Professional Handling of the Inspector

Professional handling of the inspector when he or she walks in the door to start the inspection creates the initial impression that the organization is prepared and knows what it is doing from a quality systems point of view. Included in such professional handling are the following:

- If the inspector enters the wrong door either inadvertently or intentionally, the employees must escort the inspector to the receptionist.
- The receptionist must have a prioritized list of personnel to notify when the inspector enters the reception area. The inspector should always be made to feel comfortable.
- If the official greeter is not immediately available, the receptionist should proceed to the next name on the list.
- The organization's official greeter should always check the inspector's credentials and record the number and date of issue.

Efficient and Effective Start of the Inspection

Normally, an opening meeting is conducted that includes the inspector, the Inspection Coordinator, upper management of the organization, management and supervisory personnel likely to participate or have a direct interest in the inspection, and personnel responsible for taking minutes of all inspection activities. The opening meeting is used to:

- Understand the objectives of the inspection
- Provide the inspector with information related to the organization, its history, its products and services, and the layout and functions performed in the site being inspected to the extent that the inspector is unfamiliar with these items
- Introduce the inspector to the personnel likely to supply the technical, clinical, or compliance-related information requested during the inspection
- Alert the inspector to the organization's inspection and safety policies

Efficient and Effective Conduct of the Inspection

The inspector should be accompanied at all times by the Inspection Coordinator or the delegate, a "gofer," and the official note taker. The escort should avoid having a large group of personnel follow the inspector during the inspection. The escort should be able to expedite any of the inspector's legitimate requests for access and/or information. If the inspector makes a request that appears to be beyond his or her authority or appears to be beyond the scope of the inspection, the escort should call in the appropriate organization management to discuss the request. In this situation, it is generally not a good idea to threaten to call the inspector's superiors; however, in the right situation, this is an avenue open to the organization. It is generally better to reach a compromise that allows the inspector to fulfill the inspection objectives while protecting the organization from inappropriate risk.

A good example is the case where an inspector asks to see the complaint files for a two-or-three-year period. If the inspector refuses to clarify the request as to the types or subjects of the complaints, the organization may conclude that the inspector is on an inappropriate fishing expedition. It would then be reasonable for the organization to ask the inspector for the specific objective(s) of the request and to negotiate for a more limited search of the complaint files in order to fulfill the objective(s). If this is unsuccessful, the organization might suggest that the inspector's supervisor be called in to mediate the issue. If this too is refused and no accommodation can be negotiated, the organization may refuse the request for such access to the complaint files, knowing that the refusal will likely be noted in the inspection report or may end the inspection at that point.

The escort should:

- Make sure that the appropriate organization SME answers the inspector's questions. The escort should understand the limits of his or her authority to provide information and access and should know when to call in organization management or the right SME to deal with issues outside the escort's authority or knowledge.
- Understand the organization's inspection strategy(ies) and any specific inspection objectives (for example, QMS examples that the organization would like to highlight to the inspector to show compliance with the regulatory or standards requirements).
- Be alert to the organization's QMS weaknesses and the approaches the organization intends to use to deal with these weaknesses should they be revealed during the inspection.

Employee Training

Employees likely to participate in the inspection should be trained:

- To be respectful, cooperative, and nonconfrontational
- To answer questions honestly without making claims related to the product or the QMS that they cannot substantiate
- Not to provide information beyond the scope of the questions asked
- To make sure they understand the question before answering
- Not to be afraid to ask for further explanation if they do not understand the question
- Not to be afraid to say, "I don't know the answer to that question" if it is outside their area of expertise

Respond to All Observations

It is crucial that the organization address and respond quickly and effectively to all inspector observations of QMS deficiencies and opportunities for improvement. Some responses will be made during the inspection; others will require some study and planning. Ideally, responses should be made within one or two weeks after the inspection but no later than any time limitations stated on the FDA Form 483 report or the assessor's finding report. At the conclusion of the inspection, the inspector will discuss his or her findings and issue a report on FDA Form 483. The organization should keep the following in mind:

- If the inspector's observation is not clear or is confusing, it should be discussed at the closing meeting of the inspection until both the organization and the inspector agree on its content and meaning. If the organization does not agree with the inspector's observation, the organization should respectfully inform the inspector of the disagreement and provide any data or other information that supports the organization's position. If the disagreement cannot be resolved, the organization should address the disagreement in a written response to observations submitted to the regulatory agency or the assessor organization.
- If possible, deviations or deficiencies found during the inspection should be corrected immediately, and the correction should be shown to the inspector before the conclusion of the inspection so that it can be noted in the report.
- If an observation requires time to study and to develop a corrective action, the organization should inform the inspector of this and, either during the closing meeting or in a subsequent letter, should provide a plan, including a proposed schedule, for addressing the observation.
- When forecasting the time and resources required for corrective actions, the organization should not be overly optimistic and promise unrealistic timing. If the projected deadline for finishing the promised corrective action cannot be met (for whatever reason), the inspecting authorities should be notified as soon as possible and a new deadline should be negotiated. If, however, the inspection authorities suspect that this is a delay tactic, severe consequences may result to the firm.

Follow Through as Promised

It is important that the organization complete its corrective actions or other promised actions according to the plan submitted to the regulatory agency, the registrar, or the notified body. If corrective actions have a forecast timing that extends beyond several months, it is generally a good idea to provide update reports. If it appears that certain deadlines are not going to be met, these reports can inform the agency or assessor organization of delays.

Once an FDA inspection is closed, the organization should request a copy of the investigator's Establishment Inspection Report (EIR). This report can be useful in preparing for future FDA inspections.

 **FDA Guidance**

Inspection of Medical Device Manufacturers, Program 7382.845, Issued 15 June, 2006

The inspection program described in this guidance document is intended to commence June 15, 2006, with a completion date of June 15, 2010. The guidance document can be found at http://www.fda.gov/cdrh/comp/guidance/7382.845.html.

This compliance program provides guidance to FDA field and center staffs for the inspections and administrative/enforcement activities related to the Quality System (QS) regulation (21 CFR Part 820), the Medical Device Reporting (MDR) regulation (21 CFR Part 803), the Medical Device Tracking regulation (21 CFR Part 821), the Corrections and Removals regulation (21 CFR Part 806), and the Registration and Listing regulation (21 CFR Part 807). This compliance program supersedes the program of the same name which was issued on October 1, 2000.

Scheduling Inspections of Medical Device Manufacturers

a. Priorities for QS Inspection

. . . Selection of firms to accomplish the performance goals and then remaining work plan obligations should be focused using the risk based model below:

1. Pre-Market and Pre-Clearance inspections under MDUFMA (Inspections of manufacturers of devices with a pending PMA approval will be assigned under the PMA Compliance Program 7383.001.)
2. Manufacturers of Class III devices that have never been inspected.
3. Compliance Follow Up/For Cause Inspections (See Part III B for further discussion.)
4. Manufacturers of high risk devices which can be identified by:

   A. Special Assignment from CDRH;
   B. Devices with a higher frequency of recalls and MDRs;
   C. Devices that are driven by software and those with rapidly evolving technological changes. Both of these types of devices are subject to rapid and potentially poorly controlled modifications that could affect their continued safety and efficacy; or,
   D. New devices that have not been manufactured and distributed for very long.

5. Single Use Device Reprocessors: Hospital reprocessors and third party reprocessors. See Part III of this program for further instructions related to reprocessors.

   Highest priority should be given to MDUFMA assignments and those Class III device manufacturers that have not been previously inspected. The high risk device category noted in 4) above lists suggestions to the field on how to identify firms for surveillance inspections based on a risk model.

b. Class I Device Manufacturers

All Class I devices, including those exempted from most of the Quality System regulation requirements, must comply with record keeping requirements and complaint file requirements, reporting requirements under the MDR regulation, and registration of their facility and the listing of their product. Class I manufacturers should not be routinely scheduled for inspection but should receive lowest inspectional priority unless addressed by a special, "For Cause" assignment or when a health hazard is apparent. The following link provides insight if a device is Class I exempt from QS requirements. http://www.accessdata.fda.gov/scripts/cdrh/cfdocs/cfPCD/classification.cfm.

If inspecting a manufacturer that was originally planned as a Class I QS non-exempt, Class II or III device firm, and the inspection finds that the firm no longer makes Class I QS non-exempt, Class II or Class III devices, the investigator should review the firm's complaint handling system and MDR practices, then terminate the inspection.

A. Operations

1. Inspectional Strategy

. . . The QS inspections should generally start with a walk through of the facility to become familiar with the firm's operations and general state of control. . . .

The inspection will assess the firm's systems, methods, and procedures to ensure that the firm's quality management system is effectively established (defined, documented and implemented) and effectively maintained. QS inspections should include the assessment of post-market information on distributed devices to include:

- Review of recalls
- Review of MDRs (Be alert to the fact that MDRs may contain information on recalls that have not been reported through the district under 21 CFR Part 806.)
- Review of corrections and removals
- Review of significant changes in device specifications or in the manufacturing specifications
- Follow-up on previous FDA 483 observation(s), to include the corrections, corrective actions or preventive actions for the observation(s) and the related system(s)

Available post-market information should be reviewed as a part of the preparation for the inspection, in order to facilitate efficient time spent at the facility. . . . Any problems identified as a result of the review of post-market information should be developed during the inspection.

Important Note: The review of post-market information does not mean that the investigator should open the inspection with the review of complaints and complaint information. Complaints should be reviewed within the context of the Corrective and Preventive Action sub-system according to the procedures described below in this part.

a. QS Inspections

QS inspections should generally be conducted using the Quality System Inspection Technique (QSIT). Guidance for performing an inspection is provided in the *Guide to Inspections of Quality Systems*, August 1999, also called the QSIT Guide www.fda.gov/ora/inspect_ref/igs/qsit/qsitguide.htm. . . . The table below correlates the level of inspection and the guidance on how to perform the inspections.

Inspection Level	Type of Inspection	Guide to Inspections
1	Abbreviated	QSIT—Two subsystems; Corrective and Preventive Actions (CAPA) plus Production and Process Controls (P&PC) or Design Controls
2	Comprehensive	QSIT—The four major subsystems; Management Controls, Design Controls, CAPA and P&PC
3	Compliance Follow-up*	As directed by inspectional guidance and elements of QSIT
Special	For Cause*	As directed by inspectional guidance and elements of QSIT

*Compliance Follow-up and For Cause inspections are dictated by the previous FDA 483 findings and other regulatory information and may differ from the typical QSIT approach. The inspectional guidance provided by the assignment, the district compliance branch, and/or CDRH will guide the direction of these inspections. However, elements of the QSIT Guide may also be utilized. . . .

NOTE: The Quality System regulation can be grouped into seven subsystems; however, the following four subsystems are considered major subsystems and are the basic foundation of a firm's quality management system: Management Controls, Design Controls, Corrective and Preventive Actions (CAPA), and Production and Process Controls (P&PC). MDR, Corrections and Removals, and Tracking requirements (where applicable) should be covered when covering the CAPA subsystem. The three remaining subsystems (Facilities and Equipment Controls, Materials Controls and Document/Records/Change Controls) cut across a firm's quality management system and are evaluated while covering the four major subsystems. . . .

b. Level 1 Inspections . . .

Level 1 inspections are Abbreviated Inspections.

This level of inspection (CAPA plus P&PC or Design Controls) may be used for routine surveillance and initial inspections of all firms, other than firms that manufacture Class III devices. However, it is recommended that initial inspections of Class II manufacturers utilize a Level 2 Comprehensive inspection whenever district resources permit. . . .

The following should be considered in determining whether to select P&PC or Design Controls:

- CAPA findings during the inspection;
- Subsystems covered during the previous EI. The previous EIR(s) should be reviewed to determine which subsystems were previously covered. The selection of the P&PC or Design Controls subsystem should be alternated over time so that more subsystems within a firm's overall quality management system are assessed;
- Significant changes since the previous EI. Determine if there were any design changes which required a new submission or application, or if there were any major process changes; and,
- Post market information indicating potential design problems.

The EIR must clearly state which subsystem P&PC or Design Controls was chosen and why.

Note: The adequacy of the correction(s), corrective action(s) or preventive action(s) related to any FDA 483 item(s) from the previous inspection should be covered, even if the entire subsystem will not be reviewed during the current Level 1 inspection.

c. Level 2 Inspections . . .

Level 2 inspections are Comprehensive Inspections.

Level 2 inspections will cover all four major subsystems (Management Controls, Design Controls, CAPA, and P&PC) as explained in the QSIT Guide. . . .

Level 2 inspections will be performed:

- For all initial inspections of Class III device manufacturers and where possible Class II device manufacturers
- By assignment
- For foreign inspections
- For training
- For Accredited Persons audits . . .
- When an inspection, which started out as Level 1, reveals post market information and/or objectionable conditions which cannot be adequately assessed as a Level 1 inspection. . . .
- Where district work plan resources permit (Level 2 should be considered for any inspections of Class II and Class III device manufacturers. The decision to use Level 2 inspections should be based on risk.)

Note: For more information on the Accredited Person audits see "Accredited Person Inspection Program (Medical Devices) Performance Audit Procedures" on the Division of Human Resource Development's (DHRD's) intranet website under the certification/related programs/accredited person program section.

The Level 2 QSIT approach was validated using the following inspectional sequence: Management Controls, Design Controls, CAPA and P&PC. This inspectional sequence allows the investigator to review design control issues and how the device specifications were established before reviewing the CAPA subsystem. Investigators may however start with Management Controls, followed by CAPA, Design Controls, and P&PC with appropriate linkages. Information from Design Controls and CAPA may be used to select the products and processes for inspecting production and process controls, and appropriate linkages. The subsystems may be inspected in any appropriate and justifiable sequence in order to perform a timely and effective inspection.

Selection of manufacturing processes for inspectional coverage should include the following considerations:

- CAPA indicators of process problems
- Processes used to manufacture high risk products
- Processes that have a high risk of causing product failure
- Processes that require process validation
- Processes that are new to the manufacturer
- Processes that cover a variety of process technologies and profile classes
- Common processes used in multiple products
- Processes not covered during previous inspections

It is important to thoroughly cover Purchasing Controls, to include outsourced processes, as a QSIT linkage under P&PC whenever P&PC is covered. The Purchasing Control coverage must be documented in the EIR especially if the manufacturer contracts a sterilization process or contracts the manufacture of significant components, subassemblies, or processes.

d. Level 3 Inspections . . .

Level 3 inspections are Compliance Follow-up Inspections.

Level 3 inspections are necessary after a firm was found to have . . . conditions during a previous QS inspection which [were] classified Official Action Indicated (OAI). . . . Level 3 inspections will also be performed when directed by assignment.

The QSIT Guide should be used for guidance, but the inspectional guidance provided by the assignment, the district compliance branch, and/or CDRH will guide the flow of the inspection. The district compliance officers should be contacted during Level 3 inspections to assure that:

- Appropriate inspectional areas are covered with enough depth to support any findings
- Noncompliant findings (conditions) are adequately developed and documented
- Sufficient evidence is collected to support an appropriate regulatory action recommendation . . .

If the previous inspection was a Level 2 inspection:

During domestic Level 3 inspections:

(A) Verify that adequate correction(s) and corrective action(s) have been implemented to the quality system problems previously identified.
(B) If the correction(s) and corrective action(s) were not implemented or were not implemented effectively, verify that the deficiencies continue to exist and provide adequate evidence to support a possible regulatory action.
(C) Document any additional quality system problems observed during the inspection, and provide adequate evidence to support a possible regulatory action. . . .

If the previous inspection was a Level 1 inspection:

When the previous inspection was performed as a Level 1 inspection, the other two major subsystems previously not covered must be covered in addition to the inspectional guidance. It is important that the combination of the Level 1 and Level 3 inspections cover all four of the major subsystems in order to ensure a comprehensive review of the firm's quality management system.

During domestic Level 3 inspections:

(A) Verify that adequate correction(s) and corrective action(s) have been implemented to the quality system problems previously identified; and
(B) If the correction(s) and corrective action(s) were not implemented or were not implemented effectively, verify that the deficiencies continue to exist and provide adequate evidence to support a possible regulatory action.
(C) Document any additional quality system problems observed during the inspection, and provide adequate evidence to support a possible regulatory action. . . .

e. "For Cause" Inspections . . .

For Cause inspections are carried out in response to specific information that raises questions, concerns, or problems associated with a FDA regulated firm or commodity. This information could come to the attention of FDA from any source and including but not limited to, the following:

- Results of a sample analysis;
- Observations made during prior inspections;
- Recall or market withdrawal;
- Consumer or employee complaint;
- Adverse reaction report; or,
- Suspicion of fraud.

. . . For Cause inspections are dictated by the source of information and may differ from the typical QSIT approach. These inspections are generally more in-depth in particular areas than typical QSIT inspections. . . .

For Cause inspections should be directed towards the quality problem(s), and if applicable, trace the underlying cause, assuring that appropriate correction(s) and corrective action(s) are initiated.

If a serious public health risk is encountered during a QSIT inspection, consideration should be given to performing a For Cause inspection. The district compliance branch should be consulted prior to this decision.

For Cause inspections may also be initiated at a contract sterilizer when an inspection at a device manufacturer raises questions about the adequacy of processing or quality assurance by the contract sterilizer. Likewise, an inspection at a contract sterilizer may lead to a For Cause inspection of device manufacturers if significant deficiencies are observed. The deficiencies may be an indication that the device manufacturer(s) has not assumed appropriate responsibility for the sterilization validation and processing of its own devices. . . .

f. Foreign Inspections

All foreign inspections should be conducted using the QSIT Guide under the Level 2 strategy, and any special instructions contained in the inspection assignment. The foreign manufacturer's compliance with registration and listing requirements should be covered during foreign inspections. The failure of foreign device manufacturers to list products exported to the US will subject medical devices to detention upon entry.

Foreign inspections are subject to time constraints but need to follow the instructions for a Level 2 inspection as described above. . . .

2. Inspectional Instructions

a. Required Statement(s)

The following statement should be included on each FDA 483:

This document lists observations made by the FDA representative(s) during the inspection of your facility. They are inspectional observations and do not represent a final Agency determination regarding your compliance. If you have an objection regarding an observation, or have implemented, or plan to implement, corrective actions in response to an observation, you may discuss the objection or action with FDA representative(s) during the inspection or submit this information to FDA at the address above. If you have any questions, please contact FDA at the phone number and address above.

For all medical device inspections the FDA 483 should contain the following additional statement:

The observations noted in this form FDA 483 are not an exhaustive listing of objectionable conditions. Under the law, your firm is responsible for conducting internal self audits to identify and correct any and all violations of the quality system requirements.

b. Satellite Program Areas

Some program areas are considered satellites to the four major quality management system subsystems (Management Controls, Design Controls, CAPA, and P&PC):

CAPA Satellites
- MDR
- Corrections & Removals
- Tracking

Production & Process Control Satellite
- Sterilization . . .

The following guidance should be used for determining when to cover the various programs.

QS should be covered during each inspection. Coverage is determined by the "level" of desired inspection . . .

MDR compliance should be covered during each inspection. Prior to initiating an inspection, the MDR data should be reviewed . . . to obtain information regarding the firm's current reports. Be alert to the fact that MDRs may contain information on recalls that have not been reported through the district under 21 CFR Part 806.

Corrections & Removals. Determine during all QS inspections whether the firm has initiated any corrections or removals since the previous inspection and inspect for compliance with the Corrections & Removals regulation. . . . A Corrections & Removals inspection should also be initiated when a manufacturer is reporting corrections or removals in MDR reports or Part 806 reports. Be alert to the fact that MDRs may contain information on recalls that have not been reported through the district under 21 CFR Part 806.

Tracking. A tracking inspection is recommended, for devices that were issued a tracking order, each time CAPA is covered. . . .

Sterilization. When the P & PC subsystem is being inspected, sterilization should be chosen if not covered during the previous inspection unless:

CAPA indicators of existing or potential problems are found with any other specific process; or,

Other higher risk processes exist.

c. Sampling Records

The QSIT Guide includes instructions for sampling records for review. Sampling is an important tool for reducing the time spent reviewing records while being able to make statistically based inferences about the significance of the findings. The QSIT sampling table should be used for sampling records for evaluating the firm's adherence to requirements and their procedures, not for performing data verification or analysis.

During Level 1 and 2 inspections, the review of the records may be terminated if objectionable conditions are observed before the entire sample is reviewed. A FDA 483 observation may be made that the objectionable condition was found and move on to the next part of the inspection. However, QSIT Guide instructions caution that not reviewing the entire sample may result in the loss of additional information which may be useful in understanding the potential prevalence of the objectionable condition, or the failure to identify other objectionable conditions.

During Level 3 inspections, however, the investigator and the compliance officer should work together closely to plan how sampling will be conducted. It is important for the compliance officer to be confident that the level of sampling will be sufficient to document the deficiency and support a potential regulatory action. During Level 3 inspections, it is recommended that the investigator review the entire sample of records to provide a complete picture of any deficiencies identified during sampling. . . .

3. Special Instructions Concerning Design Controls

The inspectional authority for review of design control records is derived from Section 704(e) of the Act. Such authority applies only after the establishment has manufactured the device for which the design has been under development or taken an action that precludes the argument that the product under development is not a device. Such action includes: (1) submitting to an Institutional Review Board plans for clinical investigation of the device; (2) submitting to FDA a Product Development Protocol (PDP); (3) submitting to FDA an IDE, 510(k), PMA, Humanitarian Device Exemption (HDE) or Premarket Report (PMR); and (4) changes to an already marketed device. Therefore, FDA has inspectional authority to review design control records when the device has been placed on the market or when any of the four actions above have occurred.

The above limitation does not apply to inspectional authority to review all generic design control procedures at any point in time.

Review of design controls should cover any design processes performed after June 1, 1997. The manufacturer is not required to retrospectively apply design controls to any stages in the design process that it had completed prior to June 1, 1997, unless changes have been made to the design (including changes in ownership or where the designed device will be manufactured) after June 1, 1997. . . .

There are a number of multi-establishment firms that conduct all design activities at a single facility (sometimes referred to as a research and development (R&D) center or corporate design facility). . . . Determine if the home district of the R&D center or corporate design facility has conducted a design control inspection of that facility within the previous two years. If such an inspection was conducted, it will not be necessary to conduct a design control assessment at the establishment scheduled for inspection. If an inspection was not conducted within the previous two years, issue an assignment to the home district of the R&D center or corporate design facility requesting a design control inspection.

Some manufacturers have their devices designed under contract. These manufacturers must comply with the requirements for using contractors or service suppliers under 21 CFR § 820.50 as well as ensuring compliance with 21 CFR § 820.30. The manufacturer must maintain or have reasonable accessibility to copies of a Design History File for any device that is in production.

Observations relating to Design Controls placed on the FDA 483 should be limited to the adequacy of and adherence to the procedures and/or controls established by the firm. **Do not place observations on the FDA 483 that concern the adequacy, safety, or efficacy of a particular design.** . . .

4. Special Instructions for Sterilization Processes

Sterilization Process Controls section found in the QSIT Guide is a subpart of the Production and Process Controls subsystem. The instructions for inspecting sterilization processes are applicable at the following types of facilities:

- device manufacturers that sterilize their own product
- device manufacturers that use contract sterilizers
- contract sterilizers . . .

5. Inspection of Radiation Emitting Devices

Medical Devices which are also deemed to be "electronic products" as defined by the Federal Food Drug and Cosmetic Act, Subchapter C—Electronic Product Radiation Control, section 531(2), may be inspected under this compliance program. These devices have additional Radiological Health requirements to protect the public from unnecessary radiation. . . .

When conducting QS inspections, a firm may manufacture medical devices which are capable of emitting electronic product radiation. Based on district concurrence, the firm's devices should also be assessed against the applicable standards promulgated under Chapter V, Subchapter C—Electronic Product Radiation Control of the FD&C Act. This assessment is not a QS activity and should not be reported as a QS activity. . . .

Device manufacturers subject to existing FDA performance standards (21 CFR Parts 1020–1050) should include in their device master and history records those procedures and records demonstrating compliance with the applicable standard, self-certification (21 CFR 1010), and reporting (21CFR 1002–1005).

6. Sample Collection

For QS, MDR, Tracking, and Correction and Removals violations, samples are not generally necessary to support a Warning Letter. . . .

Samples may be required to support further action beyond a Warning Letter. The investigator should work with District management and compliance branch on deciding to collect samples to support QS violations. Physical samples should not be routinely collected to support QS cases. . . .

Normally, the collection of samples for sterility issues is not to be performed during Level 1 (Abbreviated) inspections of device manufacturers or contract sterilizers. If sterility issues are in regards to packaging or seam integrity, sample collection may be needed. The following items provide guidance on sampling decisions. . . .

- Finished device samples should **not** routinely be collected and tested for sterility to prove quality system deficiencies in sterilization validation or process control. Under certain circumstances, the Center may request that samples be collected for sterility testing.

- Field examination of packaging used for sterile devices may be indicated when the assessment of packaging operations demonstrates a lack of control such that inadequate packaging is likely to occur. Examine the packages for integrity of the sterility barrier, paying close attention to seals.
- Samples of defective packaging found during a visual field examination, if regulatory action is contemplated for packaging deficiencies, consist of 20 sterilized packaged devices.
- Bioburden samples are to be collected **only** 1) when the review of the results of bioburden testing performed by the manufacturer finds unrealistically low results; and, 2) the sterilization process is a bioburden based cycle with no safety overkill element. The sample is to consist of 20 unsterilized devices.
- Biological indicators are **not** to be collected routinely. Collect 40 biological indicators only if there is reason to question the effectiveness of the indicators or under direction by the Center.
- Endotoxin samples are to be collected **only** when endotoxin control is necessary for the device and when the review of the manufacturer's test methodology suggests that the manufacturer's test results may be unrealistically low. Collect 10 sterilized devices. . . .

Guidance for Industry and FDA Staff—The Review and Inspection of Premarket Approval Application Manufacturing Information and Operations, Issued 19 June, 2006

The guidance document may be found at http://www.fda.gov/cdrh/comp/guidance/1566.html.

This guidance explains for applicants the process involved with the review of a PMA manufacturing section and inspection of the manufacturing operations described in the manufacturing section. This guidance is also generally applicable to the process involved with the review of manufacturing information in certain PMA supplements. This guidance does not address premarket notification (510(k)) submissions because a premarket inspection is not ordinarily conducted for this type of premarket submission. . . .

FDA Review of the PMA Manufacturing Section, and the Inspection Process

A. What procedure does FDA use to review a PMA manufacturing section?

. . . 3. OC/FOB [Office of Compliance Field Operations Branch] alerts the district office associated with a domestic manufacturing site identified in the PMA as to the receipt of the application. OC/FOB requests a response from the appropriate FDA district office within 7 calendar days regarding the inspection history of the manufacturing site. If there are multiple facilities involved in the manufacturing process, OC/FOB will notify all relevant districts.

The district will determine the following information concerning the manufacturing site from its records:

- the date of last inspection;
- classification of the last inspection report; and
- the similarity of the products inspected to the PMA device and similarity of the manufacturing operations inspected by FDA to those used for the PMA device under review.

Once the information is received from the district office, OC/FOB forwards the information to the assigned OC enforcement division, or to OIVD [Office of IVD Device Evaluation and Safety].

4. OC serves as the district office for any foreign facility. OC, with input from OIVD when necessary, determines whether a foreign manufacturing facility requires an inspection based on the same information noted in item 3 above.

   For foreign sites, OC/FOB notifies the Office of Regional Operations (ORO), Division of Field Investigations (DFI), and International Operations Branch (IOB) of a pending assignment. ORO/DFI/IOG coordinates the foreign site inspections for the FDA field staff. A provisional inspection assignment for a foreign facility is transmitted from OC/FOB to ORO/DFI/IOG early in the review process. . . . This early assignment is done before completion of the manufacturing section review because foreign inspections take longer than domestic inspections to organize and complete due to scheduling, travel logistics, and coordinating with foreign governments and the U.S. State Department. The longer organizational time for a foreign inspection enables the assigned OC enforcement division or OIVD to substantially review the PMA manufacturing section and to cancel the inspection if there are major deficiencies. . . .

B. What happens when OC or OIVD completes its review of the PMA manufacturing section?

. . . 2. If the review of the manufacturing section is substantially complete and there are no deficiencies in the manufacturing section, or if the deficiencies have been adequately addressed through phone calls or additional submissions, OC or OIVD will evaluate the district office's inspection history of the domestic facility. If OC or OIVD determines that FDA should conduct a QS/GMP inspection, OC/FOB will initiate an assignment with ORO [Office of Regional Operations] for a domestic inspection. OC/FOB will also confirm that the already initiated foreign inspection assignment should proceed.

3. The PMA applicant should be ready for inspection at the time of the filing of the PMA application unless the applicant states in the PMA that it is not ready. The District (or OC for a foreign facility) should contact the facility's management to alert them

to the pending inspection. At that time, the applicant should confirm that the facility is ready for inspection. The manufacturing process should preferably be in operation by the time the inspection is conducted. In any case, all process validations should be completed and the design successfully transferred into production.

4. OC/FOB plans to cancel the assigned or scheduled inspection under the following circumstances: if the PMA is determined to be not fileable; ODE or OIVD issues a major deficiency letter, denial letter, withdrawal letter, or not approvable letter; or the applicant communicates to the FDA that the manufacturing site is not ready for inspection.

If the facility is not ready for inspection, the District (or OC for a foreign facility) will ask the applicant to send a letter to the District or OC, signed by the most responsible person at the firm, indicating that they are not ready for inspection, the reason for not being ready, and when they expect to be ready. This letter will be made part of the PMA record.

The applicant should alert CDRH in writing or by real time communication in advance of when the facility will be ready for inspection. OC/FOB will then reissue an inspection assignment. . . .

C. How much time does the FDA allow for a PMA QS/GMP inspection?

Domestic Inspections: FDA field staff should complete the inspection within 45 calendar days after receipt of the inspection assignment from OC or OIVD.

Foreign Inspections: FDA field staff should complete the inspection within 60 calendar days after receipt of the inspection assignment. Please note, foreign travel requires additional time for scheduling, travel logistics, and for coordinating with foreign governments and the U.S. State Department.

An additional 30 calendar days are allotted for the field staff to write and forward a PMA application establishment inspection report to FOB for both domestic and foreign inspections.

D. What happens after the establishment inspection report (EIR) is completed by the field staff?

There are several potential outcomes from an inspection:

- If FDA concludes that there are no objectionable conditions or practices with the manufacturing operations, or any that do not justify further regulatory action, i.e., a No Action Indicated (NAI) result, then OC/FOB will notify ODE POS [Office of Device Evaluation Program Operations Staff] that the PMA approval can proceed from a manufacturing operations perspective.
- If FDA concludes that there are objectionable conditions or practices, but these do not warrant administrative or regulatory action, i.e., a Voluntary Action Indicated (VAI) result, then FDA may communicate

the objectionable conditions or practices to the applicant and recommend that the applicant voluntarily correct the deficiencies. FDA may evaluate the corrections during a subsequent inspection. As above, OC/FOB will notify ODE POS that the PMA approval can proceed from a manufacturing operations perspective.

- If FDA concludes that there are objectionable conditions or practices that warrant regulatory or administrative sanctions, i.e., an Official Action Indicated (OAI) result, then there are two possible outcomes:
  1. If the conditions or practices pertain only to the pending PMA device, then OC or OIVD will issue a deficiency letter within 30 calendar days for a non-expedited PMA and within 20 days for an expedited PMA.
  2. If the conditions or practices pertain not only to the pending PMA device but also to marketed products, then FDA may issue a Warning Letter or Untitled Letter.
- In either case, the letter will inform the addressee that no approval for a pending PMA will issue until the objectionable conditions or practices are corrected.

OC/FOB is informed of the issuance of a Warning or Untitled Letter by the issuing office. Based upon the deficiencies noted in the Warning or Untitled Letter, OC/FOB will notify ODE POS when the manufacturing operation is not satisfactory and recommend that the PMA approval be withheld. . . . If ODE or OIVD has completed its review of the PMA and concludes the PMA warrants an approval or approvable action, except for the unsatisfactory manufacturing aspects, ODE or OIVD will issue an approvable letter notifying the manufacturer of the pending GMP issues. This letter stops the review clock for the PMA.

The applicant should provide a complete response to the FDA office that issued the letter within the timeframe noted. A complete response to a deficiency, Warning or Untitled Letter begins a new 20 or 30 day FDA manufacturing section review period. . . . More than one cycle of correspondence may be needed to resolve deficiencies. Once deficiencies or violations appear to have been corrected, OC/FOB may issue a new inspection assignment, if needed, beginning a new cycle of review including the 45 or 60 day inspection as well as EIR completion and review by the District and OC or OIVD.

F. What are the most common factors that delay the review of a PMA manufacturing section or delay the inspection process?

- When OC or OIVD issues a manufacturing section deficiency letter to a PMA applicant, a timely and thorough response facilitates the review process. Until OC or OIVD receives the requested information, the review of the manufacturing section remains on hold and no inspection will be scheduled. . . .
- The manufacturing process should be in operation as soon as possible after PMA submission. As noted, all process validations should be completed and the design successfully transferred into production.

Rescheduling a PMA inspection may result in further delays of the FDA review of the PMA's manufacturing section and operations and result in an approvable pending GMP letter.

Draft Guidance: The Likelihood of Facilities Inspections When Modifying Devices Subject to Premarket Approval, Issued 5 August, 1999, Updated 13 August, 1999

This guidance document may be found at http://www.fda.gov/cdrh/comp/likehood.html.

During recent FDA/medical device industry grassroots forums, industry representatives discussed difficulties they have experienced in planning for changes related to devices with applications approved through the Premarket Approval (PMA), Product Development Protocol (PDP) or Humanitarian Device Exemption (HDE) processes. The industry representatives indicated that much of the difficulty was caused by uncertainty about FDA policies on what circumstances require submission of a PMA Supplement, when a PMA inspection may be required, or when documenting the change in the firm's files may be adequate.

FDA, with input from interested parties, developed this guidance document in an effort to help firms manage the time frames associated with implementing changes in manufacturing facilities, manufacturing methods or procedures, labeling or performance.

This guidance also identifies factors involved in deciding when a manufacturing change would ordinarily precipitate a pre-approval inspection. A determination that a pre-approval inspection would ordinarily be appropriate, however, does not preclude FDA from exercising discretion in deciding in a particular situation that a pre-approval inspection is not necessary. Conversely, the guidance document in no way limits FDA from conducting a reasonable inspection within the meaning of Section 704 of the Act at any time it deems appropriate. This guidance document is intended to reduce the confusion and concomitant delays in the implementation of a manufacturing change while maintaining necessary safeguards. Such safeguards include performing pre-approval inspections where: (a) the PMA holder has a recent history of substantial deviations from Quality System/GMP requirements; (b) the device's manufacturing has not been inspected for compliance with Quality System/GMP requirements within the last two years; or (c) the nature of the change or the inadequacy of the documentation filed with FDA necessitates a pre-approval inspection to verify the appropriateness of the change.

. . . a step-by-step description of the decision process that is necessary to determine the likelihood of an inspection.

The model encompasses three types of changes. They are:

- changes in manufacturing method or procedures (the E pathway);
- changes in the location of a manufacturing facility (the F pathway); and
- changes to the device or its labeling (the G pathway).

Changes in Manufacturing Methods or Procedures . . .

Changes in manufacturing methods or procedures for PMA devices were addressed in the Food and Drug Administration Modernization Act of 1997 (FDAMA). FDAMA modified Section 515(d)(6) of the Food, Drug & Cosmetic Act to permit a manufacturer of a device with an approved PMA to submit a 30-Day Notice describing the change and controls used to assure that the change would not adversely affect the safety or effectiveness of the device. Manufacturers can proceed with the change 30 days after receipt of the notice by CDRH unless CDRH determines that the notice is inadequate. CDRH may also convert the 30-Day Notice to a 135-Day Supplement if the notice presents complex issues or too much data to be reviewed within 30 days. A guidance document explaining the requirements for a 30-Day Notice is available on the internet at http://www.fda.gov/cdrh/blbkmem.html

FDA recognizes that some of the changes will be necessary to correct manufacturing problems that are identified by the firms' corrective and preventative action systems, or as the result of recalls. Because such changes must be implemented as quickly as possible, FDA will not normally conduct inspections as part of the review of 30-Day Notices or 135-Day Supplements.

Changes in the Locations of Manufacturing Facilities . . .

For a number of years, changes in the location of a manufacturing or sterilization facility have required inspection of the new facility to assure that it was capable of manufacturing the PMA device and was compliant with the requirements of the Good Manufacturing Practices regulation. The statutory requirement to obtain clearance for the move via a 180-day PMA Supplement has presented special problems for certain manufacturers. . . .

In 1996, FDA introduced a pilot program to facilitate the PMA Supplement review process when firms needed to change manufacturing facilities as quickly as possible. The Pilot Program for PMA Supplements, now referred to as Express PMA Supplements for Facilities Change . . . offers qualified firms an opportunity to consult with CDRH's Office of Compliance prior to initiating their move. The Office of Compliance, or the district office, as appropriate, will review the firm's protocols for validation/equipment qualification and, if necessary, offer suggestions. If the firm's protocols for validation/equipment qualification are satisfactory, or need only minor modifications, the firm will usually proceed with the move, conduct the necessary validation/qualification studies and submit the results of the studies in the PMA Supplement. If the data are satisfactory, the PMA Supplement will be approved without an on-site inspection of the new facility. . . .

Originally, FDA required an inspection of all facilities that were not being used for device, drug or biologics manufacturing at the time of the facilities change, because it had no current information on the status of the facility. Experience has shown, however, that moves to such facilities usually present only minor problems, . . . The program for Express PMA Supplements for Facilities Change now provides that moves to such facilities can generally take place without an on-site inspection of the new facility if: (1)

the PMA Supplement is in order; and (2) the original manufacturing facility received an inspection within the last two years, and there are no recent substantial deviations from the quality system/GMP requirements.

Changes to the Device or Its Labeling

. . . changes to the device may be of such magnitude that they require a new PMA instead of a PMA Supplement. This may occur when the new device has a technological basis of operation or mode of operation different from the original device and the manufacturing process for the new device differs significantly from the manufacturing process used for the original device. Typically, a new PMA application will require submission of a complete Manufacturing Section and an on-site inspection.

Future FDA Compliance Activities and Use of Standards

In an effort to increase the efficiency and effectiveness of their inspection programs, the FDA and its counterparts around the world are working together to harmonize quality system requirements and the methods for inspecting compliance with those requirements. There are memoranda of understanding between the FDA and Canada, FDA and the EU, Australia and the EU, and others.

For some time the FDA, Health Canada, the EU, Japan, and Australia have been working within the GHTF to develop guidance documents that reflect international agreement on QMS terminology, essential principles, requirements, and methods for auditing QMS compliance. Information related to proposed and approved guidance documents can be accessed from the various study group links at the GHTF Web site, http://www.GHTF.org.

The FDA is authorized under the Medical Device User Fee and Modernization Act of 2002 (MDUFMA) to accredit third parties to conduct inspections of manufacturers of class II and class III devices on behalf of the FDA. Under this program, manufacturers with a reasonably good inspection record with the FDA can request that they be inspected by an accredited party as an alternative to being inspected by the FDA. Details of the Accredited Persons Inspection Program can be found at http://www.fda.gov/cdrh/ap-inspection/ap-inspection.html.

The FDA and Health Canada have entered into a bilateral pilot program that would allow certain third-party auditors to perform single audits that can be used for compliance purposes by both agencies. The third-party auditors in this program are those accredited under the FDA Accredited Persons Inspection Program or listed as accredited auditors under the Canadian Medical Devices Conformity Assessment System (CMDCAS) program. Two Web sites have useful details of this pilot program:

- http://www.fda.gov/cdrh/ap-inspection/pmap-letter.html
- http://www.fda.gov/cdrh/ap-inspection/pmap-qa.html

It is likely that there will be continued interactions between FDA and its international partner agencies to harmonize QMS terminology and requirements. The results of these efforts will be publicized through their Web sites and their normal regulation development and publication processes.

FDA has a continuing program of recognizing international standards. This program is primarily targeted at streamlining the product approval processes by allowing manufacturers to reference and certify compliance with FDA-recognized standards in lieu of providing FDA with extensive data to review prior to product approval. Under this program, a database of recognized standards has been created. While most of the recognized standards are "vertical standards" relating to specific medical devices or groups of devices, there are a number of "horizontal standards" that contain quality and safety requirements that relate to a range of medical devices. Information related to the FDA standards recognition program can be found at http://www.fda.gov/cdrh/osel/guidance/321.html.

The FDA-recognized standards database may be accessed at http://www.accessdata.fda.gov/scripts/cdrh/cfdocs/cfStandards/search.cfm.

Within that database many of the recognized standards that relate to safety and quality can be found in the "General" or "Sterility" categories.

INDEX

D

E

F

G

H

I

L

M

N

O

P

Q

R

S

T

U

V

W